UNDERSTANDING THE FURTHER EDUCATION SECTOR

Focusing on a less well-known area of education, the Further Education (FE) sector, this book provides education studies students a chance to provoke reflection, analysis, and understanding, as well as personal and professional development in the area. Jim Crawley brings over 40 years' experience working in or with the FE sector, reflected in his committed and passionate approach alongside carefully balanced academic analysis and discussion.

This book covers subsectors of FE including colleges, skills for life, work-based learning, and offender learning and cross-sector themes such as working and managing, social justice, equality, diversity, and sustainability. This book also supports independent study and complements other topics and themes across an education studies degree.

This book is perfect for new and existing students of education studies, joint honours courses, teacher training, and those researching for a master's degree or doctorate. It is the definitive text in the field and ideal for anyone wanting to further their understanding of the FE sector.

Jim Crawley is a Visiting Teaching and Learning Fellow at Bath Spa University. He has worked in Further Education since 1974, including projects with unemployed young people to co-ordinating a national research network. He has published widely on Teaching, Professionalism, and Teacher Education all in FE and Advanced Research techniques for the wider education sector.

The Routledge Education Studies Series

Series Editor: Stephen Ward, Bath Spa University, UK

The Routledge Education Studies Series aims to support advanced level study on Education Studies and related degrees by offering in-depth introductions from which students can begin to extend their research and writing in years 2 and 3 of their course. Titles in the series cover a range of classic and up-and-coming topics, developing understanding of key issues through detailed discussion and consideration of conflicting ideas and supporting evidence. With an emphasis on developing critical thinking, allowing students to think for themselves and beyond their own experiences, the titles in the series offer historical, global and comparative perspectives on core issues in education.

Understanding Education and Economics
Key Debates and Critical Perspectives
Edited by Jessie A. Bustillos Morales and Sandra Abegglen

Understanding Contemporary Issues in Higher Education
Contradictions, Complexities and Challenges
Edited by Brendan Bartram

Education in Europe
Looking out for what the neighbours do
Edited by Tom Feldges

Pedagogies for the Future
A critical reimagining of education
Gary Beauchamp, Dylan Adams and Kevin Smith

Understanding Education Studies
Critical Issues and New Directions
Edited by Mark Pulsford, Rebecca Morris and Ross Purves

Leadership and Management for Education Studies
Introducing Key Concepts of Theory and Practice
Edited by Catherine A. Simon ad Deborah Outhwaite

New Studies in the History of Education
Connecting the Past to the Present in an Evolving Discipline
Edited by Nicholas Joseph

Understanding the Further Education Sector
History, Challenges, and Achievements
Jim Crawley

For more information about this series, please visit: www.routledge.com/The-Routledge-Education-Studies-Series/book-series/RESS

UNDERSTANDING THE FURTHER EDUCATION SECTOR

HISTORY, CHALLENGES, AND ACHIEVEMENTS

Jim Crawley

LONDON AND NEW YORK

Designed cover image: © Getty Images

First edition published 2025
by Routledge
4 Park Square, Milton Park, Abingdon, Oxon, OX14 4RN

and by Routledge
605 Third Avenue, New York, NY 10158

Routledge is an imprint of the Taylor & Francis Group, an informa business

© 2025 Jim Crawley

The right of Jim Crawley to be identified as author of this work has been asserted in accordance with sections 77 and 78 of the Copyright, Designs and Patents Act 1988.

All rights reserved. No part of this book may be reprinted or reproduced or utilised in any form or by any electronic, mechanical, or other means, now known or hereafter invented, including photocopying and recording, or in any information storage or retrieval system, without permission in writing from the publishers.

Trademark notice: Product or corporate names may be trademarks or registered trademarks, and are used only for identification and explanation without intent to infringe.

British Library Cataloguing-in-Publication Data
A catalogue record for this book is available from the British Library

ISBN: 978-1-032-74266-3 (hbk)
ISBN: 978-1-032-74264-9 (pbk)
ISBN: 978-1-003-46845-5 (ebk)

DOI: 10.4324/9781003468455

Typeset in News Gothic Std
by codeMantra

Contents

List of tables vi
List of abbreviations vii
Series editor's preface x
Introducing the book xii

1. Introducing the sector — 1
2. Further education colleges — 13
3. Managing and working in further education — 24
4. Work-based learning (WBL) — 37
5. Adult and community learning (ACL) — 50
6. Widening participation (WP) and access to higher education — 63
7. Higher education in further education (HE in FE) — 74
8. Education for social justice, equality, and diversity — 87
9. Skills for life (SfL) — 103
10. COVID-19 — 117
11. 14–19 education — 131
12. Sustainability — 147
13. Specialist colleges — 161
14. Offender learning — 175
15. Making connections – The future of further education — 186

Index *199*

Tables

4.1 Adapted from Fuller and Unwin (2019: 76–77) 45
7.1 HE in FE enrolment numbers 2017/18 to 2021/22 (Higher Education Statistics Agency, 2023: 1) 75

Abbreviations

ABE	Adult Basic Education
ACL	Adult and Community Learning
AoC	Association of Colleges
APEL	Accreditation of Prior Experiential Learning
BAME	Black and Minority Ethnicity
BHASVIC	Brighton Hove and Sussex Sixth Form College
BBC	British Broadcasting Corporation
BTEC	Business and Technology Education Council
CAT	College of Advanced Technology
CBHE	College-Based Higher Education
Cert Ed	Certificate in Education
CIC	Community Interest Company
CNAA	Council for National Academic Awards
CPD	Continuing Professional Development
DfE	Department for Education
EDSK	Education and Skills
EHoM	Engineering Habits of Mind
ESD	Education for Sustainable Development
ESFA	Education and Skills Funding Agency
ESOL	English as a second or other language
ETF	Education and Training Foundation
FAETC	Further and Adult Education Teaching Certificate
FE	Further Education
FEFC	Further Education Funding Council
FES	Further Education sector
FETL	Further Education Trust for Leadership
FEWDC	Further Education Workforce Data Collection
FSM	Free school meals
GCSE	General Certificate of Secondary Education
GFEC	General further education college
GNVQ	General National Vocational Qualification
HE	Higher Education
HEI	Higher Education Institution

HESA	Higher Education Statistics Agency
HIVE	Higher Vocational Education
HMSO	Her Majesty's Stationery Office
HNC	Higher National Certificate
HND	Higher National Diploma
ICT	Information and Communications Technology
ILEA	Inner London Education Authority
ITB	Industrial Training Board
ITP	Independent Training Provider
LA	Local Authority
Landex	Land-based colleges aspiring to excellence
LEA	Local Education Authority
LGBTQ+	lesbian, gay, bi, trans, queer, questioning, and ace
LLN	Language, Literacy, and Numeracy
LSC	Learning and Skills Council
LLDD	Learner with learning difficulty or disability
MDG	Millennium Development Goals
MSC	Manpower Services Commission
Napaeo	National Association of Principal Agricultural Education Officers
NATECLA	National Association for Teaching English and other Community Languages to Adults
NCS	National Career Service
NCVQ	National Council for Vocational Qualifications
NEET	Young person not in employment or training
NIACE	National Institute of Adult and Continuing Education
NVQ	National Vocational Qualification
OECD	Organisation for Economic Cooperation and Development
Ofqual	Office of Qualifications and Examinations Regulation
Ofsted	Office for standards in education
ONS	Office for National Statistics
PCET	Post Compulsory Education and Training
PGCE	Post Graduate Certificate in Education
PGCert	Professional Graduate Certificate in Education
PLA	Prison Learning Alliance
PSD	Personal and Social Development
QAA	Quality Assurance Agency
QCA	Qualifications and Curriculum Agency
RAE	Royal Academy of Engineering
SDG	Sustainable Development Goals
SEN	Special Educational Needs
SET	Society for Education and Training
SfL	Skills for Life
SSL	Somerset Skills and Leisure
STEM	Science, Technology, English, and Maths
TEC	Training and Enterprise Council

u3a	University of the Third Age
UCAS	Universities and Colleges Admissions System
UCU	University and College Union
UK	United Kingdom
UN	United Nations
US	United States
UTC	University Technical College
VET	Vocational Education and Training
VTCT	Vocational Training Charitable Trust
WEA	Workers Educational Association
WBL	Work-based learning
WP	Widening participation

Series editor's preface

Education Studies has become a popular and exciting undergraduate subject in many universities in the UK. It began in the early 2000s, mainly in the post-1992 universities which had been centres of teacher training. Gaining academic credibility, the subject is now taught and researched in pre-1992 and Russell Group institutions. In 2004, Routledge published one of the first texts for undergraduates, *Education Studies: A student's guide* (Ward, 2004), now in its fourth edition (Simon and Ward, 2019). It comprises a series of chapters introducing key topics in Education Studies and has contributed to the development of the subject. Targeted at students and academic staff at levels 5, 6, and 7, the Routledge Education Studies Series offers a sequence of volumes that explore such topics in depth.

It is important to understand that education studies is not teacher training or teacher education, although graduates in the subject may well go on to become teachers after a PGCE or school-based training. Education studies should be regarded as a subject with a variety of career outcomes, or indeed, none: it can be taken as the academic and critical study of education in itself. At the same time, while the theoretical elements of teacher training are continually reduced in PGCE courses and school-based training, undergraduate education studies provides a critical analysis for future teachers who, in a rapidly changing world, need so much more than simply the training to deliver a government-defined school curriculum.

Education studies is concerned with understanding how people develop and learn throughout their lives, the nature of knowledge, and critical engagement with ways of knowing. It demands an intellectually rigorous analysis of educational processes and their cultural, social, political, and historical contexts. In a time of rapid change across the planet, education is about how we both make and manage such change. Education studies, therefore, includes perspectives on international education, economic relationships, globalisation, ecological issues, and human rights. It deals with beliefs, values, and principles in education and the way that they change over time.

Since its early developments at the beginning of the century, the subject has grown in academic depth, drawing explicitly on the disciplines of Psychology, Sociology, Philosophy, History, and Economics (see Chapter 2). But it has also broadened in scope to address the many social and political questions of globalisation, international education, and perceptions of childhood.

So much of the literature on education relates to primary and secondary schooling and tertiary education in universities. Further Education (FE) is often overlooked as a sort of 'in-between' sector. This is unjust because it includes many thousands of students, young and mature, who study in an enormous range of settings. We must welcome this book that fills the gap in the study of education by setting out and analysing the full range of institutions and courses in England and Wales. You will probably be surprised at the number and variety of FE opportunities on offer for such a wide range of people in different circumstances. Its author, Jim Crawley, has spent his whole professional life in FE as a teacher, manager, and researcher, and we benefit from his knowledge and understanding in the different chapters.

As well as having a low profile in the education literature, FE has been neglected by consecutive governments, particularly in terms of its funding that has always lagged behind that of the schools and universities. Such underfunding can lead to a negative ethos in the sector: Why aren't we paid properly to teach? Why don't we have the best resource? But, as Jim shows in this book, despite underfunding, colleagues in the FE sector rise above this and see themselves as providing often unique and life-changing opportunities for the disadvantaged of all ages, helping learners to be members of a better society. At the time of writing, many working in all sectors of education feel disheartened about the future. Jim's final chapter on the future for FE inspires an optimistic view of what is possible in a warming conclusion to the book.

The International Education Studies Association (TIESA)

Many of the editors and contributors to the Education Studies book series are members of the TIESA (formerly the British Education Studies Association – BESA). Formed in 2005, TIESA provides a network for tutors and students in Education Studies. It holds an annual conference with research papers from staff and students and funds small-scale research projects.

The website offers information and news about Education Studies and two journals: *Educational Futures* and *Transformations*, a journal for student publications. Both are available without charge on the website: https://educationstudies.org.uk/

Stephen Ward, Series Editor, Bath Spa University

References

Simon, C.A. and Ward, S. (Eds.) (2019) *A student's guide to education studies*. Abingdon: Routledge.
Ward, S. (Ed.) (2004) *Education Studies: A student's guide*. Abingdon: Routledge.

Introducing the book

This book is the first in this series to focus on a part of the English education system which is generally not as well-known as the school and higher-education sectors, the Further Education (FE) sector. It is intended to provoke reflection, analysis, understanding, and personal and professional development for those studying Education Studies. The author has spent more than 40 years working in or with the FE sector, so there will be evidence of this commitment and emotion within the text at times in addition to the balanced academic analysis and discussion. This book will be helpful for new and existing students of Education Studies, joint honours courses, teacher training, and those researching for a master's degree or doctorate. It will be the definitive text in the field, and course tutors will be able to help the reader get the most from it during their study. This book will also be positively useful for supporting independent study and complementing the other topics and themes being studied. For consistency of terminology, the word 'student' will be used for those studying or training within the sector.

Features of the book include:

Chapter style and content

Fifteen accessible but authoritative chapters span a considerable range of information, history, research, and analysis about FE. The majority of chapters are about subsectors of FE, but there are also chapters that address cross-sector themes such as Managing and Working in FE or Sustainability.

A chapter structure that will:

- Define the subsector or cross-sector theme;
- Summarise the relevant student numbers and the providers involved;
- Analyse the historical development, key characteristics, and the current position;
- Discuss relevant theoretical debates and thinkers;
- Summarise the current situation of the subsector or cross-sector theme.

Sector stories

These will be real or realistic case studies or examples of organisations, students, and teachers in the FE sector, which will, as the title suggests, 'tell the story' of working, managing, and studying in the sector through a series of examples. There will usually be up to three Sector Stories in each chapter.

> **Questions for discussion**
>
> There will be at least two Questions for Discussion in each chapter. These will be included in boxes interspersed during the text.

Conclusion

A conclusion that summarises the main points with some discussion.

Summary Points

A list of four to six summary points.

Recommended reading

Items for recommended reading.

References

A chapter reference list.

Summary of chapters

1. *Introducing the sector*

    This chapter firstly defines the FE sector, then outlines its history and development and its scope and situation within English Education. The chapter considers how the range of what the more than two million students who are involved in FE study can make a coherent categorisation of the sector difficult.

    A discussion will be included of some of the less helpful ways of characterising the sector including an explanation of when and why terms including 'Education for other people's children' were coined, and how government policies, managerialism, changes, and misunderstandings have affected FE. A discussion of both the enduring characteristics and achievements of the sector as a whole and the lack of esteem in which the sector is often held conclude the chapter.

2. *Further Education Colleges*

    This chapter introduces the most well-known part of the FE sector, Further Education Colleges. There are 228 colleges in England (AoC, 2023: 3), and they provide vocational, academic, and other programmes and learning activities from entry level up to higher education for 1.6 million students. Over 930,000 adults study or train in colleges and 11,000 study higher education in a college. The chapter will expand on and explain FE college statistics, outline their history, and indicate how colleges are involved in or influence many of the FE subsectors. Research illustrating college challenges and successes will be analysed to identify where in English education FE colleges stand.

3. *Managing and working in Further Education*

    This chapter introduces models of governance which are present in the FE sector, in particular those of FE and sixth-form colleges and adult education providers, and discusses the effect sector governance has on the operation of FE organisations. The chapter then discusses the circumstances, situations, and challenges faced by leaders in FE organisations and the research that has shown how they seek to manage those challenges. The numbers of staff involved in the sector are outlined, and comments on the difficulties accessing whole-sector data are discussed. The chapter also considers models of professionalism in FE and makes use of the writings of Machiavelli to draw out some key points.

4. *Work-based learning (WBL)*

    Learning at and away from work mainly for vocational purposes is another significant part of the FE sector. Multiple types of provision are included from apprenticeships and master's courses to short tailor-made training for small businesses. In 2022–23, 166,000 people were on an apprenticeship provision in colleges (AoC, 2023: 14). A historical analysis will draw out the multiple perspectives and debates on WBL policy and practice and consider current thinking on how it can best succeed.

5. *Adult and Community Learning (ACL)*

    The chapter will explain how this area of FE has experienced a particularly difficult time in recent years, with constant reductions in funding, and, as a result, constantly reducing student numbers. Although those numbers have recently recovered to some degree, inequalities across society and this subsector still exist. It does, however, have a rich tradition of bringing leisure, vocational, and community-oriented learning to some of the most difficult-to-reach organisations, communities, and individuals. The key principles, processes, and programmes in ACL are introduced, and key moments, movements, and shifts in policy and practice are analysed.

6. *Widening participation (WP) and access to higher education*

    This chapter will introduce the history of WP within the FES and will take a particular focus on Access to Higher Education courses, which have been one of the jewels in the FE crown. From their start in the 1970s, they have grown to more than 40,000 students registered to study an Access to HE Diploma in 2020–21 (QAA, 2023: 1). The students work towards gaining access to higher education through a one-year full-time course, mainly taking place in FE colleges. The chapter will explain how the access and WP movement have had a strong influence on the philosophy of FE and wider access to learning for the more disadvantaged members of the community.

7. *Higher Education (HE) in FE*

    FE colleges have been offering Higher Education level courses since the 1960s. In the early years, these were mainly represented by technical higher-level courses for employers. The historical analysis in this chapter will address how these programmes have more recently been devised and validated in partnership with Higher Education institutions and have provided pathways for many adults in advanced learning, research, and workplace learning, with some 11,000 people studying higher education in colleges (AoC, 2023: 10). The chapter debates how similar HE in FE is to the overall 'HE experience' and whether there is a special pedagogy that relates to HE in FE.

8. *Education for social justice, equality, and diversity*

    The diversity of FE has partly led to the development of its approaches to inclusion and social justice, but there has been a long history of this as a key objective of FE. The chapter will contain a historical analysis of consistent efforts to connect the disconnected and support the

Introducing the book xv

disabled and those with learning difficulties. It will allow the reader to recognise these efforts and come to conclusions about the sector's success or otherwise in addressing and increasing inclusion and social justice.

9. *Skills for Life (SfL)*

    This chapter will contain a historical analysis of how helping adults who have not gained basic *SfL* to build their confidence has been a key aspect of FES for many years. It will outline a rich record of success within institutions alongside a challenging history of funding, policy changes, and undervaluing. Different understandings and expectations of basic skills, key skills, core skills, functional skills, and *SfL* have been present in the history and development of this area, including the more recent but essential addition of digital literacy, and these will all be discussed.

10. *COVID-19*

    This chapter will provide an analysis of the special challenges faced during the COVID-19 pandemic and the deep effects on learners, teachers, and organisations. Discussion of how staff and sector organisations have argued with research data that some deep changes relating to student support and the use of learning technology took place during the pandemic and that they should have been retained and carried forward into the future. Experiences of FE teachers on the front line during COVID-19 are a particular feature of this chapter. The chapter will also discuss whether there has been a continuation of new ideas and approaches in the FE or a return to the status quo since the pandemic.

11. *14–19 Education*

    This chapter will outline how this FE subsector has developed from courses at college for difficult school pupils to an area of provision which has grown into an important but challenging part of the overall sector.

12. *Sustainability*

    This chapter will outline how sustainability is a key development area for FE in the same way as it is for all society and the whole of education. The chapter will outline the key issues relating to sustainability in FE, how they have been addressed in recent years, and what progress has been made in Education for Sustainable Development (ESD). An analysis will be included of the extent to which the sector is taking opportunities to build upon the energy of its students and their close ties to their local communities to reduce their environmental impact in innovative ways.

13. *Specialist Colleges*

    There are 67 colleges that are not FE colleges, and they include sixth-form colleges; land-based colleges; art, design, and performing arts colleges; and specialist-designated colleges/institutes of adult learning. Institutes of Technology operate as partnerships, often between FE providers, universities, and employers. This chapter summarises the provisions, roles, and responsibilities of these colleges, how they do (or don't) fit in the broader approaches and principles of FE, what current developments are taking place, and how different (or not) specialist colleges are to general colleges.

14. *Offender Learning*

    This little-known subsector involves learning that takes place in institutions where offenders are located or in the community after they have been convicted. The pedagogy of offender learning and the challenges of reproducing the same quality of learning experience for offenders in institutions as those in colleges and other learning centres will be discussed, as will the particular challenges for teachers in this FE subsector. A consideration of possible new directions for offender learning will also be discussed.

15. *Making connections – the prospects for FE*

This book concludes with a summary of the present situation of the FE sector, with final analyses of the relationship between government and other parts of UK education, and arguments for changes to poor practice and reinforcement and greater recognition of good practice in the future. The final chapter presents a positive view for the future and makes some recommendations for change and improvement.

This extensive range of chapters aims to provide the reader with a comprehensive and detailed picture of the FE sector which will be helpful both to those studying it and those working in it.

1 Introducing the sector

This first chapter provides an introduction to the further education (FE) sector as a whole using explanation, discussion, and analysis and supports this with two sector stories about students, teachers, or those working with the sector. The chapter starts with the definition of the sector as used in this book. There follows a general overview of what the sector does and who the students, teachers, and supporting organisations are, using key statistics relating to the sector. The diversity and complexity of FE, as reflected by both the range and scope of courses and those providing them, are then considered. An outline of the history of FE in England, including key historical developments, is then introduced.

The next section on FE policy addresses the way in which the sector has faced frequent redefinition, reorganisation, name changes, misunderstandings, and greater central government control, particularly over the last 30 years. The sector has been described as "for other people's children" (Orr, 2018: 253) and as "playing with the world's largest train set" (Keep, 2006: 47), and the thinking behind these statements is outlined. The chapter conclusion argues that it is difficult to locate a set of defining principles, values, and characteristics of the FE sector as a whole and discusses why this is the case.

Defining the further education sector

As can be seen from the contents and introduction to this book, the FE sector as it is represented here has nine subsectors or areas of provision and learning activity. There is overlap, and some elements are repetitive across and within subsectors, and it is very rare to see one definition that effectively and accurately conveys the range, scope, and diversity of the sector. The definition of the FE sector in this book does, therefore, need to be broad and inclusive in scope to represent all those subsectors. The nine subsectors included are listed in the same order as they are addressed by this book.

The FE sector includes teaching and learning activity in:

- FE colleges,
- Workplace learning organisations,
- Adult and community learning centres,
- Access to higher education courses,
- Higher education in FE,

DOI: 10.4324/9781003468455-1

- Functional skills and English as a second or other language (ESOL),
- Sixth form and specialist colleges,
- Offender learning,

none of which is delivered by schoolteachers.

General sector overview

Because the following chapters will include statistics about their own subsectors, the statistics included here are mainly general, but some statistics relating to subsectors, which may be repeated later, have also been included to provide a representative picture of the size and scope of FE.

Further education and skills in government data

The Office for National Statistics further education and skills data release of July 2023 includes these statistics:

> Adult (19+) funded further education and skills (including apprenticeships) participation in England for the 2022/23 academic year was 1,612,130, which was up 6.6 per cent from 2021/22.
> Community learning participation for the 2022/23 academic year. This includes a range of non-formal courses to promote civic engagement and community development was 274,090, which was up 10.7 per cent from 2021/22.
> Of the 1,612,130 adult (19+) government-funded further education and skills learners participating in 2022/23:
>
> - Females account for 60.5% (975,880).
> - Higher level (level 4 or above) participation increased by 8.4%, to 249,670 from 230,250 in 2021/22.
> - Learners recorded as Learners with a Learning Difficulty and/or Disability (LLDD) account for 18.3% of the cohort (285,250) – an increase of 12.6% from 253,370 in 2021/22.

All statistics are from the Office of National Statistics (2023: 1).
The data used do have a comment included, which are:

Impact of COVID-19 on reporting of FE and apprenticeship data

> Historic data in this release covers periods affected by varying COVID-19 restrictions, which will have impacted on FE provision and also provider reporting behaviour via the Individualised Learner Record. Therefore, extra care should be taken in comparing and interpreting data presented in this release.
>
> *(ibid.*: 2023)

Further education colleges

The Association of Colleges also provides regular statistics about FE colleges and specialist colleges, and it is helpful to add a selection of that data here. In their '*Key Facts 2022/23*' publication, the Association of Colleges (AoC) states:

> There are 228 colleges in England. 161 general further education colleges; 44 sixth form colleges; 11 land-based colleges; 2 art, design & performing arts colleges and 10 specialist designated colleges/institutes of adult learning (September 2022).
>
> (AoC, 2023: 4)

> 611,000 16- to 18-year-olds study in colleges.
> 46,000 16 to 18-year-olds undertake an apprenticeship though colleges.
>
> (AoC, 2023: 6)

> 649,000 adults above 25-years-old are students in colleges (2021/22).
>
> (AoC, 2023: 8)

Offender learning

There are also government statistics for offender learning, this time from the Ministry of Justice. From statistics relating to 2022/23:

> 63,744 prisoners participated in courses.
> This was a 28% increase on the 49,855 prisoners participating in courses last year.
> The number of completions for Accredited Programmes in custody increased. From 1 April 2022 to 31 March 2023, 4,135 accredited programmes were completed by offenders, representing an increase of 124% compared with the previous 12-month period.
>
> Ministry of Justice (2023: 1)

Staff numbers

Returning to the Association of Colleges key facts, colleges employ '103,000 full-time equivalent people, of which 49,000 are teaching staff—64% are female; 16% are from an ethnic minority background, and 5% have a learning difficulty and/or disability' (AoC, 2023: 48).

The government Further Education Workforce Data Collection (FEWDC) is another set of data from the Office for National Statistics and includes a helpful and broad set of data from the following providers:

- General Further Education Colleges (GFECs), including tertiary colleges;
- Sixth form colleges;
- Private sector public-funded providers, often referred to as Independent Training Providers (ITPs);
- Other public-funded providers.

4 *Introducing the sector*

This includes some Higher Education (HE) providers, some Local Authority (LA) providers, and a small number of University Technical Colleges (UTCs), specialist colleges, and 16–19 free schools.

For the academic year 2021/22, the figures are:

There are an estimated 205,200 people working in the Further Education Workforce, including:

- 81,400 teaching staff,
- 50,200 support staff,
- 47,200 admin staff,
- 19,200 management staff,
- 7,100 leadership staff.
- 51.0% of teaching staff teach vocational subjects as their main subject.

Office for National Statistics (2023: 1)

These sets of statistics, both from different sources (and not entirely consistent across the data sources used), give a powerful indication of both the size and scope of the FE sector. Accessing statistics across different subsectors and organisations is a major task, and although there are good and reliable sources, aggregating them into a generally comprehensive set of data about the sector is difficult; there is no good source of fully cross-sector data at present. This is not helpful in presenting and maintaining a clear understanding of the sector.

Sector story: Large training provider of the year 2023 – The Learning Curve Group

The Vocational Training and Charitable Trust operates awards for excellence in vocational training. The Learning Curve Group, which won this award in 2023, 'demonstrated dedication to providing outstanding outcomes for their learners and transforming lives through learning. From providing exceptional opportunities through their employer networks to ensuring that they support the diverse needs of all learners, regardless of circumstances' (VTCT, 2023: 2), they provide learning opportunities for more than 200,000 individuals a year and have achieved 'both "Good" and "Outstanding" grades from Ofsted' (*ibid.*: 3). They provide programmes in hair, beauty, barbering, construction, and military preparation and 'go above and beyond to take opportunities to those who need them most, striving to remove any barriers to the accessibility of education and training along the way' (*ibid.*: 3). This is a very large organisation in FE terms, but it has the key objectives about student inclusion, support, and progression, which are characteristic of the FE sector. Their relationships with employers also represent much of the FE sector when they state that they have:

Exceptional employer relationships with renowned organisations so we can provide real-salon training, industry insights, and high standards exposure to our amazing learners. We aim to stand out from other training providers in the industry by hosting and participating in talent showcases, global competitions like World Skills, and prestigious events like London Fashion Week.

(*ibid.*: 5)

This is a very good example of a large vocational training provider within the FE sector with strong learner- and employer-related core values.

Diversity and complexity

As we have seen, there are more than 2 million students in FE, and they are studying many subjects at various locations. These include colleges, workplaces, community centres, retail premises, vocational training centres, countryside- and land-based locations and online environments, and this is only a selection. It is often the case that more than one location of study will often be involved in the whole learning experience. We have seen a sample of sector statistics, but if someone was looking to gain an idea of the sector's scope in as easy a way as possible, how might they go about it? One simple way of finding out how the FE sector appears from the outside can be by browsing the course list of any FE college. This can be easily viewed online, and it is also still possible to access a hard copy of a college prospectus if that is a preference. The example used here is a medium-sized West Country Further Education College, Bath College. When starting, as new visitors often would, by viewing their course list on their website, Bath College lists 382 courses on offer. These range from Criminology to Printmaking, from Philosophy to First Aid for Mental Health, from Motor Vehicle Repair to Counselling, and many, many more. Courses are offered from entry level and at every level up to level 5. Many courses on offer are 'funded', i.e., the students do not pay a fee directly, but there are also many with fees listed that are 'non-funded', where the student or their employer or organisation will pay a fee (City of Bath College, 2023). Most people, once they are involved and 'in the system', whether students or teachers, only need to be properly aware of their own subject area and course, and perhaps one or two other areas that may be part of their study or teaching, and it is rare that anyone needs to navigate the whole system. As a prospective new student or their friend or member of family wishing to browse what is available, this could, however, be a difficult starting point, unless it was very clear what was being looked for, and the search engine found that quickly. Browsing the course lists on college websites would often bring this many results or even more. After undertaking a search like this, the breadth of FE would be clear, but the image of a coherent and clear sector would not.

> **Question for discussion**
>
> Look at the website, prospectus, course list, or programme outlines of your local FE College or Adult Education Centre and find the answers to these questions:
>
> - How many courses and subjects are offered and at how many levels?
> - How many different payment structures are available?

There is no national curriculum for FE, even though there are some powerful influencers of the sector curriculum, including central government, funding bodies, employer associations, community organisations, training bodies, public sector, or uniformed services bodies, to name but a few. Carrying out the task to answer the question for discussion illustrates at a simple level not only how diverse the FE curriculum is, which is one of its greatest strengths, but also how dense and complicated it is, which is one of its greatest problems. The complexity contributes to making the development of a powerful cross-sector and professional identity more difficult. That the FE sector is complex and difficult to define is not a new issue, as the selection of comments from research and reports on the sector below indicate:

> Post-compulsory education and training (PCET) in England is notable for its complexity.
> (Fisher and Simmons, 2010: 7)

> The further education (FE) sector is poorly defined and understood. It has been characterised as the 'everything else' sector because of the sheer breadth of its provision.
> (Institute for Government, 2012: 1)

> The FE sector has endured constant changes through the years with a very wide scope and lack of stability in both policy and funding. This has resulted in no single clear definition for FE.
> (Edge Foundation, 2021: 4)

Hodgson *et al.* (2018: 3) provide an insightful reflection from a comparison of the whole UK FE system with others internationally when they state:

> When visitors from overseas come to look at the 'UK education system' one of the first things we have to say is that there is no single system. Education, FE and skills are areas of devolved responsibility and have developed very differently in each of the four nations. That can present challenges of coherence, for instance where an employer seeks to train apprentices in more than one nation within the UK, or a training provider wants to operate across boundaries.
>
> It also presents a unique opportunity. As with federal nations such as the US and Australia, it provides us with a potential laboratory to test and improve our education policies. Four nations share many characteristics of labour market, organisation and culture and yet are pursuing sometimes very different approaches, with a variety of outcomes.

These comments illustrate again the breadth of FE and its resulting complexity. Naming the sector is another major issue. Three different names used for the sector are used in the previous comments across four publications. They are 'Post Compulsory Education and Training (PCET)', 'FE', and 'FE and skills'. The most recent quote, from 2021, references the 'FE sector', but the official title for the sector at that time was (and still is) the 'Further Education and Skills sector'. Most publications about FE and Skills (including this one) choose to use what they consider to be the most appropriate sector name and definition for their publication, rather than using the current and official government sector title. This demonstrates an uncertainty and hesitancy about the sector name, or even a strong dislike of the name for their sector, and that is from professionals working in, or associated with FE. It would be most unusual for someone writing about the other education sectors of 'pre-school', 'primary', 'secondary', or 'higher' education, but in descriptions of FE this is commonplace.

Question for discussion

What do you believe could be done to make the awareness of and understanding about the FE sector clearer to the public at large?

A brief history of the FE sector

Given that FE subsectors have a history of their own, this section of the chapter draws together an outline of some key historical events to explain how the sector has developed. In 1563, the Statute of Artificers or the Artificers and Apprentices Act 1562 was passed, which introduced a wide range of ways of regulating the national labour market. It was an attempt to bring together the already existing apprenticeship system, which had previously been organised in a variety of ways. The master of the apprentice would have control of the seven years; the apprentice would serve up to the age of 24 years. This statute:

> Sanctioned the control a master would have over their apprentice. It was the mechanism which gave control to the master over the apprentice's livelihood. The apprentice would normally live in the same premises as their master. The master would receive payment for providing the apprentice with their training, knowledge and developing the skills of their craft.
>
> (Fletcher, 2019: 4)

In terms of FE relevance, it made apprenticeships compulsory for anyone wishing to enter a trade, and it remained as law until 1814. The apprenticeship requirement became law alongside several other measures, including imposing maximum wages, restricting workers' freedom of movement, regulating training, and fixing prices. This apprenticeship part of the statute can be seen to have offered some stability for those wishing to pursue a trade. Despite the positive aspects of the Statute, it can be seen how it also resulted in controls that were not likely to give rewards and status to tradespeople. Nevertheless, apprenticeships became 'the dominant form of work-related training up to the 1960s' (Armitage *et al.*, 2003: 245). They still play a significant part in the world of work-based learning in FE today.

In 1823, Mechanics Institutes were established, and they were providers of vocational training intended for those from disadvantaged social backgrounds. By 1826, they were working with 600,000 people. Mechanics Institutes were often sponsored by middle-class male philanthropists and intended to provide opportunities for self-improvement through adult education, and by the nineteenth century, the buildings' housing Mechanics Institutes had become visible, striking local symbols of learning, and housed leisure facilities in many parts of the country. The growing development of those learning within the institutes did result in fears among employers and others that the growing confidence of the working classes who participated could result in a workers' revolution. There never was such a revolution, but the Mechanics Institutes did make a significant contribution to what could be seen as early FE. It needs to be observed at this stage that these changes and improvements very rarely benefitted women.

The Education Act of 1944 legislated for there to be 'adequate facilities' for full-time and part-time education 'for persons over compulsory school age' and 'leisure-time occupation' (Education Act, 1944: 34). This act is seen as 'a landmark in the history of further education' (Cantor and Roberts, 2021: 2). The act raised the school-leaving age to 15 and requested (not required) local authorities to provide post-15 education in colleges. These colleges developed and grew in significant numbers and could be commercial, art, or technical colleges. This legislation produced a significant growth in FE, and colleges of Higher Education and colleges for those that catered for lower-level qualifications also grew significantly and became the beginning of what would be called a FE college today. Between 1946 and 1970, student numbers in FE grew from 1,595,000 to 3,174,000 (*ibid.*: 1).

In 1964, Industrial Training Boards (ITBs) were created with the intention of removing skill shortages and improving the quality of industrial training, as it had been concluded by the government that 'if industrial training is to be adequate, it can no longer be left to the voluntary efforts of industry' (ibid.: 11). By 1971, 27 ITBs covering 15 million workers were in place, and they were paid for by a levy on employers. By the 1990s, the situation in FE had become reasonably stable, and for many of those in FE who had experienced a strong level of independent, local FE provision within their local area, it was something of a surprise when a significant piece of legislation, the Further and Higher Education Act (Stationery Office, 1992), was implemented in 1992. FE Colleges came out of local authority control after this act, and they became independent business corporations. This was argued at the time to offer a significant increase in independence for FE, but it marked the start of what has proved to be a continuing trend of more significant involvement of central government and a growth in marketisation, managerialism, and monitoring of FE. Over time, there was a growth in the requirements to collect performance data, which were then used to provide performance indicators and to establish benchmarks against which aspects of FE could be analysed. Expectations from the government that efficiency measures would be carried out became the normal currency of expectation rather than judgements made based on professional responsibility and workplace experience and competence by those working in the sector. These changes in professional role and professional identity of the sector and its workers have been referred to as the 'terrors of performativity' (Ball, 2003: 215). Performativity is a process where workplace performance is subjected to what may be considered to be excessive and constant monitoring, and the questioning of performance and constant measuring outcomes to control and dictate performance. The 1992 act was a clear point where this approach started, and it has become more ingrained in FE (from outside) since then. To reinforce the 1992 Act, in 2003, the first inspections of the FE sector were started by the Office for Standards in Education (Ofsted).

By 1997, a labour government was in place, and education was one of their central priorities, with a manifesto commitment to 'get 250,000 young unemployed off benefit and into work' (New Labour, 1997: 1). In 1999, it introduced a major development and change to FE learning in its white paper *Learning to succeed*. In 2000, the Learning and Skills Act was introduced, and one national body – the Learning and Skills Council for England (LSC) – was created to cover all areas of non-Higher Education, post-16 education and training, plus 50 local learning and skills councils. These new organisations were given the role of developing opportunities that would encourage FE learning among post-16 teenagers and adults. They were also intended to support more tailor-made FE provision to meet local needs while also boosting national economic performance and standards.

There have been genuine and well-considered attempts to improve and develop the FE sector. One example was the *Wolf Report* of 2010. Professor Alison Wolf of King's College, London, was commissioned by the Secretary of State for Education to review vocational education. The report did find many examples of good practice from both employers and colleges with strong vocational learning taking place for 14–19-year-old students. Overall, however, the key findings of the report were that the variability of quality and consistency across vocational education was letting down the students it served. The system was seen as inflexible and inconsistent and did not always support progression to employment and further training. What was considered more important at the time, however, was that the Wolf Report judged that there were significantly more qualifications on offer than what was needed, that a significant proportion of them were of little value in the employment, further, and higher education market, and that this resulted in confusion and difficulty in equivalence, which also made progression for the students involved too complicated and difficult (Wolf, 2011). The Wolf Report recommendations included reviewing and improving the range of vocational qualifications and significantly improving the system through which vocational education and qualifications operated.

In 2007, the government introduced a requirement for new teaching staff to be suitably trained, a major shift in Initial Teacher Education for the FE sector. It then planned to revoke that change in 2012, even though it had strong support in the sector. In the end, the government introduced reforms to Initial Teacher Training qualifications and structures, and despite them including some positive elements, they led to 'confusion and concern' (Allison, 2023: 33). There were elements within the changes that were supported by the sector, but they were not sufficiently clear and coherent. Since their introduction, these changes have led to continued variation in training and a weak line of supply for new teachers in FE.

More recent FE-related initiatives have included a *Skills for Jobs* white paper (DfE, 2021). In the paper, the government proposed a 'Lifetime Skills Guarantee' alongside a 'Lifelong Loan Entitlement', which would include enabling members of the community to easily access a loan for a higher technical course or a full-length university degree. There is an assurance to make sure 'everyone has access to education and training that will help them to get a great job' (DfE, 2021: 5). Alongside this, 'upgrades to FE colleges across the country' will be made. How far these proposals have progressed is not clear at the time of writing this book, but they do illustrate what has been described as a 'constant policy churn' (City and Guilds, 2019: 1). The Association of Colleges response to the white paper was less than enthusiastic. 'The full *Skills for Jobs* white paper has a lot of detail about government plans, but it is worth noting that some parts of college activity and life are barely covered.' (AoC, 2021: 1)

Sector story – The college student – Brian

Brian has lived most of his life in Jamaica but is now living in England and has always been interested in cars and car mechanics, often helping family members and friends when repairing their cars. He would love to become a mechanic but has real difficulties with reading, writing, and maths. One of his friends suggested that he considers joining a community-based adult education English and maths course that runs at the local community centre. He goes along to an open evening, meets the tutor and some of the students, and decides to give it a try. The community centre also has access to computers and Information Technology training, and he can start on English, maths, and computer literacy within the next two weeks. As he can learn at his own pace, he moves forward steadily and increases his own confidence and competence, gaining entry-level qualifications and signing up for the next levels. These skill improvements help him get a basic job in a garage, and shows his potential and moves ahead with the higher-level qualifications as he builds his confidence there; he has started on his path to become a mechanic.

> **Question for discussion**
>
> Ask a group of approximately six people what they know about the FE sector and what it does.

The sector's policy development has been characterised by frequent and major changes, shifts in government approaches, and sector name changes. Blair (2009: 96) argues that 'the function of FE has changed as the history of the society around it has unfolded'. There has been an often remarked-upon tendency for the sector to be seen as less important than other branches of education, and there have been constant changes in ministerial responsibility on an ongoing basis for over 20 years.

'Education for other people's children' is a term coined in an article, which argued that FE colleges 'are often poorly understood by policymakers who have had little if any experience of these institutions which cater mainly to the less privileged in society' (Orr, 2018: 253). This is an unfortunate description that the FE and Skills sector has found difficult to shake off. Another categorisation of the sector came from Ewart Keep in 2006, who described the government's approach to FE as 'Playing with the biggest train set in the world' (Keep, 2006: 47). The Leader of the Opposition, Sir Keir Starmer, has also described Education in 2023 as suffering from a 'Class Ceiling', and the FE sector often recruits students who may well have already experienced that while at school or in their earlier education.

Perhaps the most significant evidence to suggest that governments do not consider FE to be important is the incredible number of changes of the minister responsible for it. City and Guilds provided a regular update on these details, and in their most recent report in 2019, they firstly commented on the overall progress of 'skills policy' as a 'constant churn of both government initiatives and skills ministers' and highlighted 'the lack of institutional memory hampering good and informed decision making' (City and Guilds, 2019: 2).

The report then goes on to outline the ministerial changes that have taken place relating to skills (This usually includes a remit for FE.):

> In our Sense & Instability publications in 2014 and 2016 we reported on the changes in responsibility for skills policy in Government at a ministerial level.
> In 2016 we reported that skills policy had been the responsibility of 65 different Secretaries of State over the last 25 years, this figure now stands at 70.
> This is in comparison, with 20 Secretaries of State up from 19 in charge of schools policy and 21 up from 19 in charge of Higher Education over the course of the same period.
> (City and Guilds, 2019: 64)

Conclusion

The discussions, descriptions, and examples in this chapter have demonstrated a number of items. The FE sector is large and complex, difficult to define, and works with a very diverse and large number of students. The sector provides opportunities for many members of the community, including vocational trainees, A-level students, adult education students, disabled young adults and adults, managers, teachers, and those who are disadvantaged. In the best providers, students in the sector will find opportunities for support, achievement, and progression, and this may be for students who have not succeeded fully in compulsory education. It is difficult to define the sector, and this is, in part, due to the breadth and depth of its provision range of learning locations and organisations, but the approaches to and achievements of its students should provide a great deal to be proud of. How much the intervention and guidance from government helps the achievement of those goals and opportunities is an ongoing question, but the overall indicators are of a less esteemed sector, which deserves better.

Summary points

- A definition and general overview are provided of what the sector does using key statistics, examples, and relevant research relating to the sector, its curriculum, its students, and its workers.
- The diversity and complexity of FE overall are explained and exemplified.
- A selection of events from the history of FE in England with comments on their impact are analysed.
- Two 'sector stories' from FE are included: one relating to an independent training provider and one relating to a student.
- A discussion of government policy in relation to the sector and its effects is introduced.
- A selection of key characteristics of the sector and its purpose are outlined, while arguing that it is very difficult to identify stated sector-wide objectives and characteristics, and there is no source of cross-sector data.

Recommended reading

Tummons, J. (2019) *PCET: Learning and teaching in the post compulsory sector*. London: Sage.

References

Allison, J. (2023) Fragmentation or focus? The precarious nature of initial teacher training within the English further education sector. *PRACTICE*, 5(1), pp. 27–40, DOI: 10.1080/25783858.2023.2177559

Armitage, A., Bryant, R., Dunnill, R., Hayes, D., Hudson, A., Kent, J., Lawes, S. and Renwick, M. (2003) *Teaching and training in post compulsory education*. Buckingham: Open University Press.

Association of Colleges (2021) *Skills for jobs white paper*. London: AoC. Available at: https://www.aoc.co.uk/news-campaigns-parliament/work-in-parliament/governments-fe-reform-agenda/skills-for-jobs-white-paper (Accessed 16 October 2023).

Association of Colleges (2023) *College key facts 2022/23*. London: AoC.

Ball, S. (2003) The teacher's soul and the terrors of performativity. *Journal of Education Policy*, 18(2), pp. 215–228.

Blair, E. (2009) A further education college as a heterotopia. *Research in Post-Compulsory Education*, 14(1), pp. 93–101.

Cantor, L.M. and Roberts, I.F. (2021) *Further education in England and Wales*. Abingdon: Routledge.

City and Guilds (2019) *Sense and instability: Executive summary*. London: City and Guilds.

City of Bath College (2023) *Course search 10/10/2023*. Available at: https://www.bathcollege.ac.uk/course/search?offset=1 (Accessed 10 October 2023).

Department for Education (2021) *Skills for jobs: Lifelong learning for opportunity and growth*. London: Department for Education.

Edge Foundation (2021) *Further education at the centre of economic and social recovery. Next steps for our plan for further education*. London: Edge Foundation.

Fisher, R. and Simmons, R. (2010) What is the lifelong learning sector? In J. Avis, R. Fisher and R. Thompson (Eds) *Teaching in lifelong learning: A guide to theory and practice*. Maidenhead: Open University Press.

Fletcher, R. (2019) *Experiential learning and experience of learning through vocational education: the trailblazer apprenticeship*. In: The Society of Legal Scholars, 110th Annual Conference, 3–6 September 2019, University of Central Lancashire.

Further and Higher Education Act (1992) London: Stationery Office.

Hodgson, A., Gallacher, J., Irwin, T., James, D. and Spours, K. (2018) *FE and skills across the four countries of the UK: New opportunities for policy learning.* London: Edge Foundation.

Institute for Government (2012) *Choice and competition in further education.* London: Institute for Government.

Keep, E. (2006) State control of the English education and training system: Playing with the biggest trainset in the world. *Journal of Vocational Education and Training,* 58(1), pp. 47–64.

Ministry of Justice (2023) *Official statistics bulletin - Published 28 September 2023. Prison education statistics and accredited programmes in custody April 2022 to March 2023.* London: Ministry of Justice.

New Labour (1997) *Because Britain deserves better.* London: The Labour Party.

Office for National Statistics (2023a) *Academic year 2022/23 further education and skills – published 20 July 2023.* London: Office for National Statistics. Available at: https://explore-education-statistics.service.gov.uk/find-statistics/further-education-and-skills (Accessed 14 October 2023).

Office for National Statistics (2023b) *Academic year 2021/22 further education Workforce.* London: Office for National Statistics. Available at: https://explore-education-statistics.service.gov.uk/find-statistics/further-education-workforce (Accessed 14 October 2023).

Office for Standards in Education (Ofsted) (2018) *Further education and skills inspection report – Bath College.* Manchester: Ofsted.

Orr, K. (2018) Further education colleges in the United Kingdom: Providing education for other people's children. In R. Latiner Raby and E.J. Valeau (Eds) *Handbook of comparative studies on community colleges and Global counterparts* (1st ed.) (Springer International Handbooks of Education). Cham: Springer International Publishing AG, DOI: 10.1007/978-3-319-50911-2_42

The Education Act 1944 (1944). London: HMSO.

Vocational Training Charitable Trust (2023) *Winner spotlight – Large training provider of the year.* Eastleigh: VTCT. Available at: https://www.vtct.org.uk/2023/09/21/winner-spotlight-ltp-of-the-year/ (Accessed 15 October 2024).

Wolf, A. (2011) *Vocational education: The Wolf report.* London: Department for Education.

2 Further education colleges

Introduction

This chapter begins with a definition of further education (FE) colleges, their place in the FE sector as the main provider overall, an indication of the purpose they strive for, and the values they claim to stand for. Data regarding students, staff, and college progress in inspections is then introduced and analysed to clarify the members of the community that study and work in FE colleges, and the way those figures have changed over a five-year period. The first sector story in this chapter is about Bath College as an example of a medium-sized institution. The section on the history of colleges highlights considerable post-war growth in student and staff numbers, early complications with developing a coherent overall system, and the first experiences of receiving limited funding whilst seeking to ensure colleges are at their best.

A historical analysis of the development of FE colleges since they became independent incorporated institutions in 1992 to the present day follows and draws out the growth in government intervention, pressure on funding, and frequent changes of ministerial responsibility. The historical analysis also outlines colleges' attempts to maintain their provision and its quality even under great duress.

The second sector story is of Ellen, an example of a female 16–18-year-old college student.

A brief comparison of English FE colleges and US Community colleges is included next, and this helps to highlight both differences and similarities between the two types of college, and also through the comparison, further emphasises the key features of FE colleges.

The last section of the chapter introduces the sector story of Norton Radstock College – a small college in an area with a relatively small population, its history, and eventual merger with a larger college.

Definition

The Education and Training Foundation (ETF) describes itself as 'the expert body for professional development and standards in Further Education (FE) and Training in England' (ETF, 2023: 1). It has produced what is one of the clearer definitions of what an FE college is, and states that 'General Further Education (GFE) Colleges are one of the main providers of further education in England and outnumber all the other types of college combined'. It continues to state that they:

> Offer a wide range of programmes. They have a strong focus on supporting learners to develop valuable workplace skills through providing technical and professional education and training.

DOI: 10.4324/9781003468455-2

Almost all offer apprenticeships and have close partnerships with employers. As well as vocational (job-based) courses, many GFE colleges offer academic (subject-based) and higher education (HE) courses.' They also have 'a wide range of learners studying on a full-time or a part-time basis. Most have completed their statutory education and are over the age of 16. However, some colleges offer courses for 14 and 15-year-olds. GFE colleges also offer adult education courses so there are learners of all ages.

(ETF, 2019: 8)

As has been discussed in Chapter 1, such clarity is somewhat rare when seeking to define FE, so this definition is welcome and is one of the more straightforward we will come across in this book.

Another helpful and more concise definition emerged from a recent study of college leaders (Azumah Dennis et al., 2019). The leaders in the study were asked, 'what is FE for?' From their answers, it was clear that they believed that the two key purposes of FE colleges were:

1) To provide opportunities for the development of individual learners;
2) To make an active contribution to society (Azumah Dennis et al., 2019: 4).

This could of course be argued to be a definition that most people would agree was appropriate for all education, but it was generated from interviews with 25 college leaders during a period of considerable pressure on resources of all kinds and considerable pressure from government in the case of this study, so it gives a strong indication of the sector ethos.

Who are the students and staff of FE colleges?

The Association of Colleges (AoC) regularly provides data about FE colleges, and a summary of data from 2017/18 to 2022/23 is set out below:

2017/18 Colleges work with 2.2 million people.

There are 181 general further education colleges.
1.4 million adults and 712,000 16–18 year olds study in colleges.

72 per cent of colleges were judged GOOD or Outstanding for overall effectiveness in their most recent inspection.

27% of students are from ethnic minority backgrounds.
17% of students have learning difficulties and/or a disability.

There are 60,000 teaching staff (AoC, 2017: 2–23).

2022/33 Colleges work with 1.6 million people.

There are 161 general FE colleges.

913,000 adults and 611,000 16–18 year olds study in colleges.

The average age of college students is 27.

91 per cent of colleges were judged Good or Outstanding for overall effectiveness in their most recent inspection.

> 23% of students are from ethnic minority backgrounds.
> 53% of students are female.
> 22% of students have learning difficulties and/or a disability.

There are 49,000 teaching staff of whom 64 per cent are female; 16 per cent are from an ethnic minority background, and 5 per cent have a learning difficulty and/or a disability (AoC, 2022: 2–25).

It can be seen from these figures that some significant differences can be identified over the five-year period since 2017/18. The most striking difference is that between 2.2 million students in 2017/18 and 1.6 million in 2022/23. Such a large reduction is very difficult to fully explain, and the AoC provides the statistics but does not comment on them. The number of adults in FE colleges has reduced more so than for 16–18 year olds (from 1.4 million to 91,300 for adults and from 712 to 611,000 for 16–18 year olds). The reasons for this decline are not entirely clear, although there has been an ongoing decline in FE student numbers during the recent years of austerity. The COVID-19 pandemic is responsible for some of the reduction, as numbers have not yet recovered from its impact. The main reason for a smaller number of colleges (181 down to 161) is that there has been a growth in college mergers. The AoC explains this by stating:

> Since the 2015 general election, there has been an increase in the number of college mergers and a new option for sixth form colleges to convert to become 16–19 academies. The government's post-16 area review programme required every college to consider their future and provided official encouragement for mergers.
>
> (AoC, 2023: 1)

There have been 78 college-to-college mergers since the 2015 general election. There will be more discussion about 16–19 academies in the chapter on specialist colleges. The increase from 72 per cent to 91 per cent in Ofsted outcomes is a very good achievement for colleges and a profile that demonstrates overall improvements in the quality of all aspects of provision, despite the difficult circumstances. The percentage of students from ethnic minorities has reduced but is broadly similar to that in schools, and the percentage of students with a disability and/or learning difficulty has increased from 17 to 22 per cent. School data is still classified as Special Educational Needs (SEN), and the current figure is 17 per cent of students.

Sector story – Bath College

A good way of finding out what a particular college does and how well it does it is to view its report from the Office for Standards in Education (Ofsted). Some of the comments from Bath College's latest Ofsted report:

> Bath College is a medium-sized general further education college, formed in April 2015 by the merger of City of Bath College and Norton Radstock College. The college has sites in Bath city

centre and at Somer Valley in North East Somerset. Approximately 2,000 learners aged 16 to 19 follow study programmes. Similar numbers of adults follow full- or part-time courses, around half with subcontractors. The college has 502 apprentices.

Learners attend the college from across Bath and North East Somerset, which has a population of 187,800. Bath is mainly prosperous, but areas of economic deprivation exist in the city and in North East Somerset. Unemployment is lower than the national level, although slightly above the wider South West region. The proportion of the population with level 2 qualifications and above is higher than that nationally, as is the proportion of pupils who achieve GCSE grade A* to C or 4 to 9 in English and mathematics at key stage 4.

(Ofsted, 2018: 2)

In terms of the Ofsted grade given, Bath College gained a 'good' rating from their inspection in January 2018. Key comments included:

- Governors, leaders, and managers have successfully created the new Bath College.
- Their clear focus on improvement has led to good outcomes for learners.
- Learners receive good teaching and learning, and managers provide a diverse range of courses and apprenticeships for learners and employers.
- A high proportion of learners achieve their qualifications, including good grades in English and mathematics GCSE.
- Learners gain very good interpersonal and practical skills, and develop appropriate behaviours and attitudes that equip them well for employment.
- The high-quality, industry-standard facilities on both sites contribute well to learners' good progress and outcomes.
- Disadvantaged and vulnerable learners, and those with additional needs, receive excellent support and practical assistance to help them overcome the difficulties they face (Ofsted, 2018: 1).

Having explained the 'official', and generally positive view of Bath College, the college's website provides a very helpful insight into how connections between the college, its staff, and the local community can be developed. Bath College has a history of training in Stone Carving and, working with its local community, developed a project to create stone carvings for the grounds of a local primary school. Stone carving students from the college worked with teachers and pupils at a local primary school to design and create stone woodland creatures that could be displayed within the school grounds. The students were able to take responsibility, develop their designs for the stone carving, and work across generations to create special items for the school environment. The stone carvings are now proudly displayed around the school grounds. The community-based project has been beneficial for students and staff of Bath College, as well as pupils, teachers, and parents at the school concerned.

The combination of the Ofsted report and the community project example shows a college with a strong vision of student support, planning and creating projects, and activities to build skills and confidence at all levels with its students, whilst also making a real contribution to the local community and business in the professional and creative way in which it works.

> **Question for discussion**
>
> Find out how many FE colleges there are within 20 miles of where you live. If there are none, extend your search to 30 miles.
>   Research enough about them to do a brief comparison of at least two colleges.
>   Make a note of the similarities and differences.

The history of FE colleges – From rapid growth to tension, pressure, and challenge

Hillier (2006: 20) observes that from early in its history FE has had 'a constant urge to ensure that the working population has the knowledge and skills to compete with other countries and to be at the forefront of technological development'. Even looking back as far as the nineteenth century, 'it can be seen that the government has always been concerned that other countries have the competitive edge, and that if we don't improve our own skills in the workforce we are doomed to economic failure'. This approach influences the whole history of FE colleges.

In Chapter1, the 1944 Education Act was discussed, with its requirements to provide adequate facilities for full-time and part-time education for persons over compulsory school age in addition to leisure-time occupation. Between the years of 1946 and 1956, a pattern of technical colleges had been developed, which consisted of three main types: regional colleges, area colleges, and local colleges. There were 22 regional colleges by 1956, and already the work in the larger regional colleges had moved towards more advanced technical levels, whilst the local college's provision had moved towards mainly non-advanced FE. As a precursor to more recent times, one barrier to the overall development of FE colleges was a lack of adequate funding. Despite this the teaching workforce increased from 4,500 to 12,000, and this was mainly in the larger colleges (Cantor and Roberts, 2021). By 1959, the Crowther Report in 1957 had highlighted the lack of opportunities for working-class school leavers and recommended that the school leaving age should be raised to 16, and that county colleges for compulsory part-time education should be created as a matter of national policy. Crowther's recommendations gained much positive comment, and the report led directly to a government white paper in 1961, which led to the majority of local colleges setting up courses for the training of 'junior technicians, craftsmen, and operatives' (Cantor and Roberts, 2021: 8). By the 1970s, more young workers who were employed in jobs with little training and who did not need qualifications joined programmes that were available in colleges for them and unemployed adults. This provided a 'second chance', and provision of this kind has now become a strong feature of FE colleges. However, FE colleges were still neither part of a national strategy nor was there any clear understanding of how to evaluate the overall quality of colleges, their programmes, or their outcomes.

By 1980, the Manpower Services Commission (MSC) had been set up to provide a more co-ordinated approach to skills development and college responsibilities. By 1990, MSC no longer existed, and direct intervention by central government with little consultation or dialogue with colleges had started to further undermine college's autonomy. Some important but harsh judgements about FE colleges were contained in an important Audit Commission Report in 1985. Hodgson *et al.* (2015: 11–12) summarised the findings, including that 'LEAs could save £50 million a year through better management and organisation' of FE colleges. They continued to state that 'more effective use of existing staff would make it possible to teach 75,000 additional students at no extra cost' (Audit Commission, 1985). Between 1988 and 1992, the Conservative Government moved towards removing FE colleges from local authority control, and this took place after the passing of the Further and Higher Education Act in 1992. This Act made colleges corporations with their own budgets, which were independent of the local authority, and this process was known as 'incorporation'. Over the following years, however, as a funding model from the newly created Further Education Funding Council (FEFC) took hold, feelings of independence started to wane. The new funding approach replaced funding per 'full time equivalent student' with funding of the 'unit of activity' that was paid for 'entry' of the student, their continuing presence or remaining 'on programme', and 'achievement' of their qualification or learning goals. The end result was that if students did not remain on course or achieve their end result, there was a significant reduction in college funding. The positive aspect of this change was that colleges needed to significantly improve student participation, support, and achievement, but it did not help to develop a unified and coherent set of FE colleges; it signalled the first in a series of policy changes, which rarely helped to make working and managing in colleges simpler. At the same time, however, the service provided to the students did begin to improve considerably, as colleges worked to ensure their students did join, remain, and achieve. This probably would not have happened, or would have happened much slower, had these funding changes not taken place.

Initially in the first year after incorporation, independence did appear to college principals to have arrived as they started to believe that controls and cuts in resources by local authorities were not taking place, and that colleges had gained a higher profile than before incorporation. From incorporation to the present day, the history of FE colleges has become:

> A story of frequent reform, fluctuating policy interest and changing policy actors and influencers. It reflects not only the shifting perspectives and priorities of policymakers in England, but also a sector almost permanently in search of itself, struggling to define its mission and purpose in a context of near-constant reform and regular political upheaval.
>
> (Keep *et al.*, 2021: 5)

Keep *et al.* (2021: 4) provide a coherent and focussed analysis of the general trends of the post-incorporation history. They argue that there has often been

> A tendency on the part of policymakers in recent times to confuse change with reform. Reform implies improvement and progress, change is just change, often for change's sake. There has been much of the latter, and relatively little of the former.

There have been many reviews, reports, and associated government initiatives, and for those working in the sector this often produces changes, adjustments, and reorganisations, which have had significant impacts and implications. Government ministers have stayed in post on average between eighteen months and two years, and they were all wishing to introduce developments 'that at the time were seen as 'the next big thing' but are now almost totally forgotten footnotes in history' (*ibid.*: 4). Overall, the

> Removal of local authority control of the polytechnics and further education colleges (via incorporation) represented one moment in what proved to be a series of decisive shifts away

from local decision making. The process has been characterised as one of delocalisation, centralisation, and nationalisation.

(*ibid.*: 5)

Despite all of these negatives, returning to the data about colleges from the start of the chapter – a good trend of improvement in Ofsted grades for colleges can be seen. This is an achievement to be particularly proud of, and it is fair to say that much of what

> …. Colleges achieve occurs despite of rather than because of the intentions and incentives set by national policy. Colleges are, to some extent at least, masters or mistresses of their own destinies, and they build upon histories and institutional legacies and trajectories that are very varied.

(*ibid.*: 6)

Sector story – Ellen – The college student

Ellen worked hard and gained a range of GCSEs at school; she has demonstrated artistic and design talent at school but has not felt confident enough to move into relevant A-Levels after completing her GCSEs. On considering her next steps, Ellen visited her local FE college. She was shown the design, fashion, and art facilities and how her study would be supported by the tutors and other staff in the college. Ellen had never felt confident with study at school and was advised that studying childcare might be a good option for her after GCSEs. Ellen chose to sign up for a Level 2 course in Fashion and Design at her local college, from which she could progress to level 3 at the end of one year and potentially progress to higher education and a degree course after that. Almost from the very start of the course, Ellen felt more confident, and felt more that she was being treated like an adult. Her tutors were very helpful and supportive; once she started undertaking assessments, she received very positive feedback and a good grade on almost every occasion in her first year. At the end of the first year, her tutors gave glowing feedback about her progress to her and her parents, and she has now progressed into year 2 as a confident young woman. When talking about her first year, she says,

> When I started, I really wasn't sure how I was going to get on at college, but the tutors, the environment and the facilities all helped me to settle in quickly and genuinely believe I could do well. College is certainly the right place for me.

A brief comparison of English further education colleges with US community colleges

To highlight more clearly the nature of English FE colleges, this section briefly compares English FE colleges with US community colleges. In a number of very important ways, the two institutions are different, particularly in the course lengths they offer, but many of the broader characteristics are similar. English FE colleges have already been defined in this chapter, and 'Education USA' – the State Department website provides this description of US community colleges:

Community colleges offer two-year programs leading to the Associate of Arts (AA) or Associate of Science (AS) degree. These colleges also have technical and vocational programs with close links to secondary/high schools, community groups, and employers in the local community. You can find large community colleges with multiple campuses in an urban/suburban setting or small campuses in a rural setting, and community colleges offer a variety of support services and cross-cultural programs, including tutoring, advising, career planning, study skills, and counselling (Education USA, 2023: 1).

Although this definition does not make it clear, it is also the case that community colleges have offered migrant, minority, and poor citizens a gateway to opportunities they may not otherwise have found. A comparative study of FE colleges and community colleges from 2012 started by drawing attention to the fact that, at the time, 'there is no recognised term for all institutions that offer mostly post-secondary education and training connected to economic, social, and personal growth' (Jephcote and Latiner Raby, 2012: 349). Key differences are that community colleges' main programme offer is two-year courses designed to bridge the students into higher education. FE colleges in Britain do not do this in quite the same way, but Jephcote and Latiner Raby (*ibid.*: 350) continue to state that 'both of these institutions share at the forefront of providing educational opportunities for non-traditional students and facilitating their progression into continuing and higher educational options'. They also argue that:

Colleges of Further Education (UK) and Community Colleges (US) have changed the post-secondary educational landscape, providing educational opportunities for large numbers of non-traditional students – especially those who are returning to learning or who are first-generation higher educational learners. The fact that access to these community college global counterparts can be gained by the broad spectrum of the population is notable. ... By allowing all students access, community college global counterparts offer a number of opportunities for students – many of whom are not university bound, and often effectively excluded from participation in higher education due, inter alia, to social status, poverty, race, ethnicity, age or gender (*ibid.*: 350).

The study helps to emphasise that the numbers of non-traditional students in both institutions are significant in the way that they 'keep open the door for learning' (*ibid.*: 361). As recent years have seen an increase in pressures on both institutions, maintaining such an open-door approach has become more difficult, and it has also become more difficult for the students involved to complete their programmes due to other external pressures. Jephcote and Latiner Raby (2012) suggest that the key challenge for both English FE colleges and US community colleges is not to ask 'who' to let in but 'how' to best service all' (*ibid.*: 361).

> **Question for discussion**
>
> Produce your own definition of what constitutes an FE college and what characteristics they would have, using what you have read in this chapter so far, and make a list of your suggestions.

Sector story – Norton Radstock College – A small college with local roots

Coal was discovered in Radstock in the 1700s and was still one of the most important industries of the town and the surrounding area of Norton Radstock, which included the nearby town of Midsomer Norton. In 1947, Norton Radstock College was opened and over the next 20 years trained and retrained miners, agricultural mechanics, and other mainly technical trades; it became a well-respected centre of mainly technical education in the local community. As is generally the case, the Radstock population was pleased to have a thriving local college, and their interest and of those in the other local towns and villages helped the college to thrive. The range of courses at the college grew so that, by the early 1980s, there were departments in engineering, business, general studies, agriculture, health and social care, and adult and community learning. The college also took on responsibility for an adult education centre at Keynsham, on the southern edge of Bristol. Courses were offered from what was level 1 at that time up to A-Level, with other advanced technical courses. There were 5,589 students when the college was first inspected in January 1999, of whom 782 were full time. The inspection report (FEFC, 1999: 2) commented that the college:

> has a number of important collaborative arrangements, including productive partnerships with the West of England TEC. It works closely with other colleges and schools in the Bath and Bristol areas, particularly in co-ordinating resources and training through effective use of IT. There are also links with two universities for the provision of higher-level qualifications in IT and teacher education. The college is actively involved in a number of community projects, including an initiative to address local economic and social regeneration funded through the government's single regeneration fund.

Despite these positive comments, some of the weaknesses observed were:

> The college should: address low achievement and poor retention in some subjects; improve the recording and use of student achievement data; ensure there is rigorous monitoring by all managers against clear targets; improve student services for part-time students; assess more accurately the quality of teaching and learning; and address weaknesses in quality assurance.
> (*ibid.*: 1)

The overall result was a mixture of four grade 2s (good) and five grade 3s (satisfactory).

As a small college in an era when colleges tended to be considerably larger than Norton Radstock, maintaining the level of quality analysis, data collection, and improvement systems was always difficult for such a small college, and, although it remained (and still does) very well respected in the local area, sustaining its existence as a small college became more difficult into the twenty-first century. By 2015, this difficulty at least partly led to an Ofsted report, which was rated inadequate, and in April 2015, Norton Radstock College merged with City of Bath college to form Bath College, as recommended by the then named Department for Business Innovation and skills. This has not however put an end to the provision of FE from a college in Norton Radstock, and since then the combined Bath College has gained a grade 2 overall, including the Norton Radstock centre. The survival of the college in a local area with a relatively small population is testimony overall to the value of FE colleges for their local communities.

Conclusion

FE colleges remain the largest and most important part of the FE sector and the main provider overall. They are involved in most of the FE sector subsectors and work with other phases of education, including secondary schools and universities. The purpose they strive for and the values they wish to stand for are not only both to help their own learners progress and achieve but also to contribute to their local area and society as a whole. The data regarding students, staff, and college progress in inspections shows some deficits and some improvements, but it is difficult to fully appreciate the effects of the COVID-19 pandemic on those statistics.

The overall system of FE colleges in England has developed considerably since the war, but it is still difficult to identify a coherent and clear structure that represents all colleges. That this is also the case globally is one of a number of conclusions that are drawn out from an English FE college and US community college comparison. A range of positive similarities and achievements with their records of access to non-traditional learners are also evident, and a strong message from their history that they have both changed society. The growth in government intervention, pressure on funding and frequent changes of ministerial responsibility are shown to have presented continuous challenges to FE colleges, but the chapter concludes with the argument that colleges still manage to achieve many of their objectives despite that pressure.

Summary points

- FE colleges are the largest and the most important part of the FE sector and the main provider overall.
- They are involved in most of the FE sector subsectors and work with other phases of education, including secondary schools and universities, and they work with 1.6 million people.
- Their objectives are to ensure their learners achieve and progress and that they contribute to the broader society.
- Over a five-year comparison period, colleges have shown a strong improvement in Ofsted inspection results.
- A clear, coherent national system identifying and supporting FE colleges does not exist, and this is also the case globally.
- There are a number of similarities and differences between English FE college and US community college comparison.
- Government intervention and frequent changes of ministerial responsibility have provided ongoing pressure for FE colleges, but they have managed to achieve a considerable proportion of their objectives despite that intervention.

Recommended reading

Keep, E., Richmond, T. and Silver, R. (2021) *Honourable histories. From the local management of colleges via incorporation to the present day: 30 years of reform in further education.* London: Further Education Trust for Leadership.

References

Association of Colleges (2017) *College key facts 2017/18.* London: AOC.
Association of Colleges (2022) *College key facts 2022/23.* London: AOC.
Association of Colleges (2023) *College mergers.* Available at: https://www.aoc.co.uk/about/college-mergers (Accessed 18 October 2023).
Audit Commission (1985) *Obtaining better value from further education.* London: HMSO.

Azumah Dennis, C., Springbett, O. and Walker, L. (2019) Further education leaders: Securing the sector's future. *Futures,* 110, pp. 1–10.

Cantor, L.M. and Roberts, I.F. (2021) *Further education in England and Wales.* Abingdon: Routledge.

Education and Training Foundation (2019) *So what is the sector? A guide to the further education system in England.* London: ETF.

Education and Training Foundation (2023) *Our vision and role.* Available at: https://www.et-foundation.co.uk/about-us/our-vision_role/ (Accessed 17 October 2023).

Education USA (2023) *Step 1 – researching your options.* Available at: https://educationusa.state.gov/your-5-steps-us-study/research-your-options/community-college#:~:text=Community%20colleges%20offer%20two%2Dyear,employers%20in%20the%20local%20community (Accessed 20 October 2023).

Further Education Funding Council (1999) *Report from the inspectorate 1998–99 Norton Radstock College.* Coventry: FEFC.

Hillier, Y. (2006). *Everything you need to know about FE policy.* London: Continuum.

Hodgson, A., Bailey, B. and Lucas, N. (2015) What is FE? In A. Hodgson (Ed.) *The coming of age for FE? Reflections on the past and future role of further education colleges in the UK.* London: UCL Institute of Education Press.

Jephcote, M. and Latiner Raby, R. (2012) A comparative view of Colleges of Further Education (UK) and Community Colleges (US): Maintaining access in an era of financial constraint. *Research in Post-Compulsory Education,* 17(3), pp. 349–366, DOI: 10.1080/13596748.2012.700177

Keep, E., Richmond, T. and Silver, R. (2021) *Honourable histories. From the local management of colleges via incorporation to the present day: 30 Years of reform in further education.* London: Further Education Trust for Leadership.

Ofsted (2018) *Further Education and skills inspection report: Bath College.* Manchester: Ofsted.

3 Managing and working in further education

Introduction

This chapter opens with an explanation of models of governance that are present in the further education (FE) sector, in particular those of FE and sixth form colleges and adult education providers, and discusses the effect sector governance has on the operation of FE organisations. The chapter then discusses the circumstances, situations, and challenges faced by leaders in FE organisations and the research that has shown how they seek to manage those challenges. It then moves on to consider three leadership styles and their potential value to FE.

The first sector story follows the career and progress of Asif and his progression to becoming an Academic Staff Governor in an FE college. The section on working in FE outlines the numbers of staff involved in the sector and comments on the difficulties accessing whole-sector data. It compares the size of the FE workforce with the considerably larger school workforce.

The second sector story in this chapter discusses the Learning and Skills Research Network (LSRN) and its 25 years of supporting research in FE. The chapter closes with a discussion of models of professionalism in FE and makes use of the writings of Machiavelli to draw out some key points.

Governance and managements arrangements

A definition of governance

Governance in the context of FE is:

- All the legal or regulatory requirements or duty, which any FE provider **must** comply with;
- Any good practice that any FE provider *should* follow, unless there is a considered and recorded reason for not doing so.

As has generally been the case in this book so far, it is difficult to identify governance arrangements that apply across the whole FE sector. This section of the chapter outlines and compares governance for FE and sixth-form colleges and adult education providers where information is readily available to provide a reasonable indication of how governance across the sector operates.

DOI: 10.4324/9781003468455-3

FE and sixth-form colleges

Governance for FE colleges and sixth form colleges was updated in 2023, and these details are drawn from that update. The status of a college is that it is a 'statutory corporation' and an 'exempt charity' (DfE, 2023: 5). Each college has a governing board, and it has four 'core functions', which are:

- Determining or, for Catholic sixth-form colleges, preserving and developing your college's educational character
- Setting and communicating your college's strategy and goals
- Holding executive leaders to account for the educational performance and quality of your college and for the performance of staff
- Exercising effective control to ensure that funds and assets are protected, your organisation remains solvent, and legal obligations are met (*ibid.*: 6)

To fulfil those core functions, the colleges have '6 main duties' (*ibid.*: 6–8) and they are to:

1. Ensure your corporation carries out its purpose for the public benefit
2. Comply with your corporation's governing document and the law
3. Act in your corporation's best interests
4. Manage your corporation's resources responsibly
5. Act with reasonable care and skill
6. Ensure your corporation is accountable

The legal requirements add explanations of further items, including governor conduct, composition of governing boards, terms of office, governor eligibility, recruiting and supporting governors, board behaviour, appraisal of governors, and further details of board roles (which include staff and student governors). There is a wide range of areas that are important within the part of governance relating to the strategy and business plan of the institution, and these include equality, diversity, safeguarding, inclusion, special educational needs, and disability. They are all expected to be 'an integral part of your strategy' (*ibid.*: 23). The key focus on planning and organising provision within the current requirements is local skills needs, as identified through detailed review and analysis. The overall model of governance indicated by the current government requirements, and the provision which results, is intended to be locally led and overlaid with a wide range of ethical, moral, equality, and diversity and community-focussed components. On absorbing and reflecting on these requirements, it is clear that FE sector governance is a complex and demanding task. Given the society-changing nature of education systems, it would be surprising if the governance requirements were not complex and demanding.

Question for discussion

Read through the governance requirements listed in the previous section, and consider what steps you would prioritise as a member of the organisation's governing body. Make a list of these steps.

26 *Managing and working in further education*

Orr, commenting on the future of FE in 2020, expressed concern that despite

> Great optimism as to the potential of FE to raise productivity and enhance social mobility this has not been achieved due to underfunding and the current system of governance. Without bold moves in both the funding and governance of FE, the sector is likely to languish.
>
> (Orr, 2020: 508)

These recent changes do appear to include that boldness to at least some degree for governance, but the underfunding issue still remains, and is likely to slow any progress.

Public providers of adult education

Bernhardt and Kaufmann-Kuchta (2023) carried out a small study comparing the governance of "Publicly Financed Adult Education" in one English and one Spanish region. Overall, they found that the governance in English adult education as represented by the region in question was 'a mixture of national and regional regulations leading to regional provision based on learners' needs' (Bernhardt and Kaufmann-Kuchta, 2023: 310), whereas the Spanish system was 'a decentralized system supporting the regional provision' (*ibid.*: 310).

They also found that, in England, at 'the national level, the main providers of basic and community education are large, nationally operating third-sector and private providers, whereas at the regional level providers are FE Colleges, local authorities, and community centers' (*ibid.*: 317). This multiplicity of providers, where not all providers are charitable, complicates governance. The inspection and reporting requirements lean heavily towards the overall national government model of governance explained earlier in this section. However, it was found in this study that this 'regional governance regime' is 'market-led with initial stakeholder involvement', which is an encouraging and more local community-focussed approach (*ibid.*: 319).

The two examples here (FE and sixth-form colleges and adult education providers) both provide helpful understandings of the key characteristics of governance in the FE sector. Bernhardt and Kaufmann-Kuchta (2023) are optimistic when they conclude that there are potentially positive governance models developing, at least in the adult education part of FE, when they state that:

In England, hierarchical and marketised coordination dominate at the national level. Annually providers' changing rules for receiving public support influence programming. At the regional level, the fast-moving and complex adult education sector seems to be in transition from a market-led regime towards a more cooperative environment (*ibid.*: 322)

They continue to argue that:

> …. In the market-led regime of England, corresponding forms of action coordination dominate and lead to providers' expected behaviours, program design, and implementation. At the regional level, however, there is structured cooperation between providers despite them lacking legal basis.
>
> (*ibid.*: 326)

Managers and leadership

Azumah Dennis et al. (2019), in their study of ten FE leadership teams, identified a complicated and dynamic management situation that FE leaders were facing, but within which they managed to exercise some professional judgements and to fulfil some of their professional aspirations. Their research:

.... concludes that while leadership actions may contribute to the further political devaluing of the sector and its designation as a labour-market skills provider, some attempts are made to preserve its wider contribution to society, offering a basis for the creation of a more socially just future for FE (*ibid.*: 1).

When interviewed, the leaders themselves not only outline many of the difficulties that FE has been encountering but also indicate very strongly how they seek to problem solve to find solutions to those difficulties. For example:

> Next year is our 125th anniversary as a college and we need to be here another 125 years, so I've just got to make sure that our college continues providing what [our county] needs to ensure that happens.
>
> (*ibid.*: 3)

and

> But actually we are really really about turning things around, FE – that is our strength. We are really about developing skills ... and about a lot of activity around supporting people where school didn't work for them, for whatever reason, and developing them back into people that are then going to go and get a job and contribute to society ... And I will argue to whoever I need to argue about to try and keep that happening really.
>
> (*ibid.*: 4)

And, even more powerfully:

> If you read the policies, it's all highly plausible, and highly doable and very aspirational. But the real day-to-day stuff they don't see. They don't see broken society, and we deal with that all of the time in FE. You deal with bits of broken society and kids that are coming out of third and fourth generation unemployment ...When you come to an area like this, and you see and hear some of things that I have to see and hear, it makes me very angry. Very angry about politicians who never see it. And don't know about it, or don't want to know about it.
>
> (*ibid.*: 4–5)

The leaders operate in an environment of

> .... A continual policy-driven tension between meeting the needs of the business and upholding the values of FE. The constant focus on measurement means that risk taking and innovation is often discouraged as teaching practice becomes progressively standardised which reduces the emphasis on 'best practice and outstanding teaching'.
>
> (*ibid.*: 7)

This research drew a number of conclusions about the situation of college leaders. The challenges involved are extreme, but their determination as leaders to help their organisations to help their community is powerfully optimistic. The research argues that the FE sector can be led and managed positively and ethically by finding that,

> .... When college leaders think about (rather than rationalise) what they are doing, they are better placed to develop alternative ways of responding to the pressures of policy. Without thinking, there is a risk that they will allow policy to foreclose the future tense, to exile those aspects of their work not premised on an economic imperative. Thinking may provide them with a basis to fight the advent of future worlds that devalue them and to engage more fiercely those actions that will assist in bringing about more desirable futures.
>
> (*ibid.*: 9)

Leadership styles

The previous sector has demonstrated the presence of positive and committed leadership skills in the people who are leading FE. This section introduces a number of leadership styles which have both advantages and disadvantages and comments on how they may be helpful to leaders in FE.

Transactional leadership

This leadership style is where a person in authority makes use of the power, which is directly linked to their position in their organisation (positional power) to achieve goals with the organisation, and to meet its governance expectations. The emphasis in an organisation would be on creating clear objectives with measurable outcomes and developing and using systems to analyse the success of those outcomes. When the objectives are not met, those involved are punished, and those involved are rewarded when they are met. The rewards for those who succeed motivate those who do to continue but the punishments for those who do not succeed in achieving the outcomes will almost always demotivate them. In this model, power is in the hands of a small group of people.

Within the FE sector, as we have described it, this leadership style may well suit the closely defined external objectives seen in the governance requirements and government policy, and it could well assist an organisation to succeed in meeting those requirements. Transactional leadership is present in FE, and a concentration of power in the hands of a small number of people can be successful if those people are highly competent. It unlikely, however, to enable an organisation to make the most of its mission and place in the sector, and to add value to its students' learning.

Transformational leadership

This leadership style pursues maximum motivation and commitment amongst the members of an organisation. The leaders develop a vision for the organisation, and this vision is shared and promoted as a higher purpose for all to strive for. The overall approach is intended to transform the motivation and efforts of all so that they all participate in a shared enterprise. When the successful change is achieved, all members of the organisation are a part of it, and rewards are shared across the organisation. Again, power is still concentrated in a small group of people, and this may often involve a charismatic leader.

Within the FE sector, this style of leadership can and does bring positive results, but it may prove somewhat difficult to sustain when the key people leading the organisation are not especially skilled at motivating their colleagues.

Distributed leadership

As the title suggests, this style of leadership distributes responsibility for planning and execution of organisational goals as a series of interconnected processes, activities, situations, and people. Leadership, irrespective of individuals' roles in the organisation, is also seen as distributed around the organisation. Everyone has a leadership responsibility, and those in senior positions in the organisation have to encourage, develop, and support that collective motivation.

There are examples of this leadership style working within the FE sector, but, given the type of external pressures found in FE, the overall collective motivation can make sustaining the overall collaboration difficult. If one part of the organisation encounters problems, it can sometimes be very difficult to get the other parts of the organisation to help.

> **Question for discussion**
>
> Reflect on your schooling, work, and life to date and ask how many leadership styles you have experienced, been involved in, or used.

Sector story – Asif – Academic staff governor (ASG)

Asif is a 26-year-old system programmer in a medium-sized retail business. He is part of a team which develops, maintains, and manages the point-of-sale system operated across the company's multiple sites. He achieved well at school and started in the company as a trainee programmer, increasing his skill levels through a specialised programme the company offers its employees in partnership with the local college. He started to supervise apprentices from that college and found that he really enjoyed this work. An opportunity arose, and he started to take on some part-time teaching at the college. He found he really enjoyed teaching and joined the ongoing teacher-training course, which was required for him to become fully qualified as a teacher. Over the next two years his teaching grew, and he secured a job as a full-time lecturer in computer systems and programming at the college. When he was on the teacher-training course, he developed a particular interest in leadership styles and in equality and diversity. He made use of an adapted teaching style that used the principles of distributed leadership and not only worked to ensure his students shared and collaborated by building their individual confidence and competence but also shared the group's collective goals and actions. His students responded well to this, and achievement in his courses grew. Asif also discovered through his interest in equality and diversity that a recent research study had highlighted:

> .... The continuing absence of governors from black and minority ethnic backgrounds on college governing boards, and that normative, invisible assumptions of how governing gets done persist, with black and minority ethnic governors often little more than a token gesture of adding diversity to the faces on the board.
>
> (Bathmaker and Pennacchia, 2023: 4)

Asif was also aware of a study on academic staff governors, which found that the situation of academic staff governors could restrict their scope as a governor because of 'insiderness; relationships, professional status', and that 'the decision-making circumstances may limit their influence in the governance of the colleges, with implications for governance quality' (Sodiq, 2022: 24). The study did, however, also make helpful recommendation to improve the situation for academic staff governors (ASGs), which included 'avoiding low-power and low-status governance roles; taking action to develop ASGs' professionality as educators; removing structural and power barriers; and allowing more opportunities for ASGs to contribute to governance' (*ibid.*: 24).

Far from being deterred by these pieces of research, Asif found that it gave him enthusiasm to be one of the people who could genuinely make a difference to the situation of ASGs to his own organisation and beyond into the sector. He stood for the position of academic staff governor in his college, was elected, and is already a member of an 'improving governance' subgroup, which reports and makes recommendations to the governing board. These have included a programme to encourage more diversity on that board, constructing a board member training programme and working with the current board on equality and diversity.

Working as a teacher in further education

From the National Office of Statistics, for the official Learning and skills sector:

There are an estimated **205,200** people working in the Further Education Workforce, including:

- **81,400** teaching staff,
- **50,200** support staff,
- **47,200** admin staff,
- **19,200** management staff,
- **7,100** leadership staff.

51.0 per cent of teaching staff teach vocational subjects as their main subject.
 5.4 per cent of teaching positions were vacant at the end of the year. **2.6 per cent** management and leadership positions were vacant at the end of the year.
 There are an estimated **3,800** governors (headcount) in General Further Education Colleges and sixth form colleges:

- **73.1 per cent** of governors were independent governors, **15.9 per cent** were staff governors, **9.7 per cent** were student governors, and **1.3%** were parent governors.
- **6.1 per cent** governor positions were vacant at the end of the year.

(Office for National Statistics, 2023a: 1)

As far as just colleges are concerned, and from the AoC, in 2022/23:

There are 103,000 full time equivalent people of which 49,000 are teachers. 64% are female; 16% are from and ethnic minority background and 5% have a learning difficulty and/or a disability.

(AoC, 2022: 48)

- The average age of college staff is 46.
- The average age of college chief executives and principals is 53.
- 8% of college chief executives and principals are from black or minority ethnic backgrounds.
- 48% of college principals are female compared to 40% secondary school head teachers and 33% university vice chancellors.

(AoC, 2022: 50)

By comparison, the school workforce is:

> 973,000 of whom 5 in 10 are teachers, 3 in 10 teaching assistants, 2 in 10 other teaching staff.
> There are 468,371 full-time equivalent teachers.
>
> Office for National Statistics (2023b: 1)

The FE data as collected does not represent the whole sector, but it can be seen that the workforce of FE is of a significant size, if somewhat smaller than the school workforce. There are also of course many other staff working in locations other than these. The Learning Curve Group, for example, as featured in a sector story in Chapter 1, have some 1,500 staff, and they are just one independent training provider, albeit a large one.

Overall, it can be seen that, firstly, up to date and coherent sector data for FE would be a very helpful improvement. Even with the readily available data, FE clearly has a large workforce and also has a workforce where progress has been made in equality and diversity as represented by the data for that workforce, from the limited data available.

Sector story – The Learning and Skills Research Network (LSRN) – Supporting research through networking

Tummons (2020: 6), when discussing professionalism in FE and the role of research for FE professionals, comments that

> .... Notwithstanding the fact that the FE sector is relatively under-researched in comparison to schools and universities, there has been a steady increase in robust empirical as well as conceptual research relating to the sector more generally, and in the specific problems of professionalism and professionalisation more specifically, in recent years.

An organisation that has contributed significantly to that growth by promoting, supporting, and sharing FE research through networking is the Learning and Skills Research Network (LSRN). It was set up by participants from a workshop on research in FE, which took place in 1996. The organisation formed in 1997 and increased network activities across regional offices and organised annual national conferences at Warwick University for seven years after that. These conferences allowed FE practitioners who were just starting on their road to being a researcher to present papers at the same workshop session as established sector experts. The LSRN become established as an organisation that teachers in the sector trusted and enjoyed working with, and it also produced a research journal, *Research in Post Compulsory Education*, a well-respected peer-reviewed journal.

The network has been operating since 1997 (over 25 years), and at the time of writing, is still operating. The purposes of the LSRN are to:

- Demonstrate the value of research and development
- Help build the capacity of the sector
- Explore ways of increasing the influence of findings

LSRN (2023: 1)

Over the years, LSRN has promoted, encouraged, and during its better off years, funded research, both small and larger, into FE. Themes that have been researched include teacher education, adult basic skills, mentoring, college leadership, technical education, employability and enterprise, and many others. Teachers working in the sector joined in small, informal network meetings, and presented either their early research ideas, ongoing progress, or final results. A number of participants became confident enough to publish their research for the first time, and many subsequently became well published researchers.

An example of how participation in this network supported important and relevant research taking place, a member of LSRN is used as an example.

Rachel – from journalist to research fellow

Rachel qualified as a lecturer in 1995 and had previously been deputy editor, features editor and reporter on a number of publications as well as a freelance journalist. She was working as a parttime lecturer in a London Adult Education centre and joined the LSRN when undertaking what proved to be the first steps in a doctorate. She completed an investigation for her Masters dissertation into the experiences of mentors supporting teacher trainees during their initial teacher training. She also developed a Masters-level CPD module to support mentors in education, training, and professional development. Her PhD thesis explored the professional development needs of English teacher trainers in the FE sector. Rachel presented at several LSRN meetings and discussed her research with other participants. Presenting at LSRN and other workshops built her confidence and helped her complete her research. She has since presented her research on mentoring and professional development at conferences in three European countries. She was also awarded a teaching fellowship at her own university, which she joined some two years ago.

In comparison with more recognised research organisations, LSRN has always had considerably fewer resources to undertake its important role. Their relatively small contributions have made a difference for teachers in FE, and it has helped them develop their professional confidence in a variety of ways. When considering the value of the LSRN over the first 12 years it operated, Hillier expressed the value of LSRN.

> Research therefore needs to be designed appropriately but also needs to be undertaken where intervention and origination of targets and goals is not a political- but a sector-led endeavour.
>
> The overall pattern of research activity in the LLS is patchy. There is far more of it today than in the past decade. We hope that the resources and commitment to this research continues to thrive. The sector and its learners need it.

(Hillier, 2010: 99)

It is fair to say that the trend of an increasing volume of research in FE has continued up to the present day, but it is also true to say the sector overall does not have sufficient resources to support research in similar ways to schools and universities.

Working in the sector as a teacher

This section of the chapter considers what the characteristics of a teaching professional in the FE sector are, and what research has suggested are models of professionalism, which are suitable for FE to aspire to and adopt. As part of a study into the professional situation of teacher educators in the FE sector, the present author (Crawley, 2014) developed a list of 'ten characteristics of a teaching professional' after having compared various existing models from previous research. They are listed below:

Ten characteristics of a teaching professional

1. Engagement in activity, which has particular and special characteristics.
2. A high personal and public status as a result of their profession, which merits payment as a result of their efforts.
3. Recognition as practising according to agreed and acknowledged codes of conduct, standards of training, competence, responsibility, and understanding.
4. Conducting their profession with honesty, integrity, and transparency within the public domain to maintain its status within its ranks and with the public at large.
5. Accepting responsibility for a social purpose within their specialism and a broader purpose in the wider community beyond that.
6. A responsibility to work with other professionals and the wider community.
7. Demonstrating autonomy within their professional practice.
8. Participating in decisions affecting their professional lives and environments, with peers and with the engagement of the wider community.
9. Subjecting their work to public accountability.
10. Selfless commitment to updating their expertise and continuous development of their field.

(Crawley, 2014: 8)

Such a list is both aspirational and comprehensive, but the question that needs to be asked in this case is: could such a model be put into practice in what has already been agreed as a complex and challenging sector? In 2017, an innovative book produced by FE professionals about FE made a number of metaphorical comparisons between Machiavelli's times and the current situation in FE. His famous work about power and politics, *The Prince,* written by Niccolò Machiavelli and published in 1532 was used for this imaginative comparison. The book draws on Machiavelli's views, and they are discussed by a series of FE professionals to highlight aspects of managing and working in the FE sector. My chapter in this book offers a way forward for teaching professionals Crawley's (2017).

The discussion opens with the following:

Machiavelli (1908: 7) argued that those who remain 'poor and scattered are never able to injure' the prince. 'Poor and scattered' is a description which just about sums up the professional situation of many working in Further Education (FE). Machiavelli also believed that a prince who had held power for some time was more likely to have loyal and well-disposed subjects than a 'new prince'.

(Crawley, 2017: 115)

The content of this chapter and others has already indicated how difficult it can be for leaders, teachers, and at time students in the FE sector to feel empowered, and that power in the system can be flowing against them. I suggest that a starting point is an 'act of connection' (*ibid.*: 116). In essence the idea of acts of connection is where FE professionals find opportunities to work together, compare their practice, research a small topic, discuss how they teach their subject, and seek developments, changes and improvements. They need to create small periods of time mainly in their own organisations to come together and make these connections. The acts of connection may just last for ten minutes at a time. If this small start and series of connections can be fostered and supported within the FE organisation it can build, as projects did with the help of the LSRN, and in the fullness of time, it can have significant results. I would sum this up as follows:

> This constitutes not so much a revolution as a process of recapturing and rebuilding localised pride and autonomy. Encouraging and positive results instil a feeling for participants that ownership has been gained of a very small corner of their particular principality, and this can lead to a natural desire for more acts of connection and growing connections.
>
> Crawley (2017: 116)

Overall, the essence of the argument in '*The Principal: Power and Professionalism in FE*' (Daley et al., 2017) is to encourage those working in FE not to be destroyed by the power of 'princes' but to join together in what has been called 'the making and taking of professionalism' (Gleeson et al., 2005). To help achieve this goal, I propose a model of professionalism called the 'connected professional', which, it is argued, could be the vehicle to take FE professionals forward. I summarise the model as follows:

There are four 'connections' which combine to make a 'connected professional' and they are:

1. The Practical Connection: The practical underpinning of teaching skills, knowledge, understanding, and application, which are essential for all teachers to be able to carry out their role.
2. The Democratic Connection: The active involvement in democratic action where practitioners work together with other colleagues towards achieving agreed common goals.
3. The Civic Connection: The active engagement in civic action with the wider community to support and enact development with and for that community. This involves moving outside of the day-to-day interactions of education and pursuing goals, activities, and developments for and with the broader community.
4. The Networked Connection: The cultivation, involvement, and sustaining of the means of active engagement with other professionals and the wider community.

To conclude, I strongly argue that ways of finding this route to professionalism in FE are essential, because:

> If we do not try to move towards acts of connection, being connected professionals and building principalities of people however, our future will continue to be disconnected and unfulfilled, and ultimately we will be unable to serve our students in the way they deserve.
>
> (Crawley, 2017: 122)

> **Question for discussion**
>
> In your own study or work, have you experienced or been involved in creating 'acts of connection'?

Conclusion

This chapter has outlined what it is like to manage and work in the FE sector. From governance to research, and staffing to training, the sector can be seen to have a range of major challenges. Leaders and teachers in the sector can, however, again be seen to still find ways of pursuing their goals and educational ideas, and to use their experience, training, and skills to solve problems caused by the tightly controlled and over-managed (from the outside) situations they encounter. A variety of leadership styles and their relevance to the FE sector are discussed.

The first sector story follows the career and progress of Asif and his progression to becoming and Academic Staff Governor in an FE college.

The section on working in FE outlines numbers of staff involved in the sector and comments on the difficulties accessing whole-sector data. It compares the size of the FE workforce with the considerably larger school workforce.

The second sector story in this chapter discusses the Learning and Skills Research Network (LSRN) and its 25 years of supporting research in FE.

The chapter closes with a discussion of models of professionalism in FE and makes use of the writings of Machiavelli and others to draw out some key points. With some assistance from support organisations outside their organisations, and from their own colleagues and organisations, it is possible for a member of staff in FE to teach, research, and develop professional practice. Research on the sector has grown significantly over the last 25 years. Inspection results are improving, and the prospects of developing 'connected professionals' can be seen to be in process, albeit not across the whole sector. To conclude, by building 'principalities of people' (Crawley, 2017: 122) there is some hope of a way forward, and there has indeed been some evidence of principalities of people making acts of connection.

Summary points

- The governance requirements of the FE sector are not only complex and challenging but are also becoming more locally focussed.
- Leaders in FE believe that the sector has an element of social justice within its goals, and they are adroit at developing problem solving approaches to support those goals.

- Open and collaborative leadership styles are difficult to adopt in the FE sector but could offer an approach for a better future.
- The FE sector has a large workforce, but it is considerably smaller than the school workforce.
- There are models of professionalism, which could enhance the professional situation of teaching professionals in FE.

Recommended reading

Daley, M., Orr, K. and Petrie, J. (2017) *The principal: Power and professionalism in FE*. London: IOE Press.

References

Association of Colleges (2022) *College key facts 2022/23*. London: AOC.

Azumah Dennis, C., Springbett, O. and Walker, L. (2019) Further education leaders: Securing the sector's future. *Futures*, 110, pp. 1–10.

Bathmaker, A-M. and Pennacchia, J. (2023) Who governs and why it matters. An analysis of race equality and diversity in the composition of further education college governing bodies across the UK. *Journal of Vocational Education & Training*, 75(1), pp. 24–42, DOI: 10.1080/13636820.2022.2126878

Bernhardt, A.C. and Kaufmann-Kuchta, K. (2023) Governance of publicly financed adult education in England and Spain–A comparison. *Adult Education Quarterly*, 73(3), pp. 310–331.

Crawley, J. (2014) *How can a deeper understanding of the professional situation of lls teacher educators enhance their future support, professional development and working context? PhD thesis*. Bath: Bath Spa University.

Crawley, J. (2017) Principalities of people – Destabilising the prince's power through 'acts of connection'. In M. Daley, K. Orr and J. Petrie (Eds) *The principal: Power and professionalism in FE*. London: IOE Press.

Department for Education (2023) *FE and sixth-form college corporations: Governance guide*. London: DfE.

Gleeson, D., Davies, J. and Wheeler, E. (2005) On the making and taking of professionalism in the further education workplace. *British Journal of Sociology of Education*, 26(4), pp. 445–460.

Hillier, Y. (2010) Critical practitioners, developing researchers: The story of practitioner research in the lifelong learning sector. *Journal of Vocational Education and Training*, 62(1), pp. 89–101, DOI: 10.1080/13636820903427553

Learning and Skills research Network (2023) *Purpose and values*. Available at: https://lsrn.wordpress.com/about/history/ (Accessed 24 October 2023).

Machiavelli, N. (1908) *The Prince*. Translated by W.K. Marriott. London: EP Dutton & Company.

Office for National Statistics (2023a) *Academic year 2021/22 further education workforce*. London: Office for National Statistics. Available at: https://explore-education-statistics.service.gov.uk/find-statistics/further-education-workforce (Accessed 24 October 2023).

Office for National Statistics (2023b) *Reporting year 2022: School workforce in England*. London: Office for National Statistics. Available at: https://explore-education-statistics.service.gov.uk/find-statistics/school-workforce-in-england (Accessed 24 October 2023).

Orr, K. (2020) A future for the further education sector in England. *Journal of Education and Work*, 33(7–8), pp. 507–514.

Sodiq, A. (2022) Academic staff governors' power and professional status in the governance of further education colleges in England. *Research in Post- Compulsory Education*, 27(1), pp. 98–127, DOI: 10.1080/13596748.2021.2011512

Tummons, J. (2020) Introduction: what does it mean to be a professional? In J. Tummons (Ed.) *Professionalism in post-compulsory education and training. Empirical and theoretical perspectives*. Abingdon: Routledge.

4 Work-based learning (WBL)

Introduction

This chapter will consider in more detail what constitutes work-based learning (WBL), how the history of further education (FE) involvement in WBL has developed, and the current situation of WBL in FE. It will draw out perspectives and debates on WBL and consider current thinking and examples of how it can best succeed in the future.

At the start of the chapter WBL is introduced and defined, and a selection of data is provided about the size and scope of this FE subsector. A historical analysis of particular historical events or developments in the history of English WBL is then presented. This includes Mechanics' Institutes, the historical development of apprenticeships, an analysis of the introduction of the National Council for Vocational Qualifications (NCVQ) and the qualifications it presided over: National Vocational Qualifications (NVQs). The first sector story of the chapter introduces Jodie, a Level 2 apprentice in customer service.

The next section of the chapter analyses the policy development associated with WBL in FE, identifies a number of challenges for the sector which have regularly featured, and considers strategies for improvement for the future of WBL in FE. Fuller and Unwin's expansive and restrictive framework for WBL then offers a positive model which could significantly improve the learning quality and content of WBL in FE.

The chapter closes with a sector story about a successful independent training provider, and how they have created and adopted an expansive learning approach which has contributed to their success.

Introducing WBL in FE

Ever since people have been working, they have needed to train others to be able to do that work, either with them or instead of them. People who contribute to other people's work also need training. In its simplest terms, there are many people learning how to work in order to ensure the work gets done, continues, and improves. When people help others to learn about work, it makes sense for at least some of that learning to take place at work, or in a situation and location which is as near to work as possible. When any of that learning takes place at work it could, at its simplest, be described as WBL. WBL, therefore, could be argued as having taken place for thousands of years. Looking back at historical events, evidence can be found of events, law changes, and more systematic approaches to WBL across England and the United Kingdom, which have been developing for more than 200 years. Most of the structures, organisations, and employers who have been involved

DOI: 10.4324/9781003468455-4

in this historical development have made their contribution to the WBL, which currently takes place in the FE sector. Some have worked better and lasted longer than others as this sector has been one of the most continuous areas of 'policy churn' across FE.

A more comprehensive and more useful definition of WBL has been offered by the Inter-Agency Group on Technical and Vocational Education and Training (IAG-TVET), which is 'work-based learning refers to all forms of learning that takes place in a real work environment. It provides individuals with the skills needed to successfully obtain and keep jobs and progress in their professional development' (IAG-TVET, 2017: 2).

How much WBL is there in England?

A helpful starting point, when searching for data on WBL, is the total number of employees in the United Kingdom. A regular survey of employees in the United Kingdom, the Business Register and Employment Survey, is undertaken by the Office for National Statistics (ONS), and the most recent data from that survey (ONS, 2023c: 2) indicates that the total number of employees in the United Kingdom in 2022 was '31.8 million; private sector employees increased by 647,300 (2.5%) and public sector employees increased by 21,700 (0.4%)'. This is from a UK population of some 67 million.

Some English-focused data is also available on the amount of WBL generally taking place in the United Kingdom. The *Employer Skills Survey* for 2022 is the source of data, and it involved:

> A large-scale telephone survey of 72,918 employers across the UK, providing labour market information on the skills challenges faced by employers. This comprised 59,486 interviews with employers in England, 3,400 interviews in Northern Ireland, 5,207 in Scotland and 4,825 in Wales. This report focuses on findings about:
>
> - Recruitment and skill-shortage vacancies;
> - Skills gaps;
> - Training and workforce development.
>
> (DfE, 2023: 1)

It is the training and workforce development figures which are relevant to this chapter. In relation to training and workforce development, the survey results are that:

> Three-fifths (60%) of employers had provided training for their staff in the last 12 months, a decrease from 66% in 2017. Half of all employers (49%) provided on-the-job training (down from 53% in 2017) and 39% provided off-the-job training (down from 48% in 2017).
>
> 60% of all employees received training in 2022, compared to 62% in 2017. The average investment in training per employee was £1,780, compared to £2,010 in 2017 (accounting for inflation).
>
> (DfE, 2023: 1)

Although this data gives neither a full nor clear picture of the size of FE-based WBL, it does give an indication of the scale of work-related training activity taking place across England, with 60 per cent of the sample of 59,486 English employers who were interviewed providing training. If these results were scaled up to the number of employees stated in the ONS data, there would be some 60 per cent of 31.8 million employees receiving training, which would be 19 million employees.

There is also some directly relevant data about WBL in FE available from the ONS (2023b).

Adult (19+) funded further education and skills (including apprenticeships) participation in England for the 2022/23 academic year was 1,612,130, which was up 6.6 per cent from 2021/22.

There is also a figure of '613,000 apprenticeships for 2021/22 within the same data release' (ONS, 2023a: 1).

The AoC has some further (and not necessarily the same) figures, which are:

In 2022/23
   611,000 16- to 18-year-olds study in colleges.
An additional 46,000 16 to 18-year-olds undertake an apprenticeship though colleges.

(AoC, 2023: 6)

166,000 people were on an apprenticeship provision in colleges.

(*ibid.*: 14)

60% of college-based apprenticeships are training in construction, planning and the built environment, and 41% in engineering and manufacturing.
   49,300 apprentices are over 25, and of that number, 25,700 are doing advanced level apprenticeships and 12,900 higher level apprenticeships.

(*ibid.*: 16)

69% of employers view that 17–18 year old college leavers are 'well prepared for work'.

(*ibid.*: 46)

As has now clearly emerged from the early chapters in this book about the FE sector, data on the different aspects and subsectors of FE is available, and it can give us a good deal of information about the particular subsector or area of work which is being considered. Overall, however, this data is rarely comprehensive, needs constant explaining, and rarely successfully represents the whole of the sector it is seeking to explain.

The data which is available does illustrate that the WBL part of the FE sector is large and that a significant proportion of employers, organisations, and interest groups are involved. The age range of students is broad, and the contribution to the nation's WBL needs is significant and ongoing. The skills training requirements of any nation are always of considerable significance, and the need for a robust, coherent WBL structure and system is clear. Unfortunately, as we have seen in Chapter 1,

When visitors from overseas come to look at the 'UK education system' one of the first things we have to say is that there is no single system. Education, FE and skills are areas of devolved responsibility and have developed very differently in each of the four nations. That can present challenges of coherence, for instance where an employer seeks to train apprentices in more than one nation within the UK, or a training provider wants to operate across boundaries.

(Hodgson et al., 2018: 3)

There will be more analysis of the FE WBL system and how it has developed later in this chapter.

A selection of significant events in the history of English WBL

As the Industrial Revolution progressed in the nineteenth century, 'large numbers of the labouring population' were 'leaving the countryside with its own culture and skills and moving into the growing towns to work in the mills' (Walker, 2017: 4). As the work in new factories and mills increased and developed, the 'middle-class educationalists thought more formal instruction was required based on the three Rs' (ibid.: 4). A range of educational establishments developed, and 'the mutual improvement society at Ramsbottom in east Lancashire for example had in 1850 about 180 members, of whom fifty were attending classes' (ibid.: 5). 'These societies brought working-class men and women together who attended classes of elementary subjects and later advanced discussions on a variety of subjects' (ibid.: 5). Mechanics Institutes were established in 1823, and they provided courses, some technical and some more general education; courses in English; lectures, access to libraries, and technical facilities such as laboratories, and buildings in which these activities could take place. By 1850, there were some 700 in existence. There are varying arguments about how successful Mechanics Institutes were, but Walker (2012: 37) confidently argues that they provided 'a firm foundation on which technical and vocational education was established by the beginning of the twentieth century and has continued to date'. Walker continues to state that 'the mechanics' institute movement was being established at a time when trade conditions were improving, thus leading to the abatement of (some of the) social strife which accompanied them, providing the necessary stability and encouragement for developing adult education' (ibid.: 38). Walker's research concludes that:

> The mechanics' institute movement was a success and did provide a firm foundation on which FE was established by the beginning of the twentieth century. Although the movement initially 'failed' to support adult working class education, its ultimate success was due to mechanics' institutes responding to the needs of industry, following the findings of the Great Exhibition of 1851. Courses and lectures were offered that were relevant to employers and employees and given national recognition through examinations offered by the Department of Science and Art, the Society of Arts and the City and Guilds London Institute.
>
> (ibid.: 41)

The development of apprenticeships

Bradbury and Wynne (2020: 319) define the terms 'apprentice' and 'apprenticeship' as follows:

> *Apprentice*: An individual who receives apprenticeship training to prepare them for a specific occupation or profession and, where applicable, End Point Assessment through an apprenticeship framework or standard.
>
> *Apprenticeship*: A job with an accompanying skills development programme, which includes the training and, where required, End Point Assessment.

The main difference between apprenticeships and education and training in a classroom or other learning location is that it will involve a significant amount of learning in the workplace in working roles within that workplace.

The Health and Morals of Apprentices Act 1802 set out a number of conditions for apprenticeships which involved spending not more than 12 hours per day on the job, and that the apprentices should be taught reading, writing, and arithmetic. Moving into the twentieth century, after the riots in England in 1981, the government wished to encourage unemployed young people into apprenticeships and other training schemes. In 2006, *the Leitch Review of Skills* (Leitch, 2006: 3) argued that 'the UK commit to becoming a world leader in skills by 2020'. This included a variety of recommendations, particularly to increase the number of apprentices to '500,000 by 2020' (*ibid.*: 14).

The number of apprentices participating in apprenticeships during the 2022/23 year was 703,670 compared to 692,920 reported for the same period in the previous year (ONSa, 2023: 1). This is all apprentices, not just those in the FE sector, but it can be seen that the Leitch recommendation has indeed been achieved. Overall, the strategy for apprenticeships has been 'wide and inclusive' (Bradbury and Wynne, 2020: 24). They also argue that 'the apprenticeship strategy has a serious commitment to developing the workforce, particularly with reference to individuals who may not previously have accessed or have had the opportunity to access formal qualifications' (*ibid.*: 328). There are, however, still barriers for apprentices, and they include low pay, low funding levels for employers and providers, difficulties accessing training away from the workplace, and disappointing achievement figures. Reddy (2017: 78) argues that 'a deal is being done when full-time students or apprentices work for low, or, as in some instances, no wages', and the deal is that 'in turn for the apprentices' long period of low-wage employment, something better has to come at the end of the toil'.

Question for discussion

What do you think that the most important WBL would be for an apprentice?
List the skills, knowledge, and experience which you feel would be the most important.

Sector story – Jodie – Level 2 apprentice

Jodie had been working part-time in a local supermarket and spending the rest of the week as a student at her local FE college. An opportunity to apply for a Customer Services Apprentice position at a local furniture manufacturer was advertised in the college's careers advice centre, and Jodie applied as she felt that the apprenticeship would provide her with the chance to continue to learn, whilst simultaneously gaining experience and relevant qualifications as a full-time apprentice. Her daily work involves talking to customers, answering their questions, and showing them around the company's showroom and products. Jodie also issues invoices and provides receipts and other documents for customers. Alongside the WBL in this particular company's type of work which has been gained, Jodie has improved her confidence, employability, Maths, English, and use of technology overall and in customer service. She receives glowing feedback from customers on her service on an ongoing basis and has also gained her Level 2 Customer Services Practitioner Award. The overall experience and learning in the workplace, and study at the local college, have proved to be a highly successful combination, and have helped maintain Jodie's high levels of motivation and commitment throughout. Since gaining the customer service award, Jodie has completed her apprenticeship and gained a job with the company, which will continue to train her to a higher level and support her in continuing WBL.

The introduction of NVQs

In 1987, the National Council for Vocational Qualifications was established to set up a national, five-level framework for 'competence-based' qualifications called National Vocational Qualifications (NVQs), and to integrate all the country's vocational qualifications into this framework. This was associated with a bold ambition to create what amounted to a national curriculum for WBL. The skills of WBL were synthesised into 'statements of competence' where each function, skill, or activity could be addressed. The process which produced these statements of competence was called 'functional analysis', and it involved identifying the functions associated with work roles and tasks at certain levels and breaking them down into their component parts. The resulting statements of competence were provided with statements of relevant 'underpinning knowledge', and the emphasis overall was on the sets of competences, rather than the theoretical aspects of WBL. The competences built up to 'elements' and then further built up to become 'units'. The units then combined into qualifications, and these qualifications were fitted into the national framework, after being accepted by the NCVQ. This was a very ambitious plan, but one which over time received a significant amount of criticism. One of the most active critics of NVQs at the time argued that the approach reduced skilled activity into small fragments with minor assessment requirements for each one, and that this 'atomised' the process of learning and combining skills and understanding, making them very difficult to reassemble into coherent and relevant WBL (Hyland, 1998). By 1997, ten years after the establishment of the NCVQ, after widespread criticisms that the 'replacement of traditional VET programmes with NVQs has led to widespread deskilling, a loss of significant theoretical content and a systematic narrowing and delimiting of vocational focus in fields such as construction' (*ibid.*: 371), NCVQ was replaced. The NVQ process, it was argued, reduced integrated professional competence into isolated fragments of competence. Demonstrating that these isolated competences could build into those required in different occupations became problematic. The Qualifications and Curriculum Authority (QCA) replaced the NCVQ in 1997, and the QCA was itself replaced in 2010 by the Office of Qualifications and Examinations Regulation (Ofqual). Ofqual does still exist at the time of writing. The establishment of NCVQ and NVQs was an important moment in the history of FE WBL, and to attempt to establish a national framework for WBL was ambitious. Some NVQs do still exist but their moment in history has passed.

Policy and development of WBL

Hodgson *et al.* (2018) report on 'FE and skills across the four countries of the UK: New opportunities for policy learning' provides a helpful critique of policy in skills development across the United Kingdom by identifying a series of policy challenges for the FE sector. The key challenges include the 'known unknowns' (*ibid.*: 41) such as 'the Fourth Industrial Revolution', which will bring a major change in the development of technology. They also include 'system historical challenges' (*ibid.*: 41) which relates to the historical status of WBL as it has developed through history in the United Kingdom. Their analysis concludes that the most directly relevant challenges for WBL are as follows:

'The Fourth Industrial Revolution'

This is the effect 'resulting from rapidly increasing technological innovation. As a part of the education and training system that is very closely aligned to the economy and its future, this is a particular area that concerns FE and skills providers'.

'The status of vocational education and training'

The 'academic/vocational divide' is a term which has long been associated with the perceived weakness between academic qualifications and vocational (i.e., work-related) qualifications. Hodgson et al. (2018: 41–42) comment on this at length because it is a major challenge for FE.

Vocational education and training are regarded as less valuable than academic education by young people and their parents. The desire to take A Levels/Highers and to gain a place at a prestigious university is still driving behaviour despite continual reforms of vocational qualifications that are designed to make them more effective and attractive. For FE and skills providers, this sometimes means that their institutions are seen as 'second best'. They are constantly having to struggle to gain funding and recognition for the important work they are doing now and will need to do in the future.

'Defining the role and purposes of FE colleges' in providing WBL

This is another historical challenge, and it has been introduced in earlier chapters. Hodgson et al. (2018: 42) argue that:

> It is often difficult to define precisely the role and purpose of FE colleges, which hampers their status and profile in public perception. National policies in all countries have further muddied the water by demanding different priorities at different times.

'Developing long-term partnerships between employers and FE and skills providers'

Historically, employers in the United Kingdom have not played the central role in the design and delivery of technical and vocational education and training that employers have in other parts of Europe ... UK employer bodies are by no means as strong or cohesive as those in other countries.

> While national government policies continue to build employers into the design and delivery of technical and vocational education and training, the approach has been primarily through exhortation, moral appeal and financial incentives rather than through legal frameworks. In this voluntarist environment, it is not surprising that employer-college partnership building remains challenging and something that has to be built up piecemeal at the grassroots level.

(*ibid.*: 42)

'Improving teaching, learning, and assessment'

In this area, there are overall improvements as has been seen in other chapters, in the Ofsted results in FE, including WBL. It is also the case, however, that 'all four countries recognised the need for both ongoing improvement and innovation, not least because of the opportunities and challenges offered by technological change' (*ibid.*: 44).

Fortunately, in addition to outlining the key challenges, Hodgson *et al.* (2018) also suggested actions that could improve the future of the FE sector, and in particular WBL. The suggested pieces of 'policy learning' recommended include the following:

More cross-sector collaboration

These collaborations could include working together to manage the Fourth Industrial Revolution by sharing experiences and understandings. Collaborations should be cross-provider collaborations and provider/employer collaborations and should include feedback from learners and other employees.

Develop more integration between national and local systems

There were some indications in Chapter 3 that local skills planning and development are beginning to emerge from the latest policies and governance arrangements for FE. For this to be fully successful, though, the national system would need to be more clearly regulated and considerably more consistent, and Hodgson *et al.* (2018) emphasise this.

Make use of the 'policy learning laboratories'

Hodgson *et al.* (2018: 46) propose a system of 'policy learning laboratories' which could draw together thinking, data, analysis, and other aspects of research and development through a process of networking and use this to focus on key issues and propose new areas for enquiry. The results of the enquiries could be shared, trialled, and potentially utilised across the sector, and could help to develop new trajectories for the whole FE sector, and in particular WBL.

Restricted and expansive learning – Fuller and Unwin (2019)

Fuller and Unwin have made a significant contribution to the ideas relating to best practices in WBL. They have found in their research that the assertion by a range of policymakers that WBL does not always have direct relevance to the broader world of work is often erroneous. They suggest that this is because providers do not always have as effective partnerships with employers as they should, and that the circumstances surrounding WBL can vary considerably. What tends to get lost in the policy discourse is that 'workplaces are not configured in the most conducive way to support and benefit from those programmes or to capitalise on the learning potential of their employees' (Fuller and Unwin, 2019: 69). They continue to argue that WBL is not only closely related to the workplace, but that:

> The most effective training programmes emerge when both providers and employers take and share responsibility for their co-production. This blending of expertise is critical for the design

and delivery of work-based learning where the Work Based becomes the predominant site for the development of occupational expertise.

(*ibid.*: 69)

This argument has been built from Fuller and Unwin's work over the last 20 years where they have established key characteristics of the environment, actions, and support needed for effective WBL. Their framework has a number of key components:

1. **The workplace as a 'site for learning'**

    This is essentially recognising and developing the locations of the workplace as a number of sites or locations which are conducive to learning. The physical workplace environments are seen as potentially 'dynamic sites of human activity providing opportunities of different types and at different levels of intensity' (*ibid.*: 71). This type of workplace can also be a site of 'employee driven innovation' (*ibid.*: 71). Fuller and Unwin do not suggest that all workplaces are learning sites at present, and that 'not all workplaces provide decent employment conditions and/or produce goods and services that properly utilise the expertise of their workforces' (*ibid.*: 71). Workplaces which are sites for learning do however exist and can make a significant difference to the learning in that workplace.

2. **The expansive–restrictive framework**

    This is a widely recognised and thoroughly researched model of WBL, and how it can happen. The framework identifies characteristics of the learning environment in the workplace, provides an opportunity for workplaces to evaluate their own situation in relation to the framework, and helps them to move towards improvement using this framework. Table 4.1 outlines the expansive–restrictive framework:

Although presented in a two-column matrix, the framework is intended to be used as a continuum and at different workplaces, and providers can readily use it to evaluate the current and developing

Table 4.1 Adapted from Fuller and Unwin (2019: 76–77)

Expansive learning environment	Restrictive learning environment
Close, collaborative working	Isolated, individualist working
Colleagues mutually supportive in enhancing teacher learning	Colleagues obstruct or do not support each other's learning
An explicit focus on teacher learning, as a dimension of normal working practices and initiatives	No explicit focus on teacher learning except to meet crises or imposed practices
Supported opportunities for personal development that go beyond institutional or government priorities	Teacher learning mainly strategic compliance with government or institutional agendas
Out-of-institution educational opportunities, including time to stand back, reflect, and think differently	Few out-of-institution educational opportunities, only narrow, short training programmes
Opportunities to integrate off-the-job learning into everyday practice	No opportunity to integrate off-the-job learning
Opportunities to participate in more than one working group	Work restricted to one departmental team within one institution

status of their workplace as a 'learning site', and how the learning across their sites operates. As an example, 'In restrictive environments, apprentices are moved as quickly as possible to being productive workers. More expansive workplaces try to ensure that short-term production pressures do not harm the longer-term goals of both the organisation and the individual' (ibid.: 75–76). Fuller and Unwin continue with the conclusion that:

> The implications of this approach for work-based programmes are considerable as they require attention to be paid to the future potential of both the workplace and the individual rather than focusing entirely on the immediate demands of a specific job role or production process.
>
> (ibid.: 76)

There are major implications within the expansive–restrictive for employers who need to recognise the value of an expansive workplace, and there are also implications for the teachers and trainers involved. They need to recognise how the workplace can support learning, and work with employers to support programme design which will facilitate an expansive learning process. They need to recognise learning opportunities within the workplace and ensure they combine with off-the-job learning (e.g., college-based) to extend WBL and enhance workplace activity. They also need to recognise, design, and support opportunities for high-quality assessment in the workplace and work with employers and students to construct learning projects. Finally, they need to seek opportunities to emphasise and develop the relationship between workplace, personal, and community learning. Fuller and Unwin (2019: 82) conclude that co-production is the process that will help expansive workplace learning to take place in the form of an extensive range of collaborations at every level, WBL sites:

> Would benefit from reflecting on the characteristics of their own workplace when thinking through the connections between the way work is organised and the potential for learning arising from work activity. This may require a new approach to the way work is organised and the design of workspaces within educational institutions to enable much greater team working, collective learning and sharing of expertise.
>
> (ibid.: 82)

Questions for discussion (based on Fuller and Unwin, 2019)
1. If you have one, what is your workplace like as a learning site?
2. If not, what is your study location like as a learning site?
3. Where would you place your study or workplace learning site in the expansive/restrictive continuum?

Sector story: Apprentify – an outstanding independent training provider

This is another sector story illustrated by reference to the organisation's most recent Ofsted inspection, which in this case took place in September 2022, with an 'outstanding' result in every area inspected. Apprentify Limited (Apprentify) is an independent training provider which specialises in providing 'apprenticeship training to the digital sector' and 'At the time of the inspection, there were 287 apprentices enrolled on apprenticeships. Most apprentices study at level 3, with the majority of enrolments in digital marketer and junior content producer apprenticeships' (Ofsted, 2022: 1). All of the teaching involved in the apprenticeships takes place online. This provider has taken considerable care in ensuring that they have 'high expectations for their staff, apprentices and employers' (*ibid.*: 2). Apprentify demonstrates best practices in managing apprenticeships, and the report states that:

> Apprentices are enthusiastic and motivated to succeed on their apprenticeship. They consistently demonstrate extremely positive attitudes to their work and their learning. Apprentices complete tasks diligently in preparation for their online training sessions, enabling them to participate fully in group discussions. During online sessions, apprentices demonstrate high levels of respect towards the views and opinions of others.
>
> (*ibid.*: 2)

The company demonstrates imaginative ways of extending WBL into an online environment because:

> Leaders develop an ambitious curriculum that meets the needs of both employers and apprentices. Leaders include additional learning to meet the needs of employers. The junior content producer apprenticeship includes topics on creating content for internal clients. Marketing executive assistant apprentices learn about the need to represent different audiences. They use this information to promote body-positive images when planning campaigns for online clothing retailers.
>
> (*ibid.*: 2)

Apprentify demonstrates a number of expansive characteristics in its provision, including close, collaborative working, mutual support of learning, opportunities for personal development, opportunities to reflect in ways which can help the apprentices to think differently, and a focus on learning as a part of normal working practices.

This example demonstrates the ways in which WBL, particularly apprenticeships, can succeed very well. The company is demonstrating very strong expertise in maintaining relationships with companies supporting and encouraging their apprentices in a highly learner-focused way; building a comprehensive curriculum and training offer with high-quality WBL and even managing to make excellent use of online learning by adopting an expansive approach: an excellent example of a training provider.

Conclusion

WBL in FE is simple to define, but much less simple to develop and manage. As with other subsectors, data on WBL is somewhat piecemeal, but the size and scope of the challenge of meeting the nation's skills needs do emerge very clearly from the data which exists. An analysis of Mechanics' Institutes finds a number of positive characteristics which became part of modern WBL in FE. Apprenticeships are shown to have a long and somewhat mixed history, but they do provide training and experience for many who may otherwise find employment difficult to come by. The introduction of the NCVQ, and the qualifications it presided over, is not one of the more successful developments in WBL in FE, but it did attempt some bold objectives.

Policy development associated with WBL in FE can be shown to be particularly challenging, with particular challenges for the sector recurring. There are strategies available which could lead to improvement for the future of WBL in FE. Fuller and Unwin's expansive and restrictive framework for WBL offers a positive model which could support future action in WBL in FE, and it is argued that WBL could significantly improve if it made more use of the co-production of an expansive learning environment and expansive learning activity.

Chapter summary points

- WBL across England involves a very large number of employees and teachers. This FE subsector is one of the largest contributors to WBL.
- Mechanics' Institutes, the historical development of apprenticeships, and analysis of the introduction of the NCVQ and NVQs have all contributed to the development of WBL in FE.
- Policy development associated with WBL in FE has contained a regularly featured number of challenges for the sector, including partnerships with employers, which are not always successful.
- There are strategies for improvement for the future of WBL in FE, and the use of the expansive and restrictive framework for WBL offers a positive example for the future.

Recommended reading

Fuller, A. and Unwin, L. (2003) Fostering work based learning: Looking through the lens of apprenticeship. *European Educational Research Journal*, 2(1), pp. 41–55.

References

Association of Colleges (2023) *College Key Facts 2022/23*. London: AoC.
Bradbury, A. and Wynne, V. (2020) Apprenticeships. In J. Tummons (Ed.) *PCET: Learning and teaching in the post compulsory sector*. London: Learning Matters.
Department for Education (2023) *Employer skills survey 2022*. London: DfE. Available at: https://explore-education-statistics.service.gov.uk/find-statistics/employer-skills-survey (Accessed 27 October 2023).
Fuller, A. and Unwin, L. (2019) Improving work based capacity as the prerequisite for Effective work-based learning: A co-production approach. In A. Bahl and A. Dietzen (Eds) *Work-based learning as a pathway to competence-based education*. Bonn: Federal Institute for Vocational Education and Training.
Hodgson, A., Gallacher, J., Irwin, T., James, D. and Spours, K. (2018) *FE and skills across the four countries of the UK: New opportunities for policy learning*. London: Edge Foundation.
Hyland, T. (1998) Exporting failure: The strange case of NVQs and overseas markets. *Educational Studies*, 24(3), pp. 369–380, DOI: 10.1080/0305569980240309
Inter-Agency Group on Technical and Vocational Education and Training (IAG-TVET) (2017) *Investing in work-based learning*. Geneva: ILO.
Leitch, A. (2006) *Prosperity for all in the Global economy: World class skills. Final Report*. Norwich: HMSO.
Office for National Statistics (2023a) *Apprenticeships and traineeships. Academic year 2022/23*. London: ONS. Available at: https://explore-education-statistics.service.gov.uk/find-statistics/apprenticeships-and-traineeships (Accessed 28 October 2023).
Office for National Statistics (2023b) *Academic year 2022/23 further education and skills – published 20 July 2023*. London: ONS. Available at: https://explore-education-statistics.service.gov.uk/find-statistics/further-education-and-skills (Accessed 27 October 2023).
Office for National Statistics (2023c) *Business register and employment survey. Employees in the UK: Provisional results 2022*. London: ONS.
Office for Standards in Education (2022) *Inspection of apprentify limited*. Manchester: Ofsted.

Reddy, S. (2017) The prince and English apprenticeships. In M. Daley, K. Orr and J. Petrie (Eds) *The principal: Power and professionalism in FE*. London: IOE Press.

Walker, M. (2012) The origins and development of the Mechanics' Institute Movement 1824–1890 and the beginnings of further education. *Teaching in Lifelong Learning*, 4(1), pp. 37–45.

Walker, M. (2017) *The development of the mechanics' institute movement in Britain and Beyond: Supporting further education for the adult working classes*. Abingdon: Routledge.

5 Adult and community learning (ACL)

Introduction

Adult and community learning (ACL) has a rich tradition of bringing leisure, vocational, and community-oriented learning to some of the most difficult-to-reach organisations, communities, and individuals and this will be discussed in this chapter. Four types of community are explained, and this is followed by an outline of the key characteristics of successful ACL in further education (FE). An explanation of the size of ACL demonstrates that there are significant numbers of people who are learning in this FE subsector in England at any given time, whether they are paying for their tuition and expecting to gain a qualification, are in formal groups or classes, enjoying leisure activities, or learning informally in community-based situations. The first sector story is about a group of 'community researchers' and their experiences.

Key periods from the history of ACL are analysed, including adult schools, an insight into the University of the Third Age (u3a), and localised ACL in the late twentieth century. The second sector story is a first-person account of the author's experience working as an 'Area Adult Education Officer' in the late 1980s. The chapter then explains how this subsector of FE has experienced a particularly difficult time in recent years, with constant reductions in funding, and, as a result, constantly reducing student numbers.

The third sector story features a current ACL provider, Somerset Skills and Leisure (SSL). The chapter closes with positive messages about some signs of improved funding, and inspiring results from a well-funded ACL initiative. Current best practices give hope that ACL could have an improving future.

What is adult and community learning (ACL)?

ACL is the most diverse of all subsectors in FE, and one reason for this is the multiplicity of locations or learning sites in which it can take place. This could include a college, an independent adult education centre, a part of a primary school used for evening classes, a field or forest school, a library, the base of a community group, a sports facility, with a group of volunteers, with a specialist adult learning organisation such as the u3a, and many more. The ethnicity, background, and circumstances of the students and their position in the community or workplace can also be almost any mixture or combination of factors, and students can be from 18 to 118 years old. Overall, ACL is a type of learning which can take place anytime, anywhere, and with anyone.

DOI: 10.4324/9781003468455-5

As seems consistently the case with FE, a subsector with this broad range of students, activities, and learning sites is always going to be difficult to clearly define, but the next section of the chapter introduces and discusses a number of definitions which are available.

Definitions

Firstly, a definition of a 'community' is needed. Craig (2011) defines three types of community:

1. **A geographical community**
   As the title suggests, this type of community would be located in a particular space or area where people are present. The community could include people with a variety of needs in a neighbourhood, a housing estate, a town, a village, an industrial estate, or many other geographical sites.
2. **A community of identity**
   This community could include people in a geographical community; they would have a variety of needs but would share an identity or aspects of a common identity. In this case, their identities or aspects of their identities would tend to connect them. The community could include recreational, gender-based, occupational, cultural, political, and ideological identities, and many more. A friendship group, sports team, political party, or trade union would be examples of communities of identity.
3. **An issues-based community**
   This community would have one or more issues which it shares and would include people with different needs, but they would be connected by one or more issues that they all consider to be important. They could include improving leisure facilities within a given location, support for the disabled, reducing climate change, organisations such as Greenpeace and Amnesty International, and many more. Issue-based communities may wish to campaign and argue their case. When considering the types of community outlined above, there may be elements of different types of community within one community, and this can complicate matters. In addition, there is a fourth, interconnected community which has been added in this book, specifically to relate to ACL in FE.
4. **A community of learners**
   This community can connect across and within all the other types of communities. Each person within such a community would have some shared and some individual needs, and they may or may not recognise the elements of community which are part of their learning. They could be members of an adult education course, a group in a series of businesses, students on formal courses, and individuals taking up informal learning opportunities. Individuals can gain a considerable amount from a community of learners, but everyone in a community of learning can also benefit when all the connections and shared interests overlap and result in shared learning and collaborative action.

Question for discussion

Think back on communities you have been or are part of.
 Can you recognise which of the four types of community you have been in, or are a part of?
 What were the advantages and disadvantages of belonging to that community, and what results or actions came from it?

The government definition of 'community learning' is somewhat narrow, and the short definition that can be found within the official ONS data of student numbers is that it 'includes a range of non-formal courses to promote civic engagement and community development' (ONS, 2023: 1).

A 2020 report from the House of Commons Education Committee defines ACL in more detail, whilst also using a different title for the subsector – 'Adult Community Learning' rather than 'Community Learning', as follows:

> Adult community learning is delivered through a diverse network of providers, including local authority adult education services, colleges, and charities. Most community learning provision is at level 2 (equivalent to GCSE level) or below, including non-formal learning which does not lead to accreditation. It covers a wide range of areas, such as English, maths, digital skills and English for Speakers of Other Languages (ESOL) qualifications, as well as learning aimed at developing employability skills and improving well-being, family-oriented programmes, and learning for leisure and enjoyment.
>
> (House of Commons Education Committee, 2020: 24)

This definition is certainly broader and does cover some relevant areas of ACL in FE, but it very much leans towards employment-related learning opportunities, and somewhat relegates the community focus to a lower status: the whole subsector is consigned to a lower level of study with the statement about most ACL being 'at level 2 (equivalent to GCSE level) or below'. This narrow and reductive government understanding of ACL has affected the importance given to the subsector in policymaking and the level of funding allocated to the sector.

Although outlined over ten years ago, Purcell and Beck's (2010) ideas around the key characteristics of successful ACL remain highly relevant. In summary, they argue that the four key characteristics of ACL are the following:

1. **A small and local focus**
   The issues, interests, needs, and characteristics of community education are usually and initially locally focused, and small in size. This provides a straightforward starting point. The local community who become involved may learn what they need by remaining local, and this indicates success, but the learning can also connect with other learning and grow larger and beyond that small, local focus.
2. **Learning involves self-reflection**
   Opportunities for participants in ACL to reflect on their learning and how it is taking place are essential for the learning to be fully absorbed, recognised, and acted on. It also helps, through collaboration with other members of the community, to broaden the learning from individual members.
3. **Learning involves plans, social capital, skills, and confidence**
   'Social capital' is a term which was brought to recent popular attention by Robert Putnam in his book 'Bowling Alone' (2001), where he argues that the links and connections in communities can be built through learning, and that they can become the 'glue' which holds a healthy community together. Building that social capital is also usually associated with individual members of communities, and whole communities increasing their skills and confidence, and then making plans for improving their own community.

4. **Learning can improve well-being and the health of individuals and communities**

    If the other characteristics of ACL are all present to some degree, the resulting learning can contribute to improved well-being amongst those directly involved as individuals, but it can also make a real difference to a community. If the learning activity continues, the improvements can be ongoing and positive for all.

What is the size of ACL?

Using the previously cited ONS data for Further Education and Skills in 2022/23 across the FE sector, community learning (this is the official government name for this subsector) data is:

> 1,612,130 adult (19+) government-funded further education and skills learners participated in 2022/23:
> Females account for 60.5% (975,880).
>
> (ONS, 2023: 1)

> Community learning participation
> 274,090
> Up by 10.7% from 2021/22

As is becoming familiar, this data gives some indication but is not comprehensive. The 1.6 million figure includes apprentices, and it is not made clear whether the 274,090 learners cited in 'community learning' are part of the overall 1.6 million or not.

The Learning and Work Institute has been undertaking the 'Adult Participation in Learning Survey' almost every year since 1996, and it provides a 'unique overview of the level of participation in learning by adults, with a detailed breakdown of who participates and who does not, over a span of more than 25 years' (Learning and Work Institute, 2022: 4). In comparison with the ONS data cited above, and the associated definition of ACL, this survey takes a very broad view of adult learning. As part of the survey, this definition is provided to the 5,000 adults aged 17 and over who take part:

> Learning can mean practising, studying, or reading about something. It can also mean being taught, instructed, or coached. This is so you can develop skills, knowledge, abilities or understanding of something. Learning can also be called education or training. You can do it regularly (each day or month) or you can do it for a short period of time. It can be full-time or part-time, done at home, at work, or in another place like college. Learning does not have to lead to a qualification. We are interested in any learning you have done, whether or not it was finished.
>
> (ibid.: 6)

The key results from the survey include the following:

> The good news is that, after a decade of declines during the 2010s, participation in learning remains back at levels last seen in the early 2000s: around two in five adults (42 per cent) say they have taken part in learning at some point in the last three years.

> Our survey also highlights stark inequalities in participation in learning. You are more likely to participate in learning if you are younger, from a higher socioeconomic group, already highly qualified, or in work. These inequalities are large and persistent. Tackling them needs to be at the heart of efforts to widen opportunity, reduce disparities, and increase prosperity.
>
> (*ibid.*: 4)

There are further interesting results, which are as follows:

> 57 per cent of adults said that they took up their main learning for their work or career. We are living longer, emphasising the benefits of lifelong learning for health and wellbeing – 35 per cent of learners said their learning had benefited their health and wellbeing. Learning can help us build connections in our community, and many enjoy learning for its own sake or the love of the subject – 22 per cent of learners said their self-confidence had improved, 13 per cent that they are more understanding of other people and cultures, and 29 per cent they now enjoy learning more.
>
> The 2022 survey shows that just over two-fifths (42 per cent) of adults are currently learning or have done so in the last three years. This is a slightly lower participation rate than 2021 (−3 percentage points) but in line with rates seen in the early 2000s after recent years of much lower participation.
>
> (*ibid.*: 4)

> Compared to 2021, participation has declined in England (−3 percentage points).
>
> (*ibid.*: 7)

This set of data is considerably more helpful than some of the other data sources which have been featured so far in this book. Some idea of numbers involved in ACL can be established from the ONS data, but the Learning and Work Institute data also tells us interesting information about who undertakes ACL, and how the data about participation can vary over time. The data on lower participation among lower socio-economic groups is concerning as ACL can bring particular benefits to those groups and individuals, but it is encouraging that participants gain confidence and enhance well-being in addition to the specific, often career-related, benefits involved.

Sector story – South West Foundation community researcher programme

In 2007, South West Foundation, an independent voluntary and community sector organisation, carried out an ACL programme which trained 200 local community members in South West England as 'community researchers'. This project was part of a larger initiative that they undertook relating to community research. The participants in the training programme were generally what are categorised in community data as members of 'deprived communities', and they attended free training so that they could become community researchers. The South West Foundation team provided sessions on the basic principles of planning, carrying out, analysing, and acting on the results of research into particular issues and problems in their local area. This approach assisted the participants to become a community of learners in the first instance, but then also to become an issues-based community.

Having identified an issue, they wished to research in their own community, groups of community researchers created the appropriate evidence, gathering tools to collect data on local issues such as facilities for children, improving play facilities and identifying problems in particular housing estates, and considering the results in order to help to solve those problems. One group first obtained a set of sweatshirts to identify themselves as a legitimate group, and then interviewed over 100 people in the local area, outside shops, outside the school, and in local parks. The main concerns which emerged from the interviews were as follows: a lack of places to meet on their estate, the lack of a crossing near the local supermarket, and issues with a local drug rehabilitation hostel which had been established in a building next to a park where their children played.

Planning, carrying out, and analysing the community research in this case built the confidence of the participants, and they presented the results in a seminar to their local councillors, housing associations, local residents, and council staff. After the successful seminar, the group were offered and then took over a local empty shop to be able to offer ongoing support and action within the local community.

The benefits to both the individuals involved and the local community were summarised by South West Foundation (2012), and they included the following:

Benefits for individuals

- The community researcher programme operated mainly in areas of greatest need, and participants have often had a history of their skills and abilities being unrecognised and under-valued. The programme has enabled those individuals to identify their own skills and value; to increase those skills and confidence and to enable them to contribute to the well-being of their communities.
- Participants became more confident in getting their views across and their voices heard.
- An unintended outcome was that a number of people who had been long-term unemployed gained positions after the training in both paid and unpaid roles in their communities.

Benefits for the wider community

- Views put forward on behalf of the community by the researchers often resulted in those views being acted upon.
- There was an increase in small community groups being established and new community resources being set up.
- Reported improvements in relationships between the local community and agencies such as housing and local authorities took place following the research programme.
- There was an actual improvement in certain measurements in the communities where the researchers became active.
- Community engagement and involvement in communities where the community researchers have been active took place.

All of the characteristics of ACL discussed earlier in this chapter can be seen to have been present in the story and success of the community researchers. They started small, built focus, and application of their learning through reflection, discussion, and analysis, and then acted on the

Extracts from the history of ACL

This section will provide examples from the history of ACL in order to illustrate how provision has developed and changed over time.

Adult schools

'The first "adult school" is said to have begun in Nottingham in 1798 to meet the needs of younger women in lace and hosiery factories. It was independent of any other organization' (Smith, 2004: 3). These schools were essentially bible classes and 'usually met on Sunday mornings and afternoons, were run by voluntary teachers, and generally their aim was to teach reading (especially the New Testament)' (*ibid.*: 3). Towards the end of the nineteenth century, the schools had broadened the selection of topics and subject areas covered, with a

> growing emphasis on discussion, fellowship, and mutual aid activities such as book or library clubs, savings banks, sick funds and temperance societies. By the end of the century there appear to have been around 350 schools involving some 45,000 participants.
>
> (*ibid.*: 4)

The majority of adult schools were run by Quakers. At their peak, by 1909–10, 'there were some 1900 schools involving over 114,000 adults' (*ibid.*: 4). Although bible study was at the centre of the schools, they also adopted 'democratic, unsectarian, and non-party methods of working' (*ibid.*: 4). As the twentieth century progressed, the numbers in adult schools dropped away, with just 2,000 participants by 1970. Smith (2004: 6) concludes that:

> Adult schools were the first dedicated educational provision for adults in Britain. Their emphasis on fellowship and the spiritual nature of education was significant and carried into other institutions. Their use of discussion and concern with democratic ways of working was an important element in the making of 'adult education method'.

The u3a (University of the Third Age)

ACL is very popular with older adults, but there is very little provision, which is directly aimed at them, or intended especially for senior citizens. The u3a, often still known as the University of the Third Age, is a charitable organisation which exists entirely to give 'enjoyment of learning of subjects of interest to' adults who are in their 'third age'. The third age is defined as being a focus on 'people who are no longer in full-time employment or raising a family' (u3a, 2023: 1). The UK u3a movement was founded in 1982, and the 'the guiding principles were to promote non-formal learning through self-help interest groups covering a wide range of topics and activities as chosen by their members' (*ibid.*: 2). The self-help interest groups can be in almost any area or subject, and a collaborative approach was at the centre of all u3as. Participation is voluntary, and 'group leaders', the teachers of the groups, would be considered equal to all in their group, and all members could take a turn at leading if they chose to. By 2023, there were:

> 1,035 u3as with nearly 400,000 members; membership costs less than £20 on average per year and is open to everyone who's not working full-time.
>
> u3a has members who draw upon their knowledge and experience to teach and learn from each other but there are no qualifications to pass – it is just for pleasure. Learning is its own reward.
>
> It's all voluntary; a typical u3a will be home to many activity groups covering hundreds of different subjects - from art to zoology and everything in between.
>
> (*ibid*.: 1)

A typical branch of u3a would have between 40 and 60 groups available and about 6–700 members. There would typically be groups in painting, current affairs, book club, foreign languages, badminton, and music making, and any person who wanted to start a group to share their own particular expertise could be given that opportunity.

The u3a movement has achieved a significant amount for older adults and their ACL, but it has also faced critiques such as that from Formosa (2019: 259) when he argues that, despite the 'benefits of participation in U3As on learners' quality of life, and social and psychological well-being … The u3as' track record in the democratisation of late-life learning – especially in terms of social class, gender, disability, and ethnic biases –leaves much room for improvement, to the extent that one can conclude that many u3as are reinforcing a degree of inequality amongst older persons in general but especially amongst the most vulnerable sectors of the ageing population.

There is little doubt that while many older adults have gained considerably in their ACL with a u3a, many other, generally less well-off or disabled older adults, do not always share those gains.

Localised ACL during the late twentieth century

Tuckett (2019: 9) argues that 'the development of educational opportunities for adults in England through much of the 20th century happened in the main through local development, responding to local demand with spasms of state interventions'. Local authorities, local charities, and local organisations developed and provided a powerful portfolio of learning opportunities for adults in their area, and reductions or removal of fees became available to a generous degree in the 1970s and 1980s. It was not unusual to be able to choose classes in floral art, politics, badminton, dressmaking, assertiveness, French, typing, and woodwork for adults with reduced vision, and literally hundreds more, just through one adult education centre. These would be for work, leisure, or personal advancement, and would run for 10, 20, or 30 weeks or for short one-day workshop sessions. There would be a new programme of learning opportunities three times a year, in autumn, winter, and summer. They would have taken place in local authority premises, FE colleges, schools, adult education centres, companies, village halls, or any other venue which would be prepared to have them.

Sector story – being an area adult education organiser in the 1980s

The author of this volume worked through the 1980s as an 'area adult education officer'. I was based in an FE college and was one of seven area adult education officers working across what was then the county of Avon. My area included Bristol, Bath, Norton Radstock, and outlying areas towards Weston Super Mare. My area also included a specialist adult education centre in Keynsham, which had been part of the local authority ACL, but which merged into my newly established area. The job involved developing and operating an annual ACL programme. There were very few restrictions on what could be included, and the financial basis of the programme was an overall balancing of income through student fees with the cost of paying tutors, who were either part-time specialists or staff already working in the college who taught adult education classes in the evening. In the 1985–86 year, the prospectus contained 72 subjects from yoga and choral singing to electronics and computers, and in the region of 300 courses. Thirty course centres were listed to accommodate the programme. There were also specialist courses to help with adult literacy and numeracy, an ongoing range of courses for unemployed adults, and community projects which included ACL in their activities as part of an 'open house' approach. This highly localised approach to provision was straightforward, and if enough people didn't enrol, the course had to close after one or two weeks. At the start of each year, I would visit classes in our centres to collect fees and make sure all were viable and operating in the correct manner, and the visits would include secondary schools (some would have 20 or more classes a week), village halls, local sports facilities, meeting rooms, libraries, and churches. Although a large proportion of the activity took place as evening classes, there was also a growing programme of daytime ACL learning opportunities. Local organisations were enthusiastic about collaborating on developing ACL provision, and there were very few restrictions in doing so. Overall, this locally focused set of provisions met most of the expectations the tutors, providers, and groups involved had about providing positive learning opportunities for their local communities. The class visits and being present at the annual enrolment event demonstrated the demand, enjoyment, and community benefit which arose from what now seems like a golden age of ACL.

Decline and recovery

ACL has experienced a difficult time in the twenty-first century. Tuckett (2019: 3) reports that between 2004 and 2011, 2 million adult learners were lost, as the numbers reduced from 4,600,000 to 2,650,000. The Institute for Fiscal Studies, in a study of 'Adult Education', also provides some stark details including the following:

There have been large falls in the numbers of adult learners and spending on adult education in the last decade.

> Total spending on adult education and apprenticeships fell by 38% between 2010–11 and 2020–21, with a 50% fall in spending on classroom based adult education. The numbers of adult learners also fell significantly particularly those taking low level qualifications, with a 50% fall in numbers taking qualifications at level 2 and below, and a 33% fall in the number of adults taking Level 3 qualifications.
>
> Total spending on adult education and apprenticeships will still be 25% lower in 2024–25 compared with 2010–11.

(IFS, 2022: 2)

Adult and community learning

There are some government plans to reverse those costs at least partially, with an 'additional 900 million in extra public spending in 2024–25' for adult education, and the introduction of entitlement to a 'lifelong loan' (*ibid.*: 2).

These are worrying figures and although another different definition of adult education is used in this report (it includes low-level qualifications; apprenticeships, sub-degree qualifications, and degrees) the loss of funding and numbers for what this chapter is calling ACL is also clear. Although endorsing some of the recent improvements in ACL funding with which the report closes, the conclusion is not overly optimistic. They argue that the new programmes for 'helping adults with few qualifications' are 'relative untested' and that 'providing effective support and training for this group is a significant challenge, but it will also be key to levelling up poorer areas of the country' (*ibid.*: 34).

Sector story – Somerset skills and learning (SSL)

SSL is a 'Community Interest Company' (CIC), which is a type of not-for-profit organisation intended to operate as a business but also contribute to their community through their activities. The philosophy and approach of this ACL provider can be seen from how it describes itself in its regular programme publication:

> We're here to support you as part of our local community.
>
> As an Adult Learning Community Interest Company (CIC), we provide many free courses through Government funding. We also reinvest any profits to make more courses and qualifications available to you, to help build your skills now and in the future.
>
> What we offer is special! We're not like college as you know it – you'll learn with like-minded people, in small, local classes or online.
>
> We have expert tutors who are committed to helping you achieve your goals and always have time for you. Your progression and success is at the heart of everything we do.
>
> We'd love to welcome you through our doors in person or virtually - see you soon!
>
> (Somerset Skills and Learning, 2023: 2)

As has been the case with other sector stories in this book, it is useful to refer to the Ofsted inspection on SSL which was rated 'good' in 2022. The inspection report describes SSL as follows:

> Somerset Skills and Learning (SSL) is a community interest company (CIC). SSL primarily provides education and training to adult learners, many of whom have barriers to learning, which aims to help them to achieve their potential in the community and at work. SSL offers a wide range of non-accredited community courses to adults ... SSL provides courses at five training centres in Somerset, online, and at community venues in targeted locations across the county.
>
> At the time of the inspection, most of the 1,000 learners are adults studying multiple community learning programmes. Most programmes are short in duration, such as, a single introductory online lesson or a few weeks of classroom-based workshops. Many learners' study with one of SSL's 19 subcontractors. The subcontractors enable SSL to provide education and training to some of the most deprived communities in Somerset.

The inspectors' comments about student experiences of adult students of SSL include the following:

> Learners of all ages are mostly well prepared for life in modern Britain. Teachers ... are knowledgeable and encourage learners to take part in discussions, such as, how democracy links to the workplace.
>
> Staff at SSL and its subcontractors understand how to help the communities they serve, focusing on the people most in need of the courses they teach.
>
> Leaders at SSL have taken great care to enter partnerships with organisations that work closely with vulnerable and disadvantaged people in Somerset.
>
> Teachers create calm and welcoming learning environments in classrooms, online and outdoors. As a result, learners feel comfortable, enjoy attending classes and feel safe.
>
> Adult learners see the health and well-being sessions as places where they can divulge safely personal information and feelings with their teacher and their peers. For example, they gain enough self-assurance to talk about what are often deep-seated issues. Adult learners increase in confidence and take part in activities that they would not previously have felt comfortable doing with other people, such as seated exercise.
>
> Learners develop a positive attitude as a result of studying the curriculum and the interaction with their peers. Much of the health and wellbeing community provision helps adult learners stay physically fit and/or mentally healthy. This is because staff in the training and community centres, used for hosting courses, are welcoming and well-practised in how to gain the confidence of people who are anxious about starting a course.
>
> (Ofsted, 2022: 2)

It can be seen from the inspection report that a good number of the key principles of ACL discussed earlier in this chapter are present.

> For example, the aim of the community learning provision is to provide vulnerable and/or disadvantaged adults with the opportunity to improve their well being while studying in a safe learning environment; ESOL learners, many of whom are Ukrainian refugees, study a curriculum which is flexible in structure and accommodates mixed ability groups successfully.
>
> (ibid.: 3)

Overall, SSL is 'a valued and respected community partner that contributes significantly to the educational and social well-being of people in Somerset' (ibid.: 3).

SSL is developing both an issues-based community and a community of learners, and they are growing community benefit in Somerset using reflection, which builds into greater personal confidence and community well-being.

Hope in catastrophic times

Despite the challenges faced by ACL in recent times and the dramatic reduction in participation in ACL, it is still possible to find projects and provisions which stand out and offer hope for the future. Purcell (2022: 22) researched an ACL project where a coalition of voluntary sector organisations combined in an initiative called 'Community Wise' to 'help people to overcome barriers to "finding their future" by helping community groups deliver creative and engaging activities in local neighbourhoods, designed to encourage people to try a new activity or learn a new skill'. The research started by recognising that 'already excluded people are becoming more marginalised' (*ibid.*: 223). Purcell interviewed participants individually and in groups, took part in project activities, observed sessions, and constructed the research in order to ensure that the perspectives of the participants were given priority. Community Wise offered 'taster' sessions in a wide range of subjects: interest groups involving men's mental health, community food initiatives, and women's support groups. Sessions took place in a wide range of locations, including village halls, community centres, cafes, school hubs, and rooms in pubs. If the taster sessions were successful, longer learning activities were developed, and subjects were added and removed through continuous negotiations with the prospective and actual students. The target for participation was 500, but over 2,200 people actually took part.

On evaluating the success of the initiative, Purcell argued that not many of the participants who had taken part in Community Wise and the research 'would be immediately suited to taking part in learning opportunities in traditional settings or groups' (*ibid.*: 235). He concludes that the learner-focused, confidence-building, and collaborative approaches of this ACL project:

> Facilitates individuals' choices to engage in meaningful-to-them activities that can accommodate the mental and physical health challenges they face; and, through the development of genuine social relationships with practitioners and peers based on mutuality, care and respect, can go some way towards ameliorating the impact of these on their daily lives.

Question for discussion

From your understanding of the content of this chapter, what would be your three main priorities to recover and strengthen ACL in FE?

Conclusion

ACL is a particularly diverse and wide-ranging subsector of FE and is as difficult to define as any, but it survives and provides learning benefits for many individuals and communities, despite experiencing reduced numbers and funding over more than the last ten years. ACL continues to offer support and learning for many adults, either within the more formal part of ACL or in the more informal learning activities which can sometimes take place within different types of community.

The four types of community and the adoption of most of the key values and characteristics can be seen in the examples of ACL discussed in the chapter, and they can also be seen in the moments from history which are introduced. Historically, the latter part of the twentieth century could be described as a good period for ACL, with many opportunities available locally which were easy to access for many members of local communities.

The particularly difficult time ACL in FE has had in the twenty-first century to date, with constant reductions in funding, and, as a result, constantly reducing student numbers, have certainly made growth and continuing existence particularly difficult. Despite this, the examples in this chapter offer positive messages and results which suggest that ACL in FE has much life in it yet, especially when positive, localised community-centred opportunities for provision are made available and undertaken by members of that community.

Summary points

- ACL makes vocational and community-oriented learning available to some of the most difficult-to-reach organisations, communities, and individuals.
- Four types of community are explained, and the four key characteristics of successful ACL are introduced.
- The size and scope of adult and community learning are as broad as any FE subsector and make ACL difficult to define overall.
- Key moments from the history of ACL provide insights into how ACL has developed over time.
- The decline of ACL in FE participation and funding in recent years has been a particularly difficult period.
- There are positive messages from more localised and community-centred projects and collaboration in ACL, and they offer some hope for the future.

Recommended reading

Putnam, R.D. (2001) *Bowling alone*. New York: Simon and Schuster.

References

Craig, G. (2011) Introduction. In G. Craig, M. Mayo, K. Popple, M. Shaw and M. Taylor (Eds) *The community development reader: History, themes and issues*. Bristol: Policy Press.
Formosa, M. (2019) Concluding remarks and reflections. In M. Formosa (Ed.) *The University of the third age and active ageing*. New York: Springer.
House of Commons – Education Committee (2020) *A plan for an adult skills and lifelong learning revolution*. London: House of Commons.
Institute for Fiscal Studies (2022) *Adult education, the past, the present and the future*. London: IFS.
Learning and Work Institute (2022) *Adult participation in learning survey 2022*. Leicester: Learning and Work Institute.
Office for National Statistics (2023) *Academic Year 2022/23 further education and skills – published 20 July 2023*. London: Office for National Statistics. Available at: https://explore-education-statistics.service.gov.uk/find-statistics/further-education-and-skills (Accessed 01 November 2023).
Office for Standards in Education (Ofsted) (2022) *Inspection of somerset skills and learning CIC*. Manchester: Ofsted.
Purcell, M.E. (2022) Hope in 'catastrophic' times: Participants' stories of nurture and transformation from an innovative community learning initiative. *Research in Post-Compulsory Education*, 27(2), pp. 219–241, DOI: 10.1080/13596748.2022.2042906
Purcell, R. and Beck, D. (2010) *Popular education practice for youth and community development work*. London: Learning Matters.
Putnam, R.D. (2001) *Bowling alone*. New York: Simon and Schuster.
Smith, M.K. (2004) *Adult schools and the making of adult education*. The encyclopaedia of pedagogy and informal education. Available at: https://infed.org/mobi/adult-schools-and-the-making-of-adult-education/ (Accessed 2 November 2023).
Somerset Skills and Learning (2023) *Learning for life: Autumn 2023*. Bridgwater: Somerset Skills and Learning.
South West Foundation (2012) *Engaging outcomes: an Evaluation Report of South West foundation's community researcher programme*. Camerton: South West Foundation
Tuckett, A. (2019) *The rise and fall of life-wide learning for adults in England*. University of Wolverhampton Repository. Wolverhampton: University of Wolverhampton.
u3a (2023) about us. Available at: https://www.u3a.org.uk/about (Accessed 3 October 2023).

6 Widening participation (WP) and access to higher education

Introduction

This chapter features the cross-sector theme of widening participation (WP) in further education (FE) and also includes analysis of the development, growth, and success of 'access to higher education' courses. After first defining WP, the chapter will illustrate the history of WP with three examples. The chapter then continues by discussing the barriers to WP and analysing how those barriers can be reduced or removed. The first sector story is about Brenda, a women returner course student.

The final sector of the chapter outlines the history and development of access to higher education (HE) courses and their major contribution to WP. A range of data on their numbers, progression to degrees, and degree success is included. The section also includes consideration of the experiences of access students, those who were teaching them, and how they contributed to the overall success. The chapter closes with the second sector story, Gavin McKay, a mature access-course student success story.

Definitions

Throughout its history, the natural target group for the FE sector has been people who have completed school or left school early, and adults who wish to continue with their lifelong learning. In more recent times, FE has also worked with 14–16-year-olds, and the majority of the people who are students in FE are in their 'post-school' period (i.e. after they have left school). Working with this group means that the FE sector needs to encourage and attract prospective students from all parts of the community who are of post-school age and persuade them to participate in FE. From the number of students across the sector and within FE subsectors which have been presented in this book in the other chapters, it can be seen that there are a large number of post-school participants who are indeed engaging with FE. Because FE is not compulsory education, however, the sector needs to encourage, persuade, and support members of the community to take part, and some are more willing or ready than others.

The process of persuading all members of the community to engage in increasing numbers with post-school learning is what has become known as the 'widening participation' movement in FE. When writing about or researching 'widening participation', the academic focus has tended to be on WP from FE to HE and researching the processes and practices which help people from under-represented groups to get to university and help them achieve and succeed whilst there. This is extremely important and has been positively supported by government policy more strongly than

DOI: 10.4324/9781003468455-6

other aspects of WP. It is not, however, the only focus of WP, particularly in this chapter, the focus is much wider. WP, as understood in this chapter, is about the following:

The efforts of government, providers, organisations, communities, and individuals to increase and deepen participation and progression in FE and from FE of all sections of the community, especially those who are under-represented and those who find participation difficult. WP also includes the approaches, techniques, principles, and practices which help members of the community to participate in FE, and the support from FE and other sectors which assists and maintains that participation and progression.

Moments from the history of WP

Really useful knowledge

Early attempts to reach 'the disadvantaged, the oppressed, the working class with relevant education' are described as 'part of the social history of the common people' and they reached 'across nations and back into the beginnings of the industrial revolution in the early 19th century' (Lovett, 1994: 3). These attempts were part of a search for what has been described as 'really useful knowledge' (Johnson, 1988), and introducing working people to that knowledge. This search:

> Occupied the attention of many social, trade union and community activists, as well as numerous committed adult educators. Many of these adult education initiatives were, in fact, social movements with a particular view of the nature of men and women and concerned to help create the sort of society which would develop their capabilities and talents to the full.
> (Lovett, 1994: 3)

One example of an organisation which was set up at least partially to engage a wider range of members of the community in 'really useful education' was the Workers' Education Association (WEA), started in 1903 with the express aim of bringing education to working-class people. The WEA was 'democratic and flexible in its teaching methods' and sought to develop 'a more critical analytical approach in its students'. Overall, the 'WEA was essentially a reformist movement' (*ibid.*: 8), and it still exists today, 120 years later. The WEA in 2023 states that 'in the last year alone, we supported 30,000 learners to achieve their goals'.

> Increasing the WEA is supporting learners to gain the skills they need to get their first job, return from unemployment and to get on in their careers. 45% of unemployed learners studying with us went on to get a job and over 60% felt more confident about getting one and knowing better what to do. 43% employed learners went on to earn more after their course.
> (WEA, 2023: 1)

Just what 'really useful knowledge' meant varied for different organisations, thinkers, educators, and philanthropists. It could relate to basic knowledge and understanding to help people succeed when working in the Industrial Revolution; it could also relate to a broader vision of workplace skills; and it could also relate to more broad knowledge about society and the roles of people within it. Overall, however, it is a title which has united a range of differing views, and it has a positive history of helping to widen participation in adult learning.

Return to work courses

Worth's (2019) research found optimistic signs in the 'Long 1970s' of 'women's mobility' and that 'post-war women returned to the education system and obtained post-secondary qualifications during the 1970s. Between 1971 and 1981, the total number of the female population with qualifications increased by 50 percent' (ibid.: 68). Before this, 'the women who attended university, just like those who passed the 11-plus exam were much more likely to be middle class' (ibid.: 68). Starting in the 'Long 1970s':

> The changing structures of post-compulsory education gave women born between the late 1930s and early 1950s an important avenue back into education. Women took up these educational opportunities in droves, especially from the early 1970s onward – a trend which has been neglected by historians. As the decades progressed, it became harder for women of the post war generation to let go of the idea of education and be satisfied with routine non-manual work. Their sense of what they wanted out of life and what they thought was possible to achieve in their careers, was shifting during this period.
>
> (ibid.: 78–79)

By the late 1980s, participation by women, especially working-class women, had slowed. During this period,

> One of the most innovative developments in further education in Britain during the 1980s was the growth of education and vocational training devised especially for adult women, in particular those who had been out of the labour market because they were for a period full-time mothers. Courses designed to help them return to work, through confidence building, the 'brushing up' of existing skills or the learning of new skills were developed in local authority colleges or in voluntary organisations.
>
> Initially they received little support or sometimes even outright hostility from further education management, which was almost totally male dominated, but through the decade such courses became increasingly respectable and established, not least because substantial funding could be attracted.
>
> (Sheridan, 1992: 213–214)

Data on how many women returner courses operated in the late 1980s and 1990s is difficult to find, but most colleges, including the one where the present author was the area adult education officer, did offer free women returner courses which were extremely popular. They were often available across three separate terms, and even during holiday periods, and in other local venues. Because of the number of courses which would have been available across England, it is reasonable to estimate that at least 5,000 women returners would have been involved in courses in English FE over the two-to-three-year period that the funding was available. The courses were free, with bookable creche places, and not only included hands-on computing, assertiveness, and job search skills as part of the course but also included career guidance, personal action planning, and personal projects to build the participants' overall confidence and well-being.

Saxby-Smith and Shepherd (2000) researched the participation of women in returner courses and found the participants regarded most content especially useful, including work placements, confidence building, communication and presentation skills, and recognising the skills they had already gained from their life experiences. One participant had

> Never been in paid employment but had set up a tenants' association and was the secretary of her son's football team. Through the course she realised that she already had a range of useful skills and an aptitude for learning.
>
> (*ibid.*: 231)

The feedback from participants also highlighted that the teachers 'co-operative, shared and experiential teaching and learning strategies' involved 'the use of team building events to develop organisational, interpersonal and problem-solving skills' (*ibid.*: 231). Saxby-Smith and Jones (2000) conclude overall that such courses 'illuminate a reality of women's lives' (*ibid.*: 232). Women returners courses made a relatively small contribution towards WP overall, but a significant, life-changing contribution to many of the participants.

The Kennedy Report

During the last two decades of the twentieth century, participation in post-16 education grew rapidly. By 1996, in the United Kingdom, 'more than 80 percent of 16-year-olds participated in some form of education or training' (Thomas, 2001: 2). There were also 'about 60 per cent of 18-year olds' (*ibid.*: 2) who also participated in education or training. Despite this increase, concern was growing that those who were continuing to participate were largely those who had already achieved in the school sector. In 1997, an important report on the history of WP in FE was published. The Kennedy Report (1997: 3) reinforced the concern introduced above by stating that:

> There has been growth, but the students recruited have not come from a sufficiently wide cross-section of the community and there is concern that initiatives to include more working-class people, more disaffected young people, more women, more people from ethnic minority groups are being discontinued because they fall through the gaps in the system. Attracting and keeping those for whom learning is a daunting experience is hard work and financially unrewarding. The effort and resources required to support such students on courses receives insufficient recognition in the current funding system.

In her critique of the situation in 1997, Kennedy argued that the incorporation of colleges, as discussed in Chapter 2, was accompanied by 'improved responsiveness to learners' needs' but that, as some providers 'competed for those students most likely to succeed', competition also 'inhibited the collaboration needed to widen participation'. FE needed to 'expand the demand for learning as a whole' (*ibid.*: 35).

Kennedy made a range of important recommendations including:

- A government campaign to create a 'learning nation';
- Redistribution of public resources 'towards those with less success in earlier learning';
- The establishment of 'a lifetime entitlement to education ... which is free for young people and those who are socially and economically deprived';

- The creation of 'a national network of strategic partnerships to identify local need, stimulate demand, respond creatively and promote learning';
- Encouraging employers to provide learning centres linked to a 'University for Industry';
- Reform of financial support to students to promote equity and 'Welfare to Work through Learning'; and
- The setting of new national learning targets and local targets for participation (Kennedy, 1997:13–14).

Although the Kennedy Report was considered to be extremely significant at the time, there were contemporary critiques. Tight (1998) in particular argued that

> While the government has now articulated the rhetoric, and begun some additional investment in the achievement, of lifelong learning, it remains to be seen how these initiatives will work out. Those working in post-compulsory education and training have been disappointed too often in the past to believe wholeheartedly that their time has come at last (Tight, 1998: 482). Despite this comment being twenty-five years old, it very similar to current comments from research and FE practitioners already featured in this book. Tight also voices concern over the emphasis on economic and employment-related learning, at the expense of other kinds of learning. His critique concludes that the movements in policy and approach in the Kennedy report offer a less than enticing vision for those it is aimed to help.
>
> Lifelong learning for all is the new imperative. Its curriculum is primarily vocational in content and intent. It is our fault if we have not participated to date. We risk social and economic exclusion if we do not participate in the future. We must pay directly for our participation.
>
> (*ibid.*: 384)

As was apparent from the data in Chapter 5, adult participation in FE has been reducing for the past ten years. At the time of writing in 2023, it is starting to recover, but under-represented groups are still under-represented, and Kennedy's vision of a 'learning nation' still remains to be fully realised.

> **Question for discussion**
> Give three reasons why WP does or doesn't matter.

Barriers to WP – why do or don't people participate?

This chapter has introduced key aspects of WP and will now consider the barriers that exist and how to overcome them. McGiveney (1990, 1996, 1999) made important contributions to the attempts to widen participation through her research, and many of her findings remain current today. McGiveney identified the key barriers to participation for the groups it was important to engage:

- **Motivation** – personal factors such as family, life situation, and a view that learning was not for them;
- **Finances** – unable to fund travel, fees, and resource costs from their own income;

- **Life circumstances** – disability, caring responsibilities, homelessness, poor mental health;
- **Lack of information** – not knowing how or where to find out about learning opportunities;
- **Institutional** – the approach and culture of providers and in particular their programmes, teachers, their support, and funding.

The literature on WP in FE is dominated by the topic of increasing participation in HE, but it is possible to identify ways of reducing the above barriers from the work of McGiveney and Thomas, and more recently Thompson (2019).

All of these strategies involve working collaboratively with local FE providers, charities, voluntary sector organisations, local authorities, and employers to reduce the barriers.

- **Motivation** – organise open, supportive, and free tasters, short courses, and events in local communities where they can be accessed;
- **Finances** – make funding for travel available, but also site activities in local easy-to-access venues;
- **Life circumstances** – ensure sites are accessible, with creche provision where necessary, and work with social services to organise and support events and activities; arrange advice and guidance support including relating to welfare benefits to be available in the venues;
- **Lack of information** – produce clear, accessible information and make it available in local communities;
- **Institutional** – work with partners to adopt a friendly, flexible, supportive, and organised approach. Identify appropriately skilled staff to work with participants. It is essential that participants feel welcome. Promote and make available progression.

These are characteristics of provision which will encourage and increase WP in FE and contribute to realising the intentions which were perhaps more powerful in the twentieth century than the twenty-first century.

Sector story – second step student – Brenda

Brenda is a 21-year-old single mum with two young children. She left school with a small collection of low-grade GCSEs, and now works part-time in a local petrol station where they are flexible about shifts which she can take. Her childcare costs each week are close to the same as her earnings, and she just survives on a small amount of state benefits. When at school, and before getting pregnant at 16, Brenda was really interested in becoming a teacher herself but did not get enough qualifications to progress to the next stage.

As Brenda is walking through the town centre, she passes the advice centre of the local voluntary organisation that often helps her with benefits and financial advice and guidance. She notices an advert for a free 'Second Step course' for women which says that the first step is coming to the course, and the second step will be to be helped to think about new directions. The ten-session free course is taking place in a community hall in town, with creche facilities, and there are six sessions. The content includes building your skills, considering what your future could hold, and working with the tutors and other participants on making progress towards the next step.

Brenda joins the course with some trepidation, but rapidly finds the other nine participants have much in common with her, and that they can support each other in solving everyday problems and looking towards the future. Brenda sees that more local learning opportunities are available at the local FE college, and that another course, also with creche facilities, starts after the Second Step course. The female course tutor is really positive and helpful, and by the end of the six weeks, Brenda has made an action plan and signed up for a basic computing course and an 'improve your maths and English' course.

After taking her first and second steps, Brenda now feels she may well have a future, even as a teacher, and is looking forward to what comes next.

Access to higher education courses

The chapter will now consider what has been a successful contributor to the cause of WP in FE and HE, and the history, content, and approaches of 'access to higher education' courses. Access to HE courses originally started in the 1970s and was aimed at people who did not have A-levels, the normal qualifications for entering HE. The course content 'traditionally combined two main features: a curriculum concerned with preparation for HE, and a course of study aimed at those excluded, disadvantaged, delayed or otherwise deterred by a need to qualify for (university) entry in more conventional ways' (Brine and Waller, 2004: 98). At the time, this was a really positive step forward for those who were under-represented in FE and HE. Access to HE courses was for mature members of the community who had not gained at least two A-levels to progress to a university place. Access was a different, highly supportive and much more person-focused route, and was in a number of ways similar to returner courses. The colleges which ran access courses negotiated a suitable curriculum with one or more local universities, and, subject to students successfully completing the course, the university concerned would offer a place. The courses gave 'mature students a yardstick against which they can measure their experience of higher education (HE); many compared favourably the "supportive" environment of the Access course with the experience of a more "anonymous" university course' (*ibid.*: 98).

By 1989, there were approximately 400 access courses in 50 local education authorities, with 6,000 students in FE colleges (Smithers and Robinson, 1989). By 2014, access to HE had grown to more than 40,000 students, and that number has been maintained, with more than 40,855 students registered to study an access to HE diploma in 2020–21 (QAA, 2023: 1).

Because of the rapid growth of access to HE courses, it became necessary to organise them more systematically on a national basis. In 1989, the Council for National Academic Awards (CNAA) established a national framework for the approval of courses. Since 1997, the Quality Assurance Agency (QAA) has been responsible for the national framework, of what is now the 'access to HE diploma'. Access courses are still intended to be:

> a course designed to respond to the need to broaden participation in HE. They assume the need for, and desirability of, increased participation by those groups which are currently under represented in HE and are built on the principle of extending opportunities for progression to HE for those adults who have benefitted the least from their past education experience.
> (James and Busher, 2018: 1)

Since their original introduction in the 1970s, access courses to specific occupational areas have proliferated, and they include access to 'Health, Public Services and Care', 'Social Sciences', and 'Arts, Media and Publishing'. Overall, there were '197 different diploma titles' (QAA, 2023: 3).

Access courses are still not only mainly provided by and in FE colleges but they are also part of the curriculum of sixth-form colleges, adult and community learning providers, and private providers. At least partly because of their success, government pressure on providers has increased, and the managerialism which has already been identified within the FE sector has also had an effect on access to HE courses. James and Busher (2018: 3–4) argue that 'courses set up to widen participation can be institutionally marginalised because performative education policies emphasise efficiency regardless of the other benefits of education'.

What was it like to study or teach on access to HE courses?

The next section of this chapter considers what the experience was like for learners and teachers on access to HE courses. In a small study of ten Access students, interviews with the students revealed that they had experienced a number of challenges and successes prior to the access course, including unsuccessful and successful previous educational experiences, financial pressures making continuing study difficult, negative peer pressure about education (in communities where progression to HE was not valued), and mixed motivation. Overall, the study found a mixture of results:

> Emerging findings reveal that (re)engaging with education and the transition from 'access student' to undergraduate student is not seamless and without challenges. Such students 'often undergo a unique and profound experience' (Hudson, 2020: 6) as they enter this new space which provides an opportunity to create new social and class-related identities. The transition to undergraduate study is easier when learners are familiar with the routines and rhythms of higher education in general and the facilities and services of a particular institution.
>
> (Hudson *et al.*, 2020: 1)

These characteristics of the support available for students in access to HE courses are referenced in other research, including Busher *et al.* (2015) who found students stated they learned better with the positive support of both their tutors and fellow students, and that 'support appeared to contribute significantly to students' individual successes and help to build their confidence as learners' (*ibid.*: 136).

When it comes to how teachers experienced teaching access to HE courses, Busher *et al.* (2015) investigated this with a piece of research involving 24 access to HE tutors from a range of colleges in the East Midlands of England. First, the tutors appeared to empathise with the students and their experiences, and this was partly because they 'had had similar experiences themselves' (*ibid.*: 128). Others preferred teaching adults and considered access to HE courses to be 'morally an important route for non-traditional learners' (*ibid.*: 129). Tutors were proud of their course and proud of their students' efforts to become 'properly independent learners and researchers' (*ibid.*: 129). Overall, the tutors recognised the course was a major challenge for the students, but both were pleased that they could help and felt rewarded by a feeling that they were helping people make positive life changes. They did recognise how the counter-productive atmosphere of college management and institutional procedures could be even more difficult for access courses than other courses, but overall 'tutors seemed to feel a moral responsibility for trying to help as many students as possible to be successful in their studies' (*ibid.*: 137), and they often succeeded with that task.

One question which has often been about access to HE courses is: 'What happens to them once they get on a degree course?' Although this has varied across the years since access courses started, at present the figures are mainly positive.

In 2021–22
88.8 per cent of Access to HE students completed their courses, in comparison with
85.1 per cent of other courses
Degree classifications were:
Access to HE students Students with other qualifications
First 25.3 per cent 26.1 per cent
2:1   32.8 per cent 37.7 per cent
2:2   18.0 per cent 13.7 per cent.

QAA (2023a: 2)

Access to HE courses is an important and successful part of the FE sector landscape and has changed the lives of many people.

Sector story – Gavin McKay

The QAA 'Access to Higher Education' website has a number of 'real stories' about access course participants, and Gavin McKay is one of those (QAA, 2023b: 1). Gavin had been working in a secondary school as their ICT manager (a non-teaching role). It was a secure and reasonably well-paid job, but Gavin had always 'wished he had followed a career in Paramedics' (*ibid*.: 2). He was 46 and had been out of education for 'a substantial number of years' (*ibid*.: 2), and it was essential to gain a relevant degree to be able to work as a paramedic. Gavin discovered that access to HE courses at his local college could gain him entry to the paramedic degree course. He began his access course in 2019 and found that 'the support from the lecturers and management team ... provided an excellent start to the initial steps and pathway to my chosen career' (*ibid*.: 3). Studying full time for a year put pressure on the family's finances, but Gavin succeeded with the support of his family, and completed the access course in 2020. At the time of writing, he is in the second year of his chosen paramedic degree. One of his tutors commented that Gavin:

> Is a testament to how dedication, commitment and ambition can unlock an individual's potential, and proof that adult learners can achieve their goals at any age or stage in life. Gavin shows us that childhood dreams of a career can come true in later life, provided you have the drive and dedication necessary to see it through.

(ibid.: 3)

Question for discussion

Access courses are for people over 19.
 Do you think they should be made available for 16–18-year-olds?

Conclusion

The cross-sector theme of WP in FE has been a strong part of the mission of FE ever since there has been FE. There have been periods of growth and periods of decline, and participation of those most disadvantaged in society is still not what society would wish it to be. There are many success stories about widening participation to and from FE, however, and these are given prominence in this chapter. The barriers to widening participation include motivation, finances, life circumstances, and providers having a positive institutional approach to WP. The ways these barriers can be reduced or removed include organising motivational events and activities, supporting students financially, providing support services and creches for students, working with partners to adopt positive approaches, and employing staff with the right skills for less conventional students.

Access to HE courses have made a major contribution to WP, and the data for this area of FE is clear, coherent, and comprehensive. It demonstrates the ongoing success of access to HE courses. The experiences of access students are often very positive, but they do also often need to overcome major life issues to succeed in their studies. Those who were teaching them find the experience extremely positive and are particularly proud of the success of their students and their contributions.

Overall, a commitment to WP is shown to be a major force and commitment in and across FE, even in times of severe difficulty.

Summary points

- Widening participation (WP) in FE is a strong part of the mission of FE.
- Participation of those most disadvantaged in society is still not what society would wish it to be.
- The history of WP does include many localised, and some national success stories about WP to and from FE.
- There are multiple barriers to widening participation but there are also institutional, local, and sector-wide ways to remove or reduce those barriers.
- Access to HE courses have made a major contribution to WP, and the data for this area of FE is clear, coherent, and comprehensive. It demonstrates the ongoing success of access to HE courses.
- The access to HE student experience is often very positive, but major life issues often also need to be overcome.
- Teaching on access courses is very popular.
- Access courses have a very important place in FE history.

Recommended reading

James, N. and Busher, H. (2018) *Improving opportunities to engage in learning: A study of the access to higher education diploma.* Abingdon: Routledge.

Any one of these three

McGiveney, V. (1990) *Education's for other people. Access to education for non-participant Adults.* Leicester: NIACE.
McGiveney, V. (1996) *Staying or leaving the course: Non completion and retention of mature students in further and higher education.* Leicester: NIACE.
McGiveney, V. (1999) *Informal learning in the community.* Leicester: NIACE.

References

Brine, J. and Waller, J. (2004) Working-class women on an Access course: risk, opportunity and (re)constructing identities, *Gender and Education*, 16(1), pp. 97–113, DOI: 10.1080/0954025032000170363

Busher, H., James, N. and Piela, A. (2015) 'I always wanted to do second chance learning': identities and experiences of tutors on access to higher education courses. *Research in Post-Compulsory Education*, 20(2), pp. 127–139, DOI: 10.1080/13596748.2015.1030235

Hudson, A., Burnell, I. and Murray, D. (2020) The place of widening participation. In S. Broadhead, J. Butcher, E. Davison, W. Fowle, M. Hill, L. Martin, S. McKendry, F. Norton, N. Raven, B. Sanderson and S. Wynn Williams (Eds) *Delivering the public good of higher education – Widening participation, place and lifelong learning*. London: Forum for Advancement in Continuing Education (FACE).

James, N. and Busher, H. (2018) *Improving opportunities to engage in learning: A study of the access to higher education diploma*. Abingdon: Routledge.

Johnson, R. (1988) Really useful knowledge 1790–1850: Memories for education in the 1980s. In T. Lovett (Ed.) *Radical approaches to adult education*. London: Routledge.

Kennedy, H. (1997) *Learning works: Widening participation in further education*. London: Further Education Funding Council for England.

Lovett, T. (1994) *Radical community education. The informal education archives*. Originally published by the YMCA George Williams College (1994). Available at: https://infed.org/mobi/radical-community-education/ (Accessed 5 October 2023).

Mc Giveney, V. (1990) *Education's for other people. Access to education for non-participant adults*. Leicester: NIACE.

Mc Giveney, V. (1996) *Staying or leaving the course: Non completion and retention of mature students in further and higher education*. Leicester: NIACE.

Mc Giveney, V. (1999) *Informal learning in the community*. Leicester: NIACE

Quality Assurance Agency (2023a) *Access to higher education. Key Statistics 2021–22*. Gloucester: QAA.

Quality Assurance Agency (2023b) *Real stories*. Gavin McKay. Student Paramedic, Swansea University. Gloucester: QAA. Available at: https://www.accesstohe.ac.uk//en/real-stories/gavin-mckay (Accessed 10 November 2023).

Saxby-Smith, S. and Shepherd, J. (2000) Promoting the participation of women returners in the workforce: guidelines for the design and delivery of returner courses, University of Surrey, UK. In A. Jackson, and D. Jones, (Eds) *Researching "Inclusion." papers from the annual conference of the standing conference on university teaching and research in the education of adults*. Nottingham: Standing Conference on University Teaching and Research in the Education of Adults.

Sheridan, L. (1992) Women returners to further education: Employment and gender relations in the home. *Gender and Education*, 4(3), pp. 213–228, DOI: 10.1080/0954025920040303

Smithers, A. and Robinson, P. (1989) *Increasing participation in higher education*. Manchester: University of Manchester.

Thomas, L. (Ed.) (2001) *Widening participation in post-compulsory education*. London: Continuum.

Thompson, D.W. (2019) Widening participation research and practice in the United Kingdom on the twentieth anniversary of the Dearing report: Reflections on a changing landscape. *Educational Review*, 71(2), pp. 182–197, DOI: 10.1080/00131911.2017.1380606

Tight, M. (1998) Education, education, education! The vision of lifelong learning in the Kennedy, Dearing and Fryer reports. *Oxford Review of Education*, 24(4), pp. 473–485, DOI: 10.1080/0305498980240404

Workers Educational Association (2023) *Looking forward to building on 120 years of experience*. Available at: https://www.wea.org.uk/news-views/news/wea-120th-birthday-ready-for-the-future# (Accessed 5 November 2023).

Worth, E. (2019) Women, education and social mobility in Britain during the long 1970s. *Cultural and Social History*, 16(1), pp. 67–83, DOI: 10.1080/14780038.2019.1574052

7 Higher education in further education (HE in FE)

Introduction

This chapter first defines HE in FE and then provides details of the large number of enrolments that this subsector has each year. Three events from HE in FE history are then analysed: the Percy report, 1944; The Dearing report, 1997; and the period after Dearing through to the present. The first sector story is about Rosina Haq, a HE in FE participant with a foundation degree in Animal Management. The next section of the chapter considers transitions to HE in FE, which includes the characteristics of HE and FE students, and the steps and approaches which need to be taken to recruit and retain them and help them complete their HE studies. Some data which give an indication of HE in FE achievement rates are also included.

The final section of the chapter considers 'HEness' (i.e. a teaching and learning experience of HE in FE which is similar to that of HE in HE), how it has developed in HE in FE, and where 'FEness' has also had a part to play. The perspectives of HE in FE teachers about teaching on HE courses bring the chapter to a close and the second sector story reflects on some further experiences of the author as an HE in FE teacher.

HE in FE – a definition

Higher level education has taken place in FE for approaching 100 years. Not unusually in the FE sector, this subsector has had various titles, including 'college-based higher education' (CBHE), 'higher vocational education' (HIVE), 'higher VET', 'Higher Education in Further Education Colleges' (HE in FECs), and 'Higher Education in Further Education' (HE in FE). As has been seen with other FE subsectors, they develop their activity and provision over an extended period, and what they are called can change regularly, dependent largely on the government in charge at any given time. Most of the provision in HE in FE, the title which is being used in this book, takes place in FE colleges, and it is a subsector which has seen particularly sustained growth for most of the twenty-first century, especially in courses which have been franchised with universities. For this chapter, Greenwood's (2010) definition is used. HE in FE:

> Refers to all those activities that relate to the management, development, delivery and assessment of higher education qualifications and programmes taught in further education colleges ... HE qualifications and programmes refer to those that are at level 4 and above in the framework for higher education qualifications.
>
> (Greenwood, 2010: 1)

DOI: 10.4324/9781003468455-7

Table 7.1 HE in FE enrolment numbers 2017/18 to 2021/22 (Higher Education Statistics Agency, 2023: 1)

FE Providers	Year 2017/18	Year 2018/19	Year 2019/20	Year 2020/21	Year 2021/22
Postgraduate	2,660	2,560	2,520	2,735	2,565
First degree	22,330	19,630	18,870	19,130	18,165
Other undergraduate	98,245	92,000	86,175	78,675	69,390
Total FE providers	123,235	114,190	107,565	100,540	90,120

How many students are there in HE in FE?

Table 7.1 gives a useful overview of number of enrolments between 2017/18 and 2021/22 at different levels of HE in FE in England.

Table 7.1 comes with this note:

> A notable reduction has been observed in learners enrolled for higher education at further education providers since 2018/19. This is partly due to some providers transferring from the further education to the higher education sector in 2018/19 and so reporting their HE provision to HESA rather than ESFA (Education and Skills Funding Agency).
>
> (*ibid.*: 1)

It can be seen from the table that enrolments have reduced over the five years from 2017/18 to 2021/22 and, although the comment above does to some degree explain this fall, the ongoing reduction is confirmed by more figures from the Association of Colleges. The AoC also publish figures relating to student enrolments in HE in FE and their characteristics, and a selection of their figures is below:

> 2021/22 110,000 people study higher education in colleges.
>
> (AoC, 2022: 10)

> 2022/23 118,000 people study higher education in colleges.
>
> (AoC, 2021: 8)

This data confirms the reduction which was apparent in the HESA data. Despite this, the number of students studying HE in FE is still significant. By way of comparison, the number of enrolments at HE providers other than FE for 2021/22 is 110,480, approximately 20,000 more than the HE in FE numbers. Enrolments with HE providers other than FE have also reduced in England over the same five years, from 128,310 in 2017/18 to 110,480 in 2021/22. Overall, as can be seen from the data, 45 per cent of all HE provisions take place in FE (Higher Education Statistics Agency, 2023: 1).

One-third of English students aged 19 and who enter HE through UCAS studied at a college (AoC, 2022: 10).

'Colleges deliver 82% of Higher National Certificates (HNCs).

Colleges deliver 58% of Higher National Diplomas (HNDs).

Colleges deliver 63% of Foundation Degrees taught in England' (*ibid.*: 12).

As has been seen before, data relating to an FE subsector does differ depending on the source, but from the data above, even when it is from a different source, it can be seen that HE in FE is almost an equal contributor in size to the HE student enrolments at HE providers.

HE in FE – key periods of history

The Percy report 1944

The 1944 Education Act has been discussed in Chapter 1, but the field of 'Higher Technological Education' was addressed by a committee chaired by Lord Eustace Percy, which was also established in 1944. It was appointed to 'consider the needs of higher technological education in England and Wales and the respective contributions to be made thereto by Universities and Technical Colleges' (Percy, 1945: 3). When published, the report recommended that:

> A strictly limited number of technical colleges should develop technological courses comparable in standard with university degree courses … full time and sandwich courses of degree standard should be established … that a number of regional advisory councils should be set up to coordinate technological studies on a regional basis under the National Council of Technology.
> (Cantor and Roberts, 2021: 3)

Overall, the Percy report is seen to have made an 'immense contribution' to the 'development of further education' (*ibid.*: 4). By 1956, there were 22 'regional colleges' and they offered a range of higher-level courses. In the mid-1950s, regional colleges were designated as 'Colleges of Advanced Technology' (CATs), and their work was almost all at higher levels, and 'included post graduate and research work' (*ibid.*: 6). They received a generous 75 per cent of their funding as grants towards this advanced level work. By the mid-1960s, they were expanded and awarded university status, which in effect started to move them out of the FE sector and into the HE sector. They had, however, contributed significantly to the development of HE in FE by this stage. In 1966, 'Polytechnics' was proposed, and by May 1971, 28 were designated. At the time, this was seen as 'the development of full-time higher education within the further education system' (*ibid.*: 9).

Britain had a binary system of HE with the old universities offering 'academic' courses, and the polytechnics serving industry and the professions. Polytechnics' courses were validated by the Council for National Academic Awards (CNAA). Heads of Polytechnics kept pestering the Secretary of State for Education to become universities, saying they were research and degree courses. But they were repeatedly reminded that Britain had a binary system. When Kenneth Clark became Secretary of State for Education in 1991, the heads of polytechnics banged on his door. This time Clark simply said, 'Oh, let's stop having this argument', two old polytechnics becoming universities and having degree-awarding powers. After 1992, therefore, polytechnics generally moved away from FE and into the HE sector, becoming universities with their own degree-awarding power. FE was left with courses which were of HE level but could not be studied up to full-time degree level.

The Dearing report 1997

One of the most important HE-related reports of the twentieth century is the Dearing report (1997). The Dearing report was established 'to make recommendations on how the purposes, shape, structure, size, and funding of higher education, including support for students, should develop to meet the needs of the United Kingdom over the next 20 years' (Dearing, 1997: 1). Although mainly known for its contribution to developing and extending HE provision in HE providers, Dearing was very positive about the opportunities offered by HE in FE. He recognised that any:

> Dividing line set between further education and higher education, or between higher education and higher-level training, is bound to be somewhat arbitrary. This is true particularly for adults - for example, when making a change of career direction a person may need access simultaneously to a range of programmes spanning both higher and further education and training.
>
> (*ibid.*: 70)

Dearing endorsed the notion of higher level, but 'sub-degree' provisions such as Higher National Certificates (one year of study at Level 4) and Higher National Diplomas (two years of study to get to Level 5) which had already been in existence for some time, as this would 'be fundamental to widening participation in higher education' (*ibid.*: 109). He did not, however, recommend that FE colleges should be able to provide all of the study involved in a degree.

As a result of the Dearing review, new two-year Level 5 'Foundation Degrees' were introduced in colleges in 2000. Lavender (2020: 294) argues that foundation degrees:

> Were to provide new and accessible routes to Higher Education. The qualifications were considered a key factor in widening participation in English Higher Education, as well as contributing to local economies and a higher qualified workforce. One key aspect of the foundation degree curriculum was that it offered higher level vocational and work-based qualifications. With this in mind, foundation degrees were developed in consultation with employers to ensure a highly relevant work based HE. To ensure the quality of such awards the degrees were also developed and validated in partnerships with universities this blend of academic and work-based or vocational provision makes foundation degrees delivered in colleges distinctive.

Since Dearing

Despite austerity measures and some degree of reduction in student numbers, HE in FE still has a very significant place in local and national FE provision. As has been seen at the start of the chapter, enrolment numbers are significant. There is also a recognisable range of local impact from HE in FE provision. The Education and Training Foundation (ETF) carried out research on the local impact of HE in FE and found that:

- College-based HE is significantly more likely to involve part-time study, and this helps local employers with upskilling their workforce as they do not need to study full time and can still work while studying.
- College-based HE students tend to be older and can often be adult returners which helps widen participation.
- College-based HE students are more likely to come from non-traditional backgrounds, including areas with a high level of deprivation, and this also helps widen participation.
- College-based HE students are more likely to be local, which contributes to the local economy and community.

- College-based HE programmes differ from those in higher education institutions in the way policy expects, which is to join first-degree courses. Students enrol for foundation degrees more so than first degrees, which not only provide increased short-term achievements but also include progression opportunities.
- More work is required to improve the quality of HE data to ensure that the full contribution of college-based HE can be demonstrated.

(Adapted from Education and Training Foundation, 2016)

The contribution of HE in FE to widening participation can be seen from this report to be significant, but there is also a strong and ongoing impact relating to local skills.

> **Question for discussion**
>
> Imagine you are in a position to choose between taking higher-level study in your local FE college, or in a university.
>   Which would you choose, and why?

Sector story – Rosina Haq – foundation degree student in animal conservation

Rosina had always been interested in wildlife and had volunteered with other members of her family in a local wildlife conservation trust as a teenager. After completing her GCSEs, Rosina was uncertain about what to study and which career to work towards. She was familiar with her local college and that it had a well-respected and well-equipped Animal Management department. After discussions with her family and a careers advisor, and a visit to a college open day, Rosina applied for, and gained a place on, a Level 3 Advanced Extended Diploma in Animal Management. This course suited Rosina very well. She learned a great deal about animal management and about the animal care sector locally, nationally, and internationally. Progression was available to a Higher Education Foundation Degree in Animal Management; Rosina took that opportunity and progressed to that two-year HE course. She enjoyed the study in college, and also the work placements with conservation groups during the course, including a marine conservation charity and a regional wildlife trust. While studying at the college, Rosina felt very well supported and that the staff were helpful, had good expertise in HE, and had high expectations of her and the other students. This was a major motivating factor in her success.

Rosina is considering progression after her college HE programme and is planning to apply to complete her degree at a nearby university. She feels confident that her future is in employment in the animal management field and would recommend her type of study to anyone else who is in a position to take advantage of it.

Transitions to HE in FE

Davison *et al.* (2022: 178) argue that the 'transition experience' for HE in FE students is:

> A search for familiarity and safety in an unfamiliar environment, the pursuit of which enables students to explore and engage more fully, developing the resources required to navigate the institution, the academic structures and conventions, and the habitus to thrive there.

Encouraging and supporting potential students in their transition first into FE, and then into HE in FE, is, therefore, an extremely important part of HE in FE. Lavender (2020) argues that there are a number of key factors involved in supporting that transition, including recognising that prospective HE in FE students will often tend to be different from the students who progress to full-time degree study at universities, and that they will often be:

- Older, and out of education for an extended period;
- Likely to have had previous negative experiences of education;
- Wishing to study part-time;
- From non-traditional backgrounds;
- From a lower socio-economic status than traditional HE students;
- Be the first member of a family to participate in HE;
- Need a study environment which they feel will be supportive.

(Adapted from Lavender, 2020)

With such a list of characteristics, it could be expected that many prospective students may well not choose to study at HE in FE at all. FE colleges have, however, developed strategies and approaches to support the transition to HE in FE. Stoten (2016) researched the reasons why 75 adults who were studying HE in FE in three FE colleges decided to do so, and his research prioritised the student voice by using interviews. He sought 'students' perceptions of university and the perceived benefits of college-based study' (ibid.: 9). After interviewing his student subjects, Stoten summarised the factors which helped them make the transition into HE in FE.

The findings suggest that the most immediate factors that impinge on students' decision-making process relate to their day-to-day context: familial responsibility, location, and convenience, as well as the perceived nature of teaching at General Further Education Colleges (GFECs). The findings also highlight the benefits of part-time study for those who have missed out or wish to return to Level 4 study (ibid.: 16).

It was also found to be the case that:

> For some students, the choice to study at a GFEC is indeed an attempt to address earlier disadvantage. For others, the decision is conditioned by the desire to improve their employability, or because of employer inducement. For a third significant group there is also a positive choice in terms of the perceived support and care available at a GFEC compared with university.
>
> (ibid.: 17)

Stoten recommends that an FE college:

> Should aim to develop its variety of HE programmes not only in terms of subject breadth but more particularly with reference to alternative modes of delivery, such as distance learning. It is within this context that innovative partnerships between college networks and local universities should be established with universities supporting curriculum innovation creatively. Such an approach would help universities engage more with sections of their local community and support colleges.
>
> (ibid.: 17)

Raven (2012: 79) argues that 'students educated in FECs do progress and that in many instances colleges are very successful in this endeavour, given that those studying with them are more likely to come from educationally and economically disadvantaged backgrounds'. He also researched the approaches which colleges make to support progression into FE and into HE in FE and found that the following approaches and strategies were seen as helpful by students.

Institution-wide interventions

- Guidance on the UCAS (university) application process, including support in preparing personal statements and advice on student finance.
- Open evenings in which those interested in Level 3 study, as well as current Level 3 students, visit the college's HE facilities and find out about opportunities to continue their studies at the same institution.
- Visits to local universities that enable participants to experience the facilities available in subjects of interest, and learn more about university life and the support available at HE.
- Provision of 'engagement days' that offer Level 3 students a range of HE subject tasters offered by the college, including in areas outside their current programmes of study.

Course-level initiatives

- Exploring with Level 3 students the HE options available in their disciplines;
- Providing guidance on the content of HE courses in the same discipline and demonstrating how the Level 3 curriculum links to these;
- Familiarising Level 3 students with the skills required for HE study, including essay writing, referencing, and presenting;
- Inviting alumni now in HE to talk to Level 3 students about their university experiences;
- Informing Level 3 students about the graduate careers associated with their subject areas;
- Arranging for guest speakers, including those now working in professions linked to their disciplines, to talk to Level 3 students about their work and learner journeys. (*ibid.*: 93–94).

Critiquing HE in FE

Avis and Orr (2016) draw attention to both some of the progress made with HE in FE and the areas of education and society which it has struggled to change. On the positive side, they argue that 'for many individuals, however, HE in FE courses can and do transform lives by opening up fields of knowledge that may explain and enhance experience' and that 'the struggle for social justice whereby students and teachers seek to collectively develop "really useful knowledge". Placing socially situated alongside really useful knowledge would serve to open up a broader vista and facilitate the formation of counter hegemonic movements' (*ibid.*: 61).

On the negative side, however, they argue that these 'hegemonic movements' have contributed to 'the systemic failure of widening participation to close the inequality gap between those who have attended HE in FE courses as against those studying at elite universities' (*ibid.*: 6). The way forward, as they argue, is 'to develop a politics that extends beyond education to wider society and that aligns itself to social movements committed to social justice and transformation' (*ibid.*: 62).

Lavender (2020: 303–304) offers a more positive overall vision of HE in FE as follows:

> The distinct contribution college-based HE makes to the lives of learners and the wider sector. These include a supportive learning environment, professional and contextually relevant curriculum, geographically accessible locations, and lower fees. It has also highlighted the contribution that providing spaces for HE in these contexts makes to the development of critical and autonomous graduates.

Completion and achievement of HE in FE

It is not straightforward to access data which summarise the achievement rates of HE in FE. The Higher Education Statistics Agency (HESA) has recently recognised this when stating:

> Detailed data on the HE taking place in universities, on a UK-wide basis, is available and easily accessible to all from HESA. However, the same cannot be said about the HE delivered by FE providers. With different government data collectors publishing reports on college HE within each UK home nation, franchising arrangements are not easily visible, and no organisation is currently integrating all these sources into one large dataset. Consequently, even though FE providers are long-standing providers of HE, relatively little is known about them as HE providers.
>
> (HESA, 2022: 1)

HESA has started to work towards solving this problem, but for the moment, the limited data which can be found on achievement levels in HE in FE is included here.

General HE student data is summarised by the 'Office for Students' each year in their annual review. The 2022 annual review provides overall statistics for student completion (i.e. successfully finishing their university degree). They are as follows:

> The completion rate for undergraduate students entering full-time first degrees in 2016–17 (first degree, full-time) is 89.2 per cent (roughly the same as for the previous four years). For their part-time counterparts it is 47.6 per cent (an increase of two percentage points from the previous year). Female full-time undergraduate first degree students have a higher completion rate than their male equivalents (91.5 per cent and 86.6 per cent respectively).
>
> (Office for Students, 2022: 1)

This data tells us that the overall completion rate for full-time study is 89.2 per cent, and for part-time study, it is considerably less at 47.6 per cent. The Department of Education also published 'National Achievement Rate Tables', with the last available data in this format for 2018/19. The achievement rate in this data for 'Level 4+' courses for 19+ Education and Training is 67.7 per cent, and this has risen from 60.7 per cent in 2016/17 (DfE, 2020: 1). There are no data for levels above four. It is difficult to compare this clearly with the overall national achievement rate for HE in the Office for Students data, and indeed, completion is roughly in the middle of the 89.2 per cent for full-time HE study and 47.6 per cent for part-time HE study at 67.7 per cent. The best interpretation of the data is that completion in HE in FE is at least reasonable but could improve.

'HEness'

HEness is about how similar to a university learning and teaching experience the student and teacher experience is in HE in FE. This section of the chapter will examine this question from both the student perspective and the teacher and organisational perspective. Firstly, there needs to be a consideration of the characteristics of a 'high quality HE experience', or 'what exactly is HEness?'

Lea and Simmons (2012), Purves *et al.* (2023), and Simmons and Lea (2013) all address this question and conclude that the characteristics of HEness include:

- Universities tend to be more autonomous institutions.
- Staff have time for research and scholarly activity.
- A 'critical mass' of HE in FE students (i.e. enough enrolments) may be difficult for some colleges.
- The higher level (Level 4 to Level 8) knowledge which is central to HE is more about 'what might be' than the Level 3 knowledge in FE, which is more about 'what is'.
- Learning at higher levels is more about developing criticality, exploring fields of study and questioning taken for granted assumptions and developing independent thinking about what may come next.
- Physical items such as a special library, HE centres, journal availability, and HE study facilities could also be considered part of HEness.
- Availability within staff teams of a discipline-based 'community of practice' (a) collection of teachers in the same discipline who can network, co-research, and develop their discipline.

Overall, on describing the characteristics of HEness, Lea and Simmons (2012) conclude that 'if HE in FE is to develop the kind of culture that HE demands, we need to ask if the right kinds of conditions exist in FE for this HEness to flourish' (*ibid.*: 184).

Other research at the time, and more recently, suggest that there has been considerable progress on HEness in FE, and that in some respects, HE in FE has become a type of 'hybrid' provision, which incorporates strengths of HEness, but also what could be described as strengths of FEness. The characteristics of this hybrid HE in FE include the following:

- High-quality, personalised student support, based on strong interpersonal staff–student relationships (Purves et al., 2023: 3).
- A desire to promote social justice through greater access and opportunities for non-traditional undergraduate learners offers a powerful motivation to many teaching in this sector (*ibid.*: 4).
- Students working more independently (HE style) but within a supportive tutorial culture (FE style); or put another way, teachers taking active responsibility in identifying independent learning needs and then providing support to meet them (Simmons and Lea, 2013: 4).
- A 'scholarship of teaching and learning' where staff and students might work together on projects which have connections with local industry and commerce; where staff and students disseminate their work locally with local industry and commerce; where students and staff work collectively on evaluating pedagogic practice; and where the development of research skills becomes a central focus within the classroom (*ibid.*: 8).
- As has been indicated in Chapter 2, research in FE has grown a significant amount in the last 20 years, particularly with the support of organisations such as the Learning and Skills Research network. It is not easy for FE staff to find the time and resources to research, but it

has grown considerably more possible than it has been. The results of this research are highly likely to be directly relevant to teachers involved in HE in FE.
- Relating the learning on HE in FE courses where possible and practical to local employment, economic, and community needs.

The views of the HE in FE teacher

Finally, King and Widdowson (2012) gathered responses from 559 staff teaching HE in FE in 30 colleges and found that their respondents:

- Regarded teaching as their main purpose and have a clear identity as teaching professionals;
- Were aware of their HE students as individuals and adopted a personalised learning approach wherever possible;
- Regarded teaching HE in FE as requiring a range of approaches and techniques responding to the needs of the subject and the experience of the students;
- Placed a high value on engaging the learners with industry-linked practical projects that were relevant to their studies and future careers. Theory was linked to practice;
- Considered that in some colleges there were difficulties in establishing a distinctive HE culture against an FE culture shaped to respond to different needs;
- Put high value on relevant CPD, defined here as including not only scholarship but professional and pedagogical updating (*ibid.*: 4).

Overall, it can be seen from the various items of research that the model of HE in FE has become something of a hybrid between FE best practice and HE best practice, and that can be seen as a particular attraction for prospective students.

Sector story – personal experience of teaching HE in FE and research and scholarly activity

The author was working in an FE college and had a teaching role on Teacher Training courses, an Access to Higher Education course, and some Adult Basic Education in literacy and numeracy. I was also head of the Department of Adult and Continuing Education. I was coordinating the city and guilds 7307 Further and Adult Education Certificate (FAETC) stages one and two teaching qualification, which was at qualification Level 4, and could be studied part-time over one academic year. A significant number of college and other staff undertook this teaching qualification, but it was not mandatory. In the 1980s, a local university offered the opportunity for the college, and my course team, to join a partnership providing Initial Teacher Education with the university as the awarding body, and five other FE colleges in the south west region as partners. This meant the course would add a second year of part-time study which would offer a Certificate in Education (Cert Ed) at Level 5, a Professional Graduate Certificate in Education (PG Cert) at Level 6, or a Post Graduate Certificate in Education (PGCE) at Level 7. Students could select which level they took the course at.

This meant an almost immediate jump from teaching level 4 to teaching levels 5, 6, and 7. At the time, I found this terrifying. I had already been undertaking research in areas of interest to me, and presenting results at FE conferences, so had become more confident with research and scholarly activity, which my college had supported me in, but this was a real challenge. Fortunately, I was already an experienced teacher, and with a great deal of effort on my part, and excellent support from the other FE college practitioners and our university award leader (and a gap of one year before the higher-level courses needed to be taught), working on the course rapidly became a weekly highlight for myself and the colleagues who were also teaching on ITE.

The partner university wished college course leaders to be qualified up to at least masters level, and I duly undertook a Master's degree, using some of my previous experience to gain credits through the process of accreditation of prior experiential learning (APEL), which was a widely used means of considering in detail what people had previously worked on, and matching this against the learning outcomes of the masters qualification so that they could gain exemption from some aspects of HE courses.

Overall, with this particular HE in FE, I'm not sure I ever quite managed to provide all the characteristics of HEness for the students, and they experienced some but not all from the partner university, but the HE in FE worked extremely well, helped teachers from under-represented groups to become qualified, and raised the status of the college as an institution.

I loved every minute of it, and felt it raised my professional standing considerably!

> **Question for discussion**
>
> Based on your reading in this chapter, from your experience of higher education to date, either in FE or in HE, which of the characteristics of HEness do you feel you have experienced?

Conclusion

HE in FE is a subsector which, like others in FE, has been named and renamed over an extended period. Its development, especially the large amount of HE in FE courses which have been franchised with local universities, has been something of an FE success story, and this can be seen from the large number of enrolments which this subsector now achieves each year. The history of HE in FE has been a transition from almost entirely vocational and technical higher-level courses in the twentieth century to considerable growth in both vocational and more academic HE courses in FE in the twenty-first century. The Dearing report, 1997 provided a major stimulus for HE in FE.

Transitions to HE in FE for students can be difficult, given that a large proportion of HE in FE students are likely to be non-traditional, mature, and with less positive experiences of education in their lives to date. FE has, however, with the support of its HE partners, developed the steps and approaches which need to be taken to recruit and retain students, and to help them complete their HE studies. This is borne out to some degree by data on HE in FE achievement rates. 'HEness' (i.e. a teaching and learning experience in HE in FE which is similar to that in HE in HE) has developed in HE in FE, and 'FEness' has also had a part to play in developing what has been called 'hybrid' provision, with the strength of both HE and FE involved. The perspectives of HE in FE teachers on teaching in HE are positive despite the pressures and differences in their working situation from many teachers in HE, and they take up the challenge of teaching HE in FE with enthusiasm.

Overall, HE in FE has multiple dimensions and is unlike HE in a variety of ways, and very similar to HE in other ways. Students appreciate the support and quality of teaching they receive, and teachers of HE in FE offer suitable and appropriate discipline knowledge, student-centred support, and teaching and local community understanding which may not always be contained to the same degree in a university.

Summary points

- HE in FE is an FE success story, which can be seen from the large number of enrolments which this subsector has each year.
- The history of HE in FE has been a transition from almost entirely vocational and technical higher-level courses in the twentieth century to considerable growth in both vocational and more academic HE courses in FE in the twenty-first century.
- Transitions to HE in FE for students can be difficult.
- FE has developed the steps and approaches which need to be taken to recruit and retain students, and to help them complete their HE studies.
- 'HEness' has developed in HE in FE and 'FEness' has also had a part to play in developing what has been called 'hybrid' provision, with the strength of both HE and FE.
- The perspectives of HE in FE teachers on teaching in HE are positive, and they take up the challenge of teaching HE in FE with enthusiasm.
- Overall, HE in FE has multiple dimensions and is unlike HE in a variety of ways, and very similar to HE in other ways.

Recommended reading

Lavender, K. (2020) College-based higher education. In J. Tummons (Ed.) *PCET: Learning and teaching in the post compulsory sector*. London: Sage.

References

Association of Colleges (2021) *College key facts 2021/22*. London: AOC.
Association of Colleges (2022) *College key facts 2022/23*. London: AOC.
Avis, J. and Orr, K. (2016) HE in FE: Vocationalism, class and social justice. *Research in Post-Compulsory Education*, 21(1–2), pp. 49–65, DOI: 10.1080/13596748.2015.1125666
Cantor, L.M. and Roberts, I.F. (2021) *Further education in England and Wales*. Abingdon: Routledge.
Davison, E., Sanderson, R., Hobson, T. and Hopkins, J. (2022) Skills for success? Supporting transition into higher education for students from diverse backgrounds. *Widening Participation and Lifelong Learning*, 24(1), pp. 165–187, DOI: 10.5456/WPLL.24.1.165
Dearing, R. (1997) *The Dearing Report (1997) - Higher Education in the learning society. Main Report*. London: Her Majesty's Stationery Office.
Department for Education (2020) *National achievement rate tables March 2020*. London: DfE.
Education and Training Foundation (2016) *The local impact of college based higher education*. London: ETF.
Greenwood, M. (2010) *Higher education in further education colleges*. York: Higher education Academy.
HESA (2022) *HESA's vision for college HE data*. Cheltenham: HESA. Available at https://www.hesa.ac.uk/blog/02-08-2022/hesa-vision-college-he-data (Accessed 13th May 2024)
Higher Education Statistics Agency (2023) *Figure 4 - HE student enrolments at HE and FE providers by level of study and HE provider type Academic years 2017/18 to 2021/22*. Cheltenham: HESA. Available at: https://www.hesa.ac.uk/data-and-analysis/sb265/figure-4 (Accessed 14 November 2023).
King, M. and Widdowson, J. (2012) *Inspiring individuals: Teaching higher education in a further education college. Exploring the pedagogy of HE delivered in an FE setting*. York: Higher Education Academy.
Lavender, K. (2020) College-based higher education. In J. Tummons (Ed.) *PCET: Learning and teaching in the post compulsory sector*. London: Sage.

Lea, J. and Simmons, J. (2012) Higher education in further education: Capturing and promoting HEness. *Research in Post-Compulsory Education*, 17(2), pp. 179–193, DOI: 10.1080/13596748.2012.673888

Office for Students (2022) *The Office for Students annual review 2022*. London: Office for Students. Available at: https://www.officeforstudents.org.uk/publications/annual-review-2022/a-statistical-overview-of-higher-education-in-england/#sectionfour (Accessed 15 November 2023).

Percy, E. (1945) *The Percy Report. Higher technological education. Report of a Special Committee appointed in April 1944*. London: His Majesty's Stationery Office.

Purves, R.M., Pulsford, M. and Morris, R. (2023) Leading undergraduate provision in further education colleges: The experiences of BA Education programme leaders. *London Review of Education*, 21(1), pp. 1–14, DOI: 10.14324/LRE.21.1.09.

Raven, N. (2012) Making a difference: Insights into effective HE progression practices in further education colleges. *Widening Participation and Lifelong Learning*, 23(1), pp. 79–101, DOI: 10.5456/WPLL.23.1.79

Simmons, J. and Lea, J. (2013) *Capturing an HE ethos in college higher education practice*. Gloucester: Quality Assurance Agency.

Stoten, D. W. (2016). Studying for a higher education qualification without going to university: an insight into students' decisions to study in post-16 colleges. *Research in Post-Compulsory Education*, 21(1-2), pp. 9–19.

8 Education for social justice, equality, and diversity

Introduction

The breadth and diverse nature of the further education (FE) sector and its students, and the position of FE in the community, have all been strong influences on the development of the sector's approaches to social justice, equality, and diversity. Social justice has been a key long-term objective of FE, and examples of this have already featured in other chapters of this book, including Chapter 3. The field of equality and diversity is extremely broad, and one chapter cannot address all aspects of FE's approach or every dimension of social justice, equality, and diversity. This chapter will therefore include a representative selection of examples in the sector which reflect the approaches, principles, challenges, and successes within this cross-sector theme. The theme will also feature to some degree in other chapters as it is a significant part of the overall approach and history of FE.

The chapter will also include a historical analysis of consistent efforts to connect the disconnected and to support the disabled and those with learning difficulties, and an analysis of the ongoing problem of NEETs (young people Not in Education, Employment or Training). The chapter will allow the reader to reflect critically on these efforts and come to conclusions about the sector's success or otherwise in addressing social justice, equality, and diversity.

The chapter begins with a discussion about definitions and how they influence society and education, including social justice, the common good, and social mobility, and offers a definition of social justice for FE. It then moves on to a selection of events in the history of social justice, equality, and diversity in FE; the Taunton Report (1864–68), the Tomlinson Report (1994–96), and social justice, equality, and diversity in 2023 are the events included.

A section on equality and diversity data follows, with some analysis and comparisons between FE and the school sector. The first sector story features National Star College which is a large, independent specialist college for students with high needs. The next section of the chapter provides examples from FE of working towards social justice, equality, and diversity across the sector, and this includes a research report from the Further Education Trust for Leadership on principles of social justice, examples of the FE sector's work in this field, and recommendations for the future of social justice, equality, and diversity in FE. The second sector story is part of this section and is about City Lit – The City Literary Institute. A summary of a small piece of research about ACL provision and mental health is then included, followed by a section on the challenges associated with NEETs and the section concludes with a summary of another small research project about the transitions of autistic students into FE.

DOI: 10.4324/9781003468455-8

The last section features the results of an important report from the Sutton Trust, an organisation which carries out research, undertakes projects, and aims to influence policy about social mobility. It offers mixed and thought-provoking results and recommendations to the FE sector on its work with social justice, equality, and diversity. The chapter conclusion returns to the FETL (2020) report, with a summary of its proposals and their possible impact on FE.

Definitions

Social justice

Social justice means different things to different individuals, groups, organisations, businesses, and politicians, or at least it can be differently interpreted and prioritised. It is difficult to imagine how different versions of the understanding of social justice could be so different that they lead to conflict, but many disagreements, conflicts, and even wars have been fought on the different parties' ideas about social justice as they see it. The purpose of this chapter is to consider what education for social justice is about and to reflect on its place in the FE sector. Atkins (2020: 43) argues that, broadly speaking 'social justice is concerned with in/equalities and creating a more equitable society (and education)'. She continues by stating that this 'means it should be of concern to anyone working in education, but particularly those of us working in FAE (Further and Adult Education), since FAE caters for many of the most marginalised and excluded learners' (*ibid.*: 43). The Further Education Trust for Leadership (FETL) argues that:

> Almost without exception, colleges of further education have an institutional history closely bound up with history of the town, city or area in which they are based. This historical identity connects colleges, physically and spatially, both to their past and to the communities they serve.
>
> (FETL, 2020: 11)

The idea of working towards 'the common good' of those communities and the community at large is also argued to be a part of social justice, and 'the common good' is understood broadly as a social situation which provides ongoing benefit to both individuals and the whole community. Social class, race, gender, and ways in which they overlap are also relevant, as are the actions taken to combat inequalities in all of these aspects of society. Overall, Atkins defines social justice as processes in society which are 'concerned with the common good, and referring to particular social and human values about equity and the way in which they are enacted by individuals and society' (*ibid.*: 44). She also adds that equity is about 'fairness, which is not necessarily the same as equality' (*ibid.*: 44).

FETL (2020: 16) continues the debate by arguing that 'social justice is a contested and politicised concept, a discursive field colonised by different interest groups from across the political spectrum'. Avis (2023) also problematises the notion of social justice within the continuing culture of managerialist and performative approaches in FE. He argues that this has shifted social justice for providers and students away from 'forms of criticality, civic and community engagement' to 'an instrumentalism that rhetorically prioritises employer needs and waged work – in other words an orientation towards learning to labour' (Avis, 2023: 443).

For this book, social justice is defined as the sharing and distribution of both the burdens and benefits of society, and this includes distributing those benefits to individuals and enhancing the connections between individuals and communities through individual, collaborative, and collective action.

Social mobility

In order to fully appreciate the characteristics of social justice in education, it is helpful to understand the term 'social mobility' as the two tend often to be part of the same conversation or argument. In England, the Social Mobility Commission was created as

> An independent advisory non-departmental public body established under the Life Chances Act 2010 as modified by the Welfare Reform and Work Act 2016. It has a duty to assess progress in improving social mobility in the UK and to promote social mobility in England.
> (Social Mobility Commission, 2023: 1)

The Commission argues that a person:

> ... Experiences social mobility – by which we mean intergenerational social mobility – when they have different life outcomes from their parents. This could mean a different income level, a different occupational class, or other differences, such as housing or education. Mobility can also be upwards or downwards.
> (*ibid.*: 13)

In 2023, the Social Mobility Commission outlined plans to broaden this definition to include 'what it means to have a "better life" than the last generation, it is better health, happiness and education that are seen as more important than money or a better job' (*ibid.*: 13).

Events in the history of social justice, equality, and diversity in FE

The Taunton Report – 1864–68

In 1864, the Schools Inquiry Commission, chaired by Lord Taunton, was appointed to inquire into the education provided in all secondary schools, an extremely far-reaching brief which resulted in 20 published volumes and some exceptionally wide-ranging proposals in 1868. Although much of the evidence in this report points towards a class-based system of secondary education, and Taunton in many ways promoted and recommended a class-based vision of social justice in education, his reports did recognise some key inequalities in secondary education at the time. He found that there 'were only thirteen girls' secondary schools in the whole of England at the time' (Gillard, 2018: 2). Taunton noticed differences and tensions between the vocational and academic aspects of education and offered a vision of secondary education, which, although class-based and offering little progression upwards for working-class pupils, did improve on what already existed and did contribute to moving the cause of social justice in education forward.

The Tomlinson Report – 1994–96

The Tomlinson Report of 1996 was another key document in the history of FE, coming out a year before the Kennedy Report in 1997 (see Chapter 6). The terms of reference of Tomlinson's enquiry were to investigate FE's

> Responsibilities towards students with learning difficulties and/or disabilities, to review the range and type of further education provision available, and to make recommendations as to how, within the resources likely to be available to it, the Further Education Funding Council can, by working with colleges and others, best fulfil its responsibilities towards these students under the Further and Higher Education Act 1992.
>
> (Tomlinson, 1996: 203)

The report's key aim was the development of a more inclusive FE sector. Its recommendations included the following:

- National staff training for inclusive learning to cover teacher training, management training, and organisational development.
- Colleges should be encouraged to produce long-term strategies and action plans on inclusive learning and to appoint inclusive learning managers.
- The Further Education Funding Council (FEFC) should provide colleges with sufficient funding to meet the costs of individual support for learning.
- Inclusive learning needs analysis on a regional basis.
- Colleges should measure their progress towards inclusive learning through self-assessment, and the provision of inclusive learning should be a criterion in their inspection.
- A framework for collaboration between the FEFC, government departments, and other agencies should be created to provide a 'seamless robe' of provision and support services and opportunities to move in and out of learning as needed.
- Colleges should be required to take more systematic account of local needs and to receive help with strategic planning to take account of under-represented groups of adult learners, including those with multiple difficulties, mental health difficulties, and emotional and behavioural difficulties.

Tomlinson's recommendations strongly helped FE move towards the concept of 'inclusive learning, which placed the responsibility for providing suitable education with the teachers, the managers and the system, which took a social model of disability rather than problematizing the student as a deficit' (Munday, 2020: 57–58). Munday gave Tomlinson credit because he:

> Aimed to improve educational opportunities for those already attending education and training ... the move towards an inclusive model of education provides teachers with the difficulty of differentiating the curriculum but also opportunities to harness the individual differences that can enrich the learning experience of all involved. Inclusive education perceives diversity as part of human nature and as such the education institution (and not the student) has to adapt in order to provide education for all.
>
> (ibid.: 58)

Although the FE sector has found it difficult in the twenty-first century to sufficiently fund and deliver inclusive education, the Tomlinson Report did make a considerable contribution to efforts in FE working towards social justice, equality, and diversity, particularly in the area of student support.

Social justice, equality, and diversity in 2023

Avis (2023), in a wide-ranging and stark analysis of vocational education and training (VET) and social justice, draws attention to

> The continued significance of poverty and disadvantage in the lives of many people in the UK. These inequalities are currently being deepened as a result of the current crisis surrounding the increasing cost of living and growing rates of inflation.
>
> (*ibid.*: 448)

He cites the Social Mobility Commission (2022: 49) who warn that:

> ... A situation is emerging that is quite new in modern British history, and one that could have far-reaching socio-political consequences ... younger generations of men and women now face less favourable mobility prospects than did their parents, or their grandparents: that is, are less likely to experience upward mobility and more likely to experience downward mobility.

Avis argues that, despite the difficult current circumstances which currently prevail in relation to social justice and social mobility, the Social Mobility Commission's view from 2020 now has even greater importance.

> Disadvantaged students aged 16 and over tend to cluster in further education – often the poor relation to schools and universities. The sector is underfunded and under-valued. With the right support and a concerted effort to rebuild its reputation, however, this sector could transform lives for the better.
>
> (*ibid.*: 36)

Question for discussion

What do you think are the most pressing social justice issues facing society today, and how could education improve them?

Equality and diversity

Given the experiences so far in this book of attempts to locate comprehensive, cohesive, and accessible data about the FE sector, and comparisons with other education sectors, the reader will not be surprised to hear that finding comparative data across the school and FE sectors is not straightforward. There are some statistics available which can help with analysis and comparison, and the next section considers these.

The AoC includes a section of data on equality, diversity, and inclusion in their College Key Facts publication, and the 2022/23 data is below:

16–18-year-olds Adults
23 per cent Students from ethnic minority 24 per cent
background
46 per cent Female students 60 per cent
26 per cent Students with learning difficulties 17 per cent
And/or disability

(AoC, 2022: 28)

21% of students in colleges have a learning disability and / or disability.
46,000 college students are aged 60 and over.
18% of 16–18-year-olds in colleges claimed free school meals at age 15.
9% of 16–18-year-olds in maintained schools and academies claimed free school meals at age 15.

(*ibid.*: 30)

The Office for National Statistics data on the FE and Skills sector also provides some relevant sector wide statistics.
Females account for 60.5% of all students (975,880).
Learners recorded as having a Learning difficulty/disability (LLDD) account for 18.3% of the cohort (285,250), an increase of 12.6% from 253,370 in 2021/22.

(ONS, 2023: 1)

By way of comparison, the 2022 school 'Special Educational Needs' (SEN) data is:

Over 1.5 million pupils in England have SEN.
The percentage of pupils with an EHC (educational health care) plan has increased to 4.3%, from 4.0% in 2022.
The percentage of pupils with SEN but no EHC plan (SEN support) has increased to 13.0%, from 12.6% in 2022.

(ONS, 2023: 1)

The comparisons which can be made are limited but include that the ONS (2023) data on FE and Skills for LLDD in 2022/23 is 18.3 per cent or 285,250, which is a higher percentage than schools. The AoC data indicates that 18 per cent of 16–18-year-olds claimed free school meals in colleges, as opposed to 9 per cent of school pupils. This would support the Social Mobility Commission's (2020) view that students with more disadvantages tend to 'cluster' in FE.

There is also some helpful data on college support for staff and student equality and diversity.
83% of colleges increased resources spent on mental health between 2017 and 2020.
95% of colleges have staff trained in Mental health first aid.
71% of colleges have trained all staff in mental health awareness.
100% of colleges have structures in place to support staff mental health and wellbeing.

(AoC, 2022: 36)

Sector story – National Star College

The description of National Star College in its most recent Ofsted inspection, which took place in January 2023, is:

> National Star College is a large independent specialist residential and day college for students with high needs that is part of the National Star registered charity. The college recruits students from 48 local authorities and has sites in Cheltenham, Hereford and Wales. At the time of the inspection, there were 208 students in scope, attending the Cheltenham and Hereford sites. Students are aged 16 to 25, with most being 19 years or over. Students at National Star College have complex physical disabilities and medical conditions, including autism spectrum disorder and other learning, behavioural, sensory, or physical disabilities.
>
> (Ofsted, 2023: 1)

The college offers study pathways for its students, including the key themes of 'personal development'; 'engaging with the world around you' and 'work outcome and personal development'. Recently, they have also added a Level 3 diploma in adult care as an apprenticeship, with 15 apprentices, all 19 or over. Therapeutic interventions and specialist support for students are an integral part of the provision. The inspection report makes a number of positive comments about the inclusive curriculum and culture of the college, stating that 'staff at all levels in the organisation promote a culture that encourages students and apprentices to respect equality and diversity, embrace differences and ensure inclusive practice' (*ibid.*: 2). The report continues:

> Leaders, managers, governors and trustees have invested significantly in resources for students with high needs. Students benefit from a highly effective specialist therapy team and an emotional and well-being team. They also have access to a range of facilities that enhance their learning experience, such as a golf course, a farm, a swimming pool, a hydrotherapy pool, a rebound room and polytunnels.
>
> (*ibid.*: 3)

Another significant contributor to the equality and diversity approaches at National Star College is that:

> Teachers and therapists work collaboratively to identify accurate starting points for students on most programmes. They use this information to develop individual timetables that include therapies, life skills and enrichment to meet students' education, health and care plan outcomes and long-term aspirations.
>
> (*ibid.*: 4)

A good example of how National Star College provides inclusive learning in innovative ways is the case study featured on their website 'Alexa for independence' (National Star College, 2023: 1). Alexas are 'smart speakers' used domestically to play music, set timers, and control some household devices. This project at National Star College teaches and helps students to use Alexas to 'support their learning and environment' (*ibid.*: 1). For example, they allow students to record a spoken commentary to a simple household task such as making a pizza or preparing a drink. This recording can then be used as support on the next occasion that the task is done, as it can be played back.

Students have also been able to progress using the Alexas to turn on TVs, lighting and more, and the training and participation in this project gives them both more life confidence and confidence with technology. One of the college therapist's comments that the students' use of the Alexa 'allows them independence, a sense of control over their world and the impact to use the same technology as their peers to increase their quality of life' (*ibid.*: 1).

Overall, National Star College offers a positive example of an FE sector institution which has social justice, equality, and diversity firmly at the centre of its values and practices.

Working towards social justice, equality, and diversity across the FE sector

FETL – Leadership, FE, and social justice

FETL (2020: 12) cites examples of 'strategies drawn on by leaders to develop and sustain a values driven approach shaped by a commitment to social justice'. The report summarises (Duckworth and Smith, 2019) in stating that:

> Teachers in colleges are engaging with students not as "consumers" or "clients" or "bums on seats" but as human beings with an ability to learn and connect educational experiences to hope and plans for the future. In addition, the report reveals how teachers seek to overturn the damage caused to students' learner identities in negative prior educational experiences, when they incorporate students' biographical experiences into the curriculum and when they strive to establish egalitarian relations within their classrooms.
>
> (FETL, 2020: 31)

FETL (2020) also argues that the case studies used in their report:

> Illustrate how further education learning environments work to promote an ethos of egalitarianism – usually explicitly. Students' backgrounds are taken into account, while their thoughts, views and practices are valued and seen as an important curriculum resource from which to move forward. In such a context, teachers emerge as transformative leaders, subverting the 'symbolic violence' inflicted on their students in their earlier experience of education'.
>
> (*ibid.*: 32)

The sector story which follows is based on one of those case studies.

Sector story – City Lit – The City Literary Institute

The FETL research cited in the previous section included the creation of three case studies which were produced as examples of how FE institutions can demonstrate a strong commitment to social justice, equality, and diversity. Extracts from the City Lit Institute case study are used in this sector story. The case study begins with some description and background of City Lit:

> City Lit – the City Literary Institute – was established through the wave of investment and innovation in adult non-vocational education that took place in London in the aftermath of World War I.

Five literary institutes were founded with funding from London County Council, which sought to develop new provision "for the needs of a large number of students who seek education other than vocational", with "a coherent programme of studies related to leisure, and an adult setting". City Lit was set up in 1919 and is the only institute that survives.

(*ibid.*: 69)

The college has charitable status and is a community learning provider located in Holborn, in central London. Its offer emphasises inclusion and the idea of 'learning together' – putting the social and collective aspects of learning at the heart of its mission. The organisational set-up of the organisation does have advantages over an FE college, and it:

'Caters for adults only and maintains a balance between fee-paying courses and community learning. This means that just under half of its income comes from the Education and Skills Funding Agency (ESFA). It also means that the college's student body straddles social divides and includes people from a wide range of socioeconomic backgrounds. City Lit's status as an Institute for Adult Learning ... means that it is able to run courses that do not lead to a qualification and, as a corollary, it sits outside the system of metrics based on achievements and the regime that links funding to achievement.

(*ibid.*: 70)

The 2019 student data for City Lit was:

72 per cent of students were aged between twenty-six and sixty-five-years-old.
68 per cent of students were female.
23.7 per cent declared themselves to be Black and Ethnic Minority Ethnicity (BAME)
51 per cent were employed and 32 percent not in employment.
Nine per cent of students identified themselves as having a disability and or learning difficulty.
The total number of (part-time) students was 36,500.

FETL (2020: 70–71)

The research methodology which was used involved a preliminary survey; more than one visit; interviews and focus groups with participants; collected documents and data sources and video recordings. A summary of the key results relating to City Lit and social justice, equality, and diversity included comments that:

- A commitment to social justice is embedded in the culture of the college, and the results can be seen as furthering social justice.
- The college has funding arrangements which are more generous than general FE colleges, and this means social justice goals can be central to the institute's purpose with less pressure than an FE college.
- Governors, staff, and leadership are united in the college's mission and egalitarian approaches, and they are also part of the organisational culture.
- Students are accepted as who they are, and their biographies are an important part of the curriculum.

96 Education for social justice, equality, and diversity

- The timing of when and where learning takes place is fluid and flexible.
- Learning together is considered to be as important as learning as individuals.

(Adapted from FETL, 2020)

In the concluding sections of their research, FETL (2020: 124) argue that:

> In a college setting in which social justice values are most fully realised, the pedagogical goals reach beyond college walls. There is a selflessness and altruism in the everyday cultural practices of the college. The college is, in that sense, primarily a vehicle for bringing about change at the level of the individual but also in society more broadly.

Question for discussion

What do you think are the most important characteristics of social justice in education?

Adult and community learning (ACL) and mental health

Lewis (2014) undertook research into a small ACL project relating to mental health by holding focus groups with students in provision for adults with mental health issues. The provider was the Workers' Educational Association (WEA) (see Chapter 6), and there were some 36 participants. There were 21 women and 15 men, and 23 participants were aged between 41 and 60 years. The content of the courses included a wide range of 'self-help' themes such as social support, relaxation, meditation, confidence-building, stress management, and assertiveness. In addition, some participants were also attending courses in other subjects, including literacy, computing, and maths. More than half of the participants had few or no educational qualifications, although eight had gained qualifications at Level 3 or above. The results of the research provided a range of ways in which the courses had enhanced self-esteem and self-confidence. The process of building confidence and working with other students and the tutor built a 'sense of common humanity' (Lewis, 2014: 363). One student commented that:

> The issues I had were not being able to accept myself. Always feeling rejected and things like that where coming to this class I don't feel rejected and I don't know if there's other people been in the same situation....

(*ibid.*: 365)

Evaluating the research overall, Lewis (2014) argues that the learning involved clearly had a social justice focus, and that:

> The adult learning was helping to address mental health and educational inequalities across dimensions of social class, age and gender and to address social isolation and exclusion as key social determinants of poor mental health and subjective well-being ... Many of those attending had been initially educationally disadvantaged. Furthermore, breaking isolation and generating social support was found to be a particularly significant benefit for older participants and

women with caring responsibilities, whereas agency freedom in terms of speaking out about and standing up to violence and abuse was of particular importance for the mental health of women participants, many of whom had experiences in this area.

(*ibid.*: 370)

16–24-year-olds not in education, employment, or training (NEETs)

The percentage of 16–24-year-olds NEET in April to June 2023, in the United Kingdom, was estimated at 11.6 per cent. This is up 0.3 percentage points from the previous quarter and up 0.5 percentage points compared with pre-COVID-19 levels (October to December 2019). The increase is entirely driven by young males whose NEET rate from April to June 2023 was estimated at 12.2 per cent. This is up 1.1 percentage points, both on the previous quarter and compared with pre-COVID-19 levels. In contrast, the NEET rate amongst females remained stable at 11.0 per cent. Of the estimated 794,000 16–24-year-olds who were NEET, 427,000 (54 per cent) were male and 367,000 (46 per cent) were female.

A small research study by Avila and Rose (2019: 60) explores 'the perceptions of professionals working with young people who are NEET (Not in Employment, Education or Training) about their role in young people's trajectories'. The situation of NEETs has been 'a growing concern in Western economies and has been at the forefront of government agendas for the last 30 years' (*ibid.*: 60). Overall, 'the educational provision dedicated to NEETs is often described as providing low-value qualifications, and practitioners who work with NEETs are considered to have a lower status than other teaching professionals' (*ibid.*: 60). The central issue at the heart of attempts to reduce the number of NEET young people is:

> That NEET young people are likely to be so due to their socioeconomic status, the circumstances of difficulty that surround their lives or an educational system that is not promoting social mobility. Yet programmes designed to re-engage and train young people, in assuming that unemployed youth are at fault for their own inactivity, also assume they have a lot of agency in overcoming their circumstances.

(*ibid.*: 64)

Avila and Rose asked 25 participants about their work with NEET young people, including six interviews. Strategies for helping NEET young people to progress included providing a safe space where participants could be given the time to review their actions, thoughts, and attitudes, and to consider moving on towards employability and employment. Despite the NEET practitioners' clear desire to help solve the lasting problem of NEET young people, Avila and Rose (2019: 80) concluded that they were working in:

> An educational framework that, on the surface, aims to support disadvantaged young people to improve outcomes, but that, at its core, positions NEET young people in-line with explanations of poverty that view the individual as ultimately responsible for their own circumstances.

(*ibid.*: 80)

98 Education for social justice, equality, and diversity

Encouragingly though, the practitioners involved still maintained a sense of social justice when explaining that:

> Their jobs were no longer just to deliver increasingly punitive work-based interventions that positioned young people negatively, instead their task was to 'heal' through encouragement, help and support. Ultimately, practitioners just wanted to 'get a magic wand and make everything better for everyone' (P4), and in doing so they would be supporting young people into a re-engagement route to work.
>
> (*ibid*.: 76)

Transitions of autistic students into FE

Shepherd (2022) carried out research into the rarely researched areas of autistic students progressing to FE from special education. Shepherd explored the transition experiences of six autistic young people over a 12-month period as the young people moved from three special schools to a first year at five FE colleges in England. Their special schools had a maximum of 250 students, whilst the colleges had a minimum of 5,000 students. 'They progressed to a range of courses and qualification levels according to their prior attainment but also, according to the level of social support they required at college' (*ibid*.: 882). Data was 'collected from 40 interviews with parents, teachers, careers advisers and college tutors as well as from documentary and observational evidence' (*ibid*.: 882). It was not expected that the research data would lead to generalisations, but that they do 'provide detailed, illustrative accounts of transition experiences from multiple perspectives, including those of autistic students thus addressing a knowledge gap' (*ibid*.: 883).

The research identified three areas of transition: 'as induction', 'as development', and 'as becoming', and this was based on avoiding a deficit model of autism and disability. Transition as induction proved difficult for students and family alike, and Shepherd found that:

> Overall, while there was clear evidence of transition planning in the 'induction' category, there were also significant limitations when the quality of transition visits and transition plans was unreliable. There were also significant omissions not least in the abdication of institutional responsibility over the summer break.
>
> (*ibid*.: 885)

With regards to the transition to development stage, autistic students 'challenges in managing time, social interaction and having higher parental dependency than their peers' (*ibid*.: 887). Regarding development:

> The institutions in the study appeared to lack capacity to make adaptations and show double empathy when it came to travel training, supporting time management and recognising the essential interdependence of autistic students with their parents or carers. These findings correspond to a narrow interpretation of transition, linked to a limited time period and an undifferentiated view of personal development.
>
> (*ibid*.: 887)

Education for social justice, equality, and diversity 99

The final transition as becoming was also problematic, as the 'social needs of the six students were not sufficiently attended to in the transition process, and this had an impact on their progress at college and inhibited their potential becomings' (*ibid.*: 888). The colleges did not sufficiently acknowledge:

> This lived reality of autistic students and understanding of the impact of the social and educational environment on their anxiety the research suggests, like Bellini (2006), that the provision of social support at times of transition is fundamental for autistic students.
>
> (*ibid.*: 888)

Overall, this research highlights powerfully the complex, sensitive, and demanding necessities of working towards greater social justice, equality, and diversity in FE colleges. The students featured in this research did not have a particularly positive experience, and Shepherd argues that 'Previous studies have shown that transition is problematic for many students, not just those with autism and intellectual disabilities'; and that 'autistic students may experience distinctive challenges in navigating even small changes in their everyday lives, let alone major life changes such as the move to college' (*ibid.*: 889).

Shepherd concludes that her research:

> Demonstrates the responsibilities of educational institutions to make environmental adaptations that encompass not only the structural barriers reflected in 'tick-box' approaches to transition but also question what capabilities institutions have, or need to develop, in order to enable students to navigate change in ways that ensure that all students can thrive.
>
> (*ibid.*: 889)

Going further

An important report on 'further education, disadvantage and social mobility' was published by the Sutton Trust in late 2021. The report aimed 'to look at previous cohorts of learners, to demonstrate the extent to which the FE sector, and FE colleges in particular, have been successful in leading to well-paid employment, and facilitating progression to HE' (Sutton Trust, 2021: 5). This is essentially social mobility as it has already been discussed in this chapter. The report argues that:

> Whether FE Colleges can boost social mobility therefore depends on whether young people from a more disadvantaged background have better outcomes relative to their more advantaged peers in FE Colleges than in Sixth Form Schools. If this is the case, then FE Colleges, where the disadvantaged are more likely to attend, can play in key role in narrowing differentials across socio-economic backgrounds.
>
> (*ibid.*: 5)

The findings of the research included:

- More young people from a disadvantaged background attend an FE college rather than school.
- Within FE colleges young people from a more disadvantaged background, as indicated by eligibility for free school meals (FSM), are more likely to be studying for lower-level qualifications at Level 1 or below, relative to the non-FSM group.

- By the age of 28, the earnings gap between those more disadvantaged background who attended FE colleges earn 15 per cent less than other students.
- The difference in earnings is accounted for by the characteristics of the students.
- In terms of progression to HE, FE colleges are more successful in terms of improving the chances of their students from more disadvantaged backgrounds.

(Adapted from the Sutton Trust, 2021).

By focusing on young people, the scope of this report does not include FE's work with a large proportion of their students, i.e. adults. The progress of social justice in terms of social mobility with young people is noticeable, but less than could be the case. The progress with adults may well produce more optimistic results.

Conclusion

This chapter has outlined efforts to connect the disconnected and support the disabled and those with learning difficulties, in the cause of social justice, equality, and diversity. The sector's success in some areas is clear, but it is also clear that significant challenges still exist, particularly in an environment which is not getting any easier for FE.

FETL (2020) sought that their report would 'enable colleges to enact leadership that is orientated towards achieving social justice, as defined in this report' (*ibid.*: 128). Their recommendations included:

- **Funding** – colleges' positions need to be privileged and not disadvantaged in terms of educational funding. The case at present is that FE has less funding than other sectors of education, and that the 'students with the most needs (both educational and socio-economic) should have access to more funding, rather than less, as is currently the case, and this should be a fundamental principle of further education nationally' (*ibid.*: 128–129).
- **Curriculum and teachers** – the 'divided and divisive curriculum' (*ibid.*: 129) needs to be broad and not reduced to vocational education for the working class. Academic courses, community learning, and HE in FE all need to be retained and developed. The sector needs to value and nurture 'teachers who empathetic and skilled in managing educational relationships that are sincere and caring, and in which the teacher's belief in the students fosters their self-belief and confidence' (*ibid.*: 129).
- **Governors** – need to be more 'representative of the communities they serve and who have a professional background in (further) education where possible' (*ibid.*: 129).
- **Time and space** – pressure on producing results quickly and compressing course content and curriculum needs to be reconsidered including course length and funding. Building new, large college learning sites and retaining and developing use of more learning sites in local communities is urgent.
- **A new localism** – The more recent moves towards localism are welcomed and this 'new direction of travel' (*ibid.*: 131) needs to continue.

FETL (2020) makes a sound case for the elements which need to be in place if FE is to continue its ongoing search for social justice, equality, and diversity.

Education for social justice, equality, and diversity

Summary points

- Social justice is a complex and contested field, and clear definitions are important.
- The Taunton Report, the Tomlinson Report, and the post-COVID-19 pandemic followed by a cost-of-living crisis are all significant milestones in FE's progress towards social justice, equality, and diversity.
- A variety of research, reports, and commentaries suggest that FE colleges are constrained in their progress towards social justice, equality, and diversity because of their funding and because of pressure from the government of the day for them to concentrate on VET for young people rather than the full range of their activity. ACL and more independent, community-focused providers appear to be able to offer successful models of practice which colleges are seeking to operate but find it difficult.
- Recommendations for change and improvement have been made from the sector which will further take forward the cause of social justice, equality, and diversity in FE, but the government needs to accept these recommendations, fund them, and strongly support FE in taking them forward.

Recommended reading

Atkins, L. (2020) Social justice and education. In J. Tummons (Ed.) PCET. *Learning and teaching in the post compulsory sector*. London: Sage.

References

Association of Colleges (2022) *College Key Facts 2022/23*. London: AOC.
Atkins, L. (2020) Social justice and education. In J. Tummons (Ed.) PCET. *Learning and teaching in the post compulsory sector*. London: Sage.
Avila, T.B. and Rose, J. (2019) When nurturing is conditional: How NEET practitioners position the support they give to young people who are not in education, employment or training. *Research in Post-Compulsory Education*, 24(1), pp. 60–82, DOI:10.1080/13596748.2019.1584439
Avis, J. (2023) In pursuit of equity vocational education and training and social justice. *Research in Post-Compulsory Education*, 28(3), pp. 439–459, DOI: 10.1080/13596748.2023.2221119
Bellini, S. (2006) The development of social anxiety in adolescents with autism spectrum disorders. *Focus on Autism and Other Developmental Disabilities*, 21(3), pp. 136–145.
Duckworth, V. and Smith, R. (2019) *Transformative teaching and learning in further education: summative report*. London: UCU.
FETL (Further Education Trust for Leadership) (2020) *Leadership, further education and social justice*. London: FETL.
Gillard, D. (2018) *Report of the schools inquiry commission 1868. Background notes*. Available at: https://www.education-uk.org/documents/taunton1868/index.html (Accessed 19 November 2023).
Lewis, L. (2014) Responding to the mental health and well-being agenda in adult community learning. *Research in Post-Compulsory Education*, 19(4), pp. 357–377, DOI: 10.1080/13596748.2014.955364
Munday, D. (2020). Diversity in the PCET sector. In J. Tummons, (Ed.) PCET. *Learning and Teaching in the Post Compulsory Sector*. London: Sage.
National Star College (2023) *Alexa for independence case study*. Available at: https://www.nationalstar.org/sharing-knowledge/knowledge-hub/edtech-case-studies/alexa-for-independence/ (Accessed 20 November 2023).
Office for National Statistics (2023) *Academic year 2022/23 further education and skills – published 20 July 2023*. London: Office for National Statistics. Available at: https://explore-education-statistics.service.gov.uk/find-statistics/further-education-and-skills (Accessed 20 November 2023).
Office for Standards in Education (2023) *Inspection of National Star College – report*. Manchester: Ofsted.

Shepherd, J. (2022) Beyond tick-box transitions? Experiences of autistic students moving from special to further education. *International Journal of Inclusive Education*, 26(9), pp. 878–892, DOI: 10.1080/13603116.2020.1743780

Social Mobility Commission (2020) *Monitoring social mobility 2013–2020*. Available at: https://www.gov.uk/government/publications/monitoring-social-mobility-2013-to-2020/monitoring-social-mobility-2013-to-2020 (Accessed 20 November 2023).

Social Mobility Commission (2022) *State of the nation 2022 – People and places*. London: Social Mobility Commission.

Social Mobility Commission (2023) *State of the nation 2023 – People and places*. London: Social Mobility Commission.

Taunton Report (1868) *Report of the schools inquiry commission. Volume I*. London: HM Stationery Office.

The Sutton Trust (2021) *GOING FURTHER. Further education, disadvantage and social mobility*. London: The Sutton Trust.

Tomlinson Report (1996) *Inclusive learning. Report of the learning difficulties and/or disabilities committee*. Coventry: The Further Education Funding Council.

9 Skills for life (SfL)

Introduction

This further education (FE) subsector is one which has been subject to challenge, change, and pressure on an ongoing basis ever since learning opportunities were provided, which were intended to help members of the community to develop and improve the essential skills they needed for life. Which skills, in particular, are designated 'skills for life' (SfL) has been subject to debate, controversy, and continuous politicisation, with the skills involved in the vocational and employment part of life at one end of the range of views and skills involved at the living or domestic part of life at the other. Everyone, whatever their particular position, tends to agree that SfL are important, but it is surprising how rarely this agreement turns into coherent, generous, reasonable, and sustained funding and government support. Governments consistently argue that they wish to improve, for instance, the literacy of the nation, but when it comes to prioritising funding and attention for this amongst the many challenging areas needing funding, SfL rarely finds itself at the front of the queue for resources. SfL could be described as the Cinderella subsector of the Cinderella sector, despite colleges and other FE providers regularly demonstrating they work successfully to improve the SfL of students who often start from a position of considerable disadvantage. There have been many new government plans to improve the literacy and numeracy of the nation, and they contain measures and approaches which sometimes do look hopeful. Regularly, however, these policies and plans have not succeeded in significantly improving the SfL of the nation.

The chapter will not include details and discussion about General Certificate of Secondary Education (GCSE) resits taken in colleges by young people, as this will be addressed in Chapter 11, FE for 14–19-year-olds.

The chapter will firstly provide a definition of SfL, with discussions about the different understandings and expectations. Titles including basic skills, adult basic skills, key skills, core skills, functional skills, language, literacy, and numeracy (LLN), social skills, essential skills, and SfL have all featured in the history and development of this subsector, and a historical analysis will draw out these multiple changes. Examples from the history of SfL are the 'On the Move' literacy campaign from 1975; the Moser Report of 1999, and the 'action for English for speakers of other languages (ESOL) campaign of 2011.'

The chapter then continues with data on the numbers of students on SfL courses and how that has changed in recent years. The first sector story reflects on the Youth Media Project from 1976, and the author's role in that project. The chapter finishes with examples of SfL in action, which explore the experiences of students and teachers studying and teaching SfL, and provides examples of research and projects which have built a body of critique, good practice, and characteristics of successful SfL work in action.

DOI: 10.4324/9781003468455-9

Definitions

When looking for definitions of SfL, the first task is to understand what skills are involved. A limited definition would include only literacy and numeracy, or perhaps English and maths. A broader definition, and one which has been used regularly, is LLN. A very broad definition would include literacy skills, numeracy skills, digital skills, problem-solving skills, communication skills, working with others, and presentational skills. These have all been featured at some point as part of SfL in FE, and social skills could also be added. Within this chapter, and this book, SfL will include literacy, numeracy, digital literacy, and social skills. The definitions of each of these components of SfL are the following.

Literacy

The heart of literacy is 'language and understanding' (Smith, 2020: 67). It is more than just 'a set of skills that can be acquired step by step' (*ibid.*: 67) but is rather part of the 'context in which it operates, and that these contexts shape what literacy is, depending on to which purposes, settings and participants it can be located' (*ibid.*: 67). Literacy needs to be recognised as existing within a social situation and 'the fundamental skills of reading, writing, and communicating, both verbally and in written form, cannot be detached from the context in which they function' (*ibid.*: 69). Overall, literacy is seen as a socially operating capability and not an instrumental set of competences, which need to be learned in order to satisfy certain requirements. For this chapter and this book, the definition of literacy is capability with the skills, understanding, and application of reading, writing, and communicating, both verbally and in writing, to help individuals, groups, and society to be able operate in a range of social, work, and personal contexts.

Numeracy

Numeracy, as with literacy, has definitions which focus on occupational and personal competences as 'basic skills of computation' or a 'less prestigious equivalent to mathematics', but more positively, as 'the foundation skills acquired at a young age by schoolchildren, on which more complex mathematical knowledge can later be built' (*ibid.*: 72). This more instrumental approach to numeracy emphasises the use of mathematics to be able to function effectively at work. The social model of numeracy, however, argues that numeracy is 'a crucial body of skills, knowledge and understanding that provides a lifelong learner a way of better understanding the world around them' (*ibid.*: 72). Overall, in this chapter and this book, an adapted version of Smith's (2020) definition is used, which is that numeracy is capability with a set of number skills, understanding, and application that, once attained, underpin mathematical faculties that are important for functioning in employment and wider society.

English for speakers of other languages

NIACE (2006: 3) argues that 'confidence in English language opens doors and helps people engage in and contribute to civil society', whereas 'lack of fluency in the language condemns many people to poverty' (*ibid.*: 3). Participants in ESOL provision are often immigrants who are seeking to 'integrate successfully, to fulfil their potential and to avoid marginalisation or disenfranchisement' (Brown,

2017: 47). The 'provision of ESOL programmes to develop English language skills is therefore important for avoiding ghettoization and promoting social inclusion' (*ibid*.: 47). As can be seen in these remarks, ESOL has been argued to be another important contributor to social justice. As with other definitions in this section, understandings about ESOL provision, and the need for it have also been focussed on the more instrumental end of employment and skills, with a strictly vocational focus, and the field of immigration is itself fraught with many competing arguments which have often not helped the ESOL cause. The definition of ESOL used in this chapter and this book uses an extract from the Scottish Executive's 2007 'Adult ESOL Strategy for Scotland', which intends to provide opportunities for 'all Scottish residents for whom English is not a first language' to acquire 'the language skills to enable them to participate in Scottish life: in the workplace, through further study, within the family, the local community, Scottish society and the economy' (*ibid*.: 4).

Digital literacy

Pangrazio *et al*. (2020: 442) introduce their literature review of 'what is digital literacy' with the statement that the:

> Digitalisation of everyday life has had significant implications for education. Given the recent proliferation of digital devices and educational software, schools and educators are still grappling with how to integrate technologies into the curriculum and prepare students for their (digital) futures.
>
> (*ibid*.: 443)

Although this review does not directly address itself to FE, what it has to say is directly relevant for FE, and importantly the writers emphasise the need for localised understandings of digital literacy because they consider 'a standardised approach to digital literacies is problematic' (*ibid*.: 443). As with literacy and numeracy, definitions of digital literacy range between the instrumental, which concentrate on 'digital competence, digital skills or digital proficiency' (*ibid*.: 454) where the approach to teaching digital literacy will be to 'focus on building new skills that can be applied to digital technologies in a functional way' (*ibid*.: 455). For those wishing to address digital literacy as a social practice, 'students' everyday practices' (*ibid*.: 454) and their existing knowledge, experience, and understanding need to be connected to the digital tasks and activities within the educational curriculum. At the end of their review, Pangrazio *et al*. (2020: 456) ask the question about priorities for the understanding and defining of digital literacy, and whether 'the goal of digital literacies is to create productive workers in the "knowledge economy" or, in a more sophisticated fashion, address active engagement with democratic citizenship'. This book adopts the more expansive definition of digital literacy, defining it as a process which includes the skills, knowledge, and capability involved in being able to experience work, education, life, and personal development with the assistance of digital technologies.

Social skills

Social skills was a popular term in the 1970s and 1980s, and the techniques and approaches to developing social skills were used in particular within some government schemes of the time as a means of helping young people develop and improve some of the attitudes and capabilities which they needed in order to gain employment. As with the other definitions in this section, there were instrumental and social understandings of just what life and social skills meant and included.

Mintz et al. (2012: 54) suggest that such skills can be argued as 'relating to the facility of interacting with other people, and include skills such as appropriate communication, learning social norms, regulating one's own behaviour, and understanding its impact on others'. The Sutton Trust (2017), although calling social skills 'essential skills', make a sound case for including an understanding of social skills as including 'the attitudes, skills and behaviours that are thought to underpin success in school and work, and include the ability to respond to setbacks, work well with others, build relationships, communicate effectively, manage emotions, and cope with difficult situations' (ibid.: 7). Because the term social skills include the word 'social', definitions tend to recognise the social aspects of skills which will be included, in addition to those which will be relevant for work. During the 1970s and 1980s, many government schemes included social skills training with some success, even though the primary objective was generally to move people on towards employment. The definition in this chapter and book of social skills is the skills, knowledge, and capability involved in empowering people to take action to promote positive social relationships, ask for help, develop healthy relationships, protect themselves, and be able to live in and interact with society in harmony.

Drawing these definitions together, SfL can now be defined as a combination of literacy, numeracy, digital literacy, and social and life skills, which combine as they develop to improve the confidence of individuals, groups, and communities in themselves and their relationships with their community, their work, other individuals and groups, and the world in general.

Question for discussion

In your education to date, which aspects of SfL do you feel were included in the curriculum and how helpful to you was that?

Examples from the history of SfL in FE

What's in a name?

SfL, as previously mentioned earlier in this chapter, is a subsector which has experienced very frequent (even for the FE sector) naming and renaming. SfL is also a field where historically adults will appear at times to be the clear SfL policy focus, and on other occasions, 16–18-year-olds appear to be the clear SfL policy focus. There are, of course, also occasions when both are the principal policy focus. This makes clear analysis of policy on a historical basis difficult. To help the reader, a timeline of different agencies responsible, and terms used to describe SfL, and their focus is below.

(a). Primarily aimed at adults
   1980 The Adult Literacy and Basic Skills Unit was created, and the principal term used was 'Adult Basic Education'.
   1995 The Basic Skills Agency was created, and the principal term used was 'Basic Skills'
   1999–2003 The Moser report was produced, and the principal term used was 'Skills for Life'. The National Strategy for Adult Literacy and numeracy skills (DfES, 2001) also added 'ESOL' English for Speakers of Other Languages to SfL policy.

2001–10 The Learning and Skills Council was in existence and the principal term used was 'Adult Basic Skills'.

2021 A report from the Learning and Work Institute (2021) (not a government agency) was published and the principal term was 'basic skills'.

(b). Primarily aimed at 16–18-year-olds (including apprentices)

1979–2000 – core skills

1996–2012 – key skills mainly as components for young adults in General National Vocational Qualifications (GNVQs) – even referred to as 'generic skills' in Task Force Report (DfEE, 2000)

From 2004 – Functional skills

2019 – reformed functional skills

On the move – 1975

When compulsory schooling began in 1944, it did not include everyone learning how to read and write. There were some examples of education for SfL, then known as 'adult basic education' (ABE) during the 1950s and '60s, but this was a local provision and was often taught by volunteers. In an article written in 1995, Jones and Marriott summarised some of the social attitudes which had allowed such skills to become a low priority for society at the time. They describe the response of education to adults lacking SfL as 'minimal' and:

> Rooted in the attitudes of the times: approach to policy and administration; expectations of the "welfare state"; beliefs about the causes and consequences of poor attainment, and in particular an association in the public mind with low intelligence and delinquency.
>
> (Jones and Marriott, 1995: 337)

By the early 1970s, adult education was coming more to the fore, but the organisations who were providing adult education did little for SfL, as they felt there was no demand. By 1973, it was recognised that there were 'two million functionally illiterate people in England and Wales' (ibid.: 349), with very few of them getting any help or assistance from education providers. Recognition was growing that something needed to be done, and the BBC agreed to work with the relevant bodies to produce an adult literacy campaign. By 1974, the Inner London Education Authority (ILEA) was making provision in 29 of their 30 adult education institutions, and in October 1975, the BBC programme 'On the Move' began to broadcast 'on Sundays, in a carefully judged slot immediately following the early news bulletin' (ibid.: 350). The programme was not only popular but also included a referral service, where people could call and be referred to a contact in their own local authority. An evaluation of the 'Move on' project argued that 'without the BBC's initiatives, progress towards nationwide provision would have been more limited despite any increasing campaigning at the grassroots' (ibid.: 350). This innovative and helpful initiative is generally credited with making a significant difference, and Jones and Marriott (1995: 351) conclude that:

> The consolidation of literacy and basic skills in the normal programme of adult education across England and Wales, must obviously be counted among the noteworthy additions to the educational system in recent times. The increase in student numbers from 5000 in 1973 to 110,000 in 1985,64 and the continuing high level thereafter make the point adequately.

Significantly, Jones and Marriott do not give most of the credit to the education sector, but the:

> Voluntary agencies and public broadcasting – not the functionaries of the educational system – took the lead in luring illiterates into the open, and in devising the organizational and pedagogical welcome which proved itself robust enough to be naturalized throughout the system.
>
> (*ibid.*: 352)

The Moser Report

The International Adult Literacy Survey carried out by the OECD (Organisation for Economic Co-operation and Development) in 1996 revealed that the UK had low literacy and numeracy levels in comparison with other OECD member countries. In response to this survey, in 1998, Lord Claus Moser was appointed to:

- Review the current situation regarding different kinds of provision, co-ordination, good practice, and how to increase and disseminate it;
- Consider funding models for SfL;
- Suggest ways of increasing the volume, effectiveness, and quality of all SfL learning opportunities.

He estimated in his report (Moser, 1999: 2) that perhaps as many as 7 million people - have more or less severe problems with basic skills, in particular with what is generally called 'functional literacy' and 'functional numeracy'. Moser recommended a national strategy for Adult Basic Skills, with the aim of 'helping half a million adults a year by 2002' (*ibid.*: 6). A range of initiatives from the Labour government were introduced to implement changes as recommended by Moser. They were included in the 'Skills for Life Strategy for England' and are summarised in FETL (2021) as follows:

- National standards for literacy, language, and numeracy;
- A core curriculum framework, materials, and tests;
- New qualifications and professional standards for basic skills teachers;
- National targets for the number of adults the strategy aimed to reach and the number of formal qualifications to be gained.

(Adapted from FETL, 2021)

These actions:

> ... Grew out of the recognition that improving adult basic skills brings multiple benefits to employers, individuals, families and wider society. Improved literacy, language and numeracy skills are of crucial importance in raising Britain's standing in international measures of educational achievement and in promoting social participation and social mobility, as well as being a vital means of enhancing the UK's global economic competitiveness,
>
> (*ibid.*: 20)

Overall, much positive SfL development and improvement in provision took place at least partly as a result of Moser's report, but somewhat disappointingly, just five years later, the 'Skills for Life survey' found that:

Although the number of adults with literacy skills below Level 1 had fallen since the introduction of Skills for Life, the survey revealed that 5.2 million adults still had literacy skills below this level compared to the Moser estimate of seven million in 1999. The number of adults with numeracy skills below Entry Level 3 had fallen only slightly to 6.8 million.

(ibid.: 23)

The action for ESOL campaign 2011

This section of the chapter presents an example of 'democratic, active professionalism among FE teachers, the Action for ESOL campaign' (Peutrell, 2015: 139). It is an important example, both in the field of ESOL and in the professional identity and practice of those teaching in FE. In November 2010, the government of the time published plans for significant cuts in ESOL provision. This prompted a campaign which has been described as 'unique in the recent history of FE' (ibid.: 139). Extra restrictions were planned on who could access ESOL provision; the funding rate for ESOL provision was reduced; funding for workplace ESOL was removed; and fees were changed from free to between £400.00 and £1,200.00. This news was even more of a surprise, because of 'the widely accepted view that English language skills were crucial to integration in a practical sense, or with the consensus among mainstream politicians that migrants had an obligation to learn English' (ibid.: 140). In January 2011, Action for ESOL was launched. A supporting statement at the time from the National Association for Teaching English and other Community Languages to Adults (NATECLA) stated:

> Adequate and sustained funding of ESOL is not a luxury, it is an essential public service. This was recognized by Skills for Life, the national strategy for the improvement of adult literacy and numeracy. Thousands of migrants achieved levels of English which enabled them to join the jobs market, access training and participate more fully in their local communities'.
>
> (NATECLA, 2023: 1)

The campaigners had a very strong argument, and they pursued it through 'eight months of intense work by teachers, researchers, students and members of refugee and migrant welfare and rights groups, until the government announced a near U-turn just as the academic year was due to start' (Peutrell, 2015: 143). The character of the campaign was professional, personal, and provided an almost perfect model of a campaign by radical social movements. It included:

> ... A national petition; letter writing; briefings; rallies, demonstrations and lobbies; local and national alliance building; gaining the support of sympathetic politicians and councillors and the endorsement of public figures, trade unions and civic organisations; producing local impact studies; arranging radio and television interviews; and making use of the range of social media, including practitioner e-bulletins. It was urgent but it was also celebratory and, at times, carnivalesque. Events included picnics, teach ins, silent protests, noisy protests and giving out food.
>
> (ibid.: 143)

Students were also at the centre of the campaign, and they marched, spoke, made banners, and appeared on specially made videos online. It was clear from their contribution that they wanted to learn English, and these cuts would 'make this impossible' (ibid.: 145).

Peutrell argues that 'one of the most distinctive features of the campaign was the ESOL Manifesto (Action for ESOL, 2012), a statement of the campaign's beliefs, values and demands' (*ibid.*: 146). The manifesto was not only positive but also recognised and critiqued problems with ESOL provision at the time. It proposed placing the values of 'community adult education' (*ibid.*: 148) at the heart of ESOL, the need for teachers as professionals to go beyond the limitations of the classroom, and to work collaboratively with their colleagues, students, and communities to influence and shape policy. Overall, Peutrell reflects that as teaching professionals we 'should refuse the passivity of compliant professionalism, loosen institutional identities and create our own spaces for thought and action' (*ibid.*: 153). The Action for ESOL campaign showcases the professionalism of ESOL teachers, the commitment of actively engaged students, and the capacity to influence government on occasions where a strong case for change is powerfully presented.

How many SfL students are there?

The Learning and Work Institute (2021) has a very helpful report on ways forward with 'basic skills', and the report contains a good analysis of data on student participation in recent years. Extracts from the data and analysis follow:

> Research indicates that learning below Level 2 can result in a 7pp increase in individuals' employment rate and support learners in accessing better quality work, including increased job satisfaction, pay and security. The economic case for basic skills is equally strong with a social return of £17 for Entry Level and £22 for every £1 invested in Level 1 provision, in the case of younger learners (19–24 years old).
>
> (*ibid.*: 4)

'An estimated 9 million working-age adults in England have low basic skills in literacy or numeracy, of which 5 million have low skills in both' (*ibid.*: 4).

'An estimated 11.7 million people lack digital "life" skills. England is 15th out of 31 OECD countries in literacy skills and 19th in numeracy skills' (*ibid.*: 4):

> The high level of basic skills needs is compounded by adult participation in English, maths and ESOL plummeting by 63, 62 and 17 per cent respectively since 2012. Participation has fallen across every Mayoral Combined Authority in England. On current trends it would take 20 years for all adults with low literacy or numeracy to participate in learning.
>
> (*ibid.*: 4)

> In part this reflects the Government halving the Adult Education Budget from 2011–12 to 2019–20. Funding in England fell from £2.8 billion in 2011–12 to £1.5 billion in 2019–20, a 52 per cent fall in real terms. At the same time, funding rates per learner were frozen and funding for organisations who would often refer adults to basic skills provision, such as local authorities and community groups, was reduced too.
>
> (*ibid.*: 4)

While much policy is focused on Level 3 and above, 18 per cent of adults aged 19-64 are not qualified to at least Level 2. A foundation of basic skills is both a good thing in its own right and an essential underpinning to progress to higher learning.

(*ibid.*: 5)

The data above is extremely disappointing, as it is now over 20 years since Moser reported and the SfL Strategy was launched. The situation is even more disappointing when the evidence for the benefits of SfL provision is explained. The Learning and Work Institute makes a number of helpful proposals about the future of SfL in FE, and a selection of these will feature in the chapter conclusion.

The chapter now moves on to examples of SfL provision, the ways in which they have made helpful contributions to SfL in England, and what the experiences of the students and teachers have been.

Sector story – The youth media project – 1976

In 1976, when this story takes place, the author was just gaining early experience in the FE sector. After a brief spell of working in part-time youth work in Bristol, I gained a one-year post as a 'Project Leader' on a Manpower Services Commission (MSC) funded project called the Youth Media Project. The MSC was an organisation given a central role in employment and training by the Conservative government in 1973. This particular project was created by a local group of organisations, including the local FE college, the county youth service, and careers service, and it was co-ordinated by the college vice principal's department. The other Project Leader was an experienced media professional who had also undertaken some youth work, and the project was intended to:

- Provide work experience and training for a group of approximately 16 unemployed 18-year-old to 21-year-old young adults.
- Devise and deliver training in employability, job search, work preparation, social skills, literacy, and numeracy.
- Provide careers advice and guidance via a local authority careers officer who was attached to the project.
- Provide training in basic media production skills including video camera use, designing programmes, interviewing, editing, and finishing short video productions.
- Showing the completed videos to audiences of local FE students and others and discussing the content.
- Provide support for participants to help with personal and training issues.
- Work towards all participants gaining employment or further training from the project.

The project did have some distinctive features. Firstly, participants were paid for attending, and this was the case for a range of the schemes of the time. The amount was based on trainees in the industry, so was relatively generous for government schemes at the time, and extremely generous for most schemes since. The second was the use of video and the media generally as a tool to develop SfL and work-related skills. The media skills were to be used as a vehicle for developing all the other skills involved, especially SfL and employability skills. This was nearly 50 years ago and was a true innovation at the time. It would be entirely contemporary as an idea now when technology and digital media are often used as a vehicle to develop other skills. I claim no credit for the idea, as I joined once the project was designed, but being involved as a project leader/ trainer was very rewarding, and very interesting, and we did even find ourselves on local TV when two social- and life-skills gurus of the time, James Priestley, and Philip McGuire, visited to run a session. Very exciting times! In terms of the results of this project, the group of students had a variety of skills, attitudes, and issues and some interestingly challenging personalities, but as the project progressed, they became a good team and demonstrated good improvements in most of the project areas. There were problems, as some had difficult histories, but they were almost always solved, and a number of interesting and helpful videos were made around the local area and shown to appreciative audiences. By the end of the one year of the project, almost all the participants had jobs or training to go into, and the project was extended for another year with another group. This was my first job, full-time job as a teacher, and it really did make a difference to the people involved, including me!

Examples of SfL in action

Functional skills in mathematics

Dalby and Noyes (2022: 432), when discussing functional skills mathematics, commented on how 'for a time, Functional Skills mathematics flourished and was becoming valued by stakeholders'. Unfortunately, an ongoing problem with functional skills in mathematics as part of FE SfL provision is the difficulty of integrating functional skills with the established GCSE curriculum. Dalby and Noyes argue that 'Mathematics education in England's Further Education colleges is entangled in the academic-vocational divide, where qualifications for vocational education have often been … shaped more by academic values than by vocational purposes' (*ibid.*: 435). They continue to argue that the 'young people for whom such qualifications are designed have arguably not been served well by regular qualification reforms' (*ibid.*: 435). Their research included two empirical studies in FE colleges involving documenting the views of managers, teachers, and students about teaching and learning approaches and experiences.

Initially, amongst teachers, managers, and students, there was enthusiasm for 'Functional Skills as a suitable qualification for 16–18-year-old students in vocational education due to the relevance of the skills'. By the second study, however, after a gap of five years, participants had 'identified deficits in Functional Skills mathematics' (*ibid.*: 442). There was broad agreement that an alternative qualification was needed. On the positive side, 'teachers have consistently reported that the classroom approaches engendered by the Functional Skills mathematics curriculum tend to make mathematics more relevant to low-attaining vocational students, which can help improve student motivation, increase engagement and reduce negative attitudes' (*ibid.*: 447). A key issue with functional skills mathematics is that the 'challenge of achieving consensus about a curriculum when there are multiple views of the type of mathematics that is most appropriate for post-16 students to develop is a chronic one' (*ibid.*: 449). Despite what appears a difficult future for functional skills mathematics, FE has managed to have made a difference to some participants because 'Functional Skills mathematics has helped to engage many students by making mathematics more relevant' (*ibid.*: 449–450).

Literacy connections

Sligo *et al.* (2019) undertook research into the work of literacy tutors, their beliefs, and their experiences in New Zealand with apprentices and their teachers and employers. The general working situation of literacy tutors as described in the research is similar to literacy tutors working in FE-based SfL in England. The research aimed to evaluate aspects of apprentices' literacy support, how well the support helped with the workplace application of literacy and the teaching and provision could be improved. The researchers interviewed tutors, managers/supervisors in the workplace and apprentices to provide data relating to the value of their training, progress with literacy knowledge and workplace application, and 'recommendations for future training' (*ibid.*: 113). The results provided an example of the tensions between more instrumental and work-related expectations of literacy learning (from the apprentices and their employers) and more socially situated expectations of literacy learning (from the tutors). The tutors were used to working with adults, and what connected the tutors was that they:

> Believed that literacy abilities were associated with new opportunities in community and workplace settings for their clients. In their minds, every citizen had a right to literacy and thus it was a moral imperative in their task to advance social justice, as they saw it, for them to help their learners become competent in reading and writing. They saw capabilities in literacy as empowering to people who typically possessed few resources in their lives and who in the tutors' experience were often economically and socially marginalised.
>
> (*ibid.*: 115)

The apprentices appreciated the supportive and helpful approach of their tutors, but were in work situations where the outcomes of their programmes which would help them in the workplace were their main priority. They:

> Had a strong personal sense of the importance of building their own literacy, which their experience of defeat at school made most unlikely, it would have been massively difficult or else impossible for them to hold this position in the face of what other influential people in their industries believed.
>
> (*ibid.*: 116)

What connected the apprentices was the need to achieve 'what the workplace required of them in terms of literacy practice' (*ibid.*: 117). Sligo *et al.* (2019) explained the differences between themselves and the students as follows:

> Whereas tutors had assumed that lifelong learning and ongoing progress in textual literacies were important in access to social justice and full societal participation, and were good things in their own right, the apprentices, managers and trade training coordinators were quite clear in their minds that improved textual literacy was just a means of helping apprentices to progress towards the aspirational goal of being accepted within an industrial community.
>
> (*ibid.*: 117)

114 *Skills for life*

Over a period of time, however, the tutors recognised that their professional capability and motivation to support the students in their own aims led to adjusting their own views to arrive at:

> … A new frame of reference and grounded them in their work. Their experience with the apprentices taught them to reimagine their work, as a way to build apprentices' literacy skills in tandem with supporting their learners' entry into the occupations they so strongly craved to join. The tutors started to visualise their goal of social justice in a different light, recognising how justice for the apprentices might be achieved by their being accepted into secure positions.
>
> (*ibid.*: 123)

As a result of this shift in the tutors' strategy, the apprentices' confidence grew to a considerable distance beyond where it had been when they started the programme, and their employers' objectives, their tutors' objectives, and their own objectives were all achieved.

Sector story – Melanie – 'Getting on'

Melanie had a difficult time at home and at school when she was a child. Her parents had mental health issues, the household was often chaotic, and Melanie was left to fend for herself. She tried hard at school, but always seemed to be one or two steps behind her classmates. She got on well with some of the teachers but left with few qualifications or friends. She took on two jobs to make ends meet, both with cleaning companies, and had become a supervisor of the local council's cleaning team by the age of 21. One of the other people in the cleaning team talked to her during a break about going back to school 'but a school for people our own age'. This was, in fact, a trade union workplace scheme called 'Getting on', which was aimed at providing literacy and numeracy support for adults, confidence building, career development, and digital literacy.

The course fitted into Melanie's work schedule, and she joined to work towards Level 2 qualifications. Her literacy tutor, Christine, was impressed by Melanie's hard work and determination and recognised a particular talent for writing in her coursework. Melanie had often dreamt about writing a novel, and Christine encouraged her to write her own story as a starting point. Not only did Melanie complete this, and then a novel, but it was published and set her off on a career as a writer. Participation of SfL learning did not just improve Melanie's literacy skills, it gave her an opportunity to dream, and then opened doors towards achieving her dream.

Within this chapter, Melanie's story shows the importance of workplace SfL provision and how providing accessible learning opportunities in SfL can be a starting point for so much more.

> **Question for discussion**
>
> How digitally literate are you, where did you learn those skills and how helpful are they in work, study, and life?

Conclusion

There have been major successes and major disappointments in SfL in FE, but there are some excellent proposals for how the future of SfL can be improved which are in the public domain.

The Learning and Work Institute (2021) firstly summarises some of the key benefits of SfL, and they include:

- SfL learning results in a range of positive personal and social outcomes and helps participants to progress to further learning.
- Increased levels of SfL have a direct relationship to economic and employment success.

(Adapted from Learning and Work Institute, 2021)

What will increase participation in SfL is:

- Tailored recruitment and engagement which are relevant to different students' needs;
- Providing strong and effective social and practical to students such as childcare and transport;
- Tailored course content towards students' interests and needs;
- Working with employers to find models of provision which also suit them.

(Adapted from Learning and Work Institute, 2021)

Summary points

- SfL in FE includes literacy, numeracy, ESOL, digital literacy, and social skills.
- The history of SfL has been one of regular name changes and challenges.
- On the move campaign from 1975, the Moser Report from 1999, and the action for the ESOL campaign illustrate this.
- SfL student numbers have been reducing in recent years, and the comparative position of the UK in terms of global measures is not strong.
- Examples of functional skills in mathematics, literacy connections, and a sector story demonstrate some key aspects of SfL in action.
- Students' needs have always been at the heart of SfL for teachers and providers, which is why they have been successful despite external problems.
- Ways forward with SfL have been proposed and are focussed on students' and employers' needs.

Recommended reading

Peutrell, R. (2015) Action for ESOL: Pedagogy, professionalism and politics. In M. Daley, K. Orr and J. Petrie (Eds) *Further education and the twelve dancing princesses*. London: Institute of Education Press.

References

Action for ESOL (2012) *The ESOL manifesto. A statement of our beliefs and values*. London: Action for ESOL.
Brown, S. (2017) Mixed messages (or how to undermine your own policy): ESOL provision in the Scottish FE sector. In M. Daley, K. Orr and J. Petrie (Eds) *The principal: Power and professionalism in FE*. London: UCL Institute of Education Press.
Dalby, D. and Noyes, A. (2022). The waxing and waning of functional skills mathematics. *Journal of Vocational Education & Training*, 74(3), pp. 434–453.
DfEE (2000) *Skills for all: Proposals for a national skills agenda*. London: Department for Education.
DfES (2001) *'Skills for life'. The national strategy for adult literacy and numeracy skills*. London: Department of Education and Skills.

Further Education Trust for Leadership (2021) *Skills for life: A new strategy for English, Maths, ESOL and digital. Learning from the past to improve in the future. Next Stage 2021–2031*. London: FETL

Jones, H.M.F. and Marriott, S. (1995) Adult literacy in England, 1945–75: Why did it take so long to get 'On the Move'? *History of Education*, 24(4), pp. 337–352, DOI: 10.1080/0046760950240405

Learning and Work Institute (2021) *Getting the basics right. The case for action on adult basic skills*. Leicester: Learning and Work Institute.Mintz, J., Branch, C., March, C. and Lerman, S. (2012) Key factors mediating the use of a mobile technology tool designed to develop social and life skills in children with Autistic Spectrum Disorders. *Computers in Education*, 58(1), pp. 53–62.

Moser Report (1999) *Improving literacy and numeracy: A fresh start*. London: Department of Education and Employment.

National Association for Teaching English and other Community Languages to Adults (2023) Available at: https://www.naldic.org.uk/eal-advocacy/eal-news-summary/221210.html (Archived website) (Accessed 29 November 2023).

NIACE (National Institute for Adult and Continuing Education) (2006) *More than a language…: NIACE committee of enquiry on English for speakers of other languages (Executive summary)*. Leicester: NIACE.

Pangrazio, L., Godhe, A. L., and Ledesma, A. G. L. (2020). What is digital literacy? A comparative review of publications across three language contexts. *E-learning and Digital Media*, 17(6), pp. 442–459.

Peutrell, R. (2015) Action for ESOL: Pedagogy, professionalism and politics. In M. Daley, K. Orr, and J. Petrie (Eds) *Further education and the twelve dancing princesses*. London: Institute of Education Press.

Scottish Executive (2007) *The adult ESOL strategy for Scotland*. Edinburgh: Scottish Executive.

Sligo, F., Tilley, E., Murray, N. and Comrie, M. (2019) Community of practice versus community of readers: The literacy tutors' dilemma. *Journal of Vocational Education & Training*, 71(1), pp. 108–125, DOI: 10.1080/13636820.2018.1464052

Smith, M. (2020) Literacy and numeracy in the post compulsory sector. In J. Tummons (Ed.) *PCET. Learning and teaching in the post compulsory sector*. London: Sage.

The Sutton Trust (2017) *LIFE LESSONS: Improving essential life skills for young people*. London: Sutton Trust.

10 COVID-19

Introduction

This chapter starts by reminding the reader of what happened to further education (FE) and society at large over the time of the COVID-19 pandemic. The chapter uses accounts from the time, research, and reflection to remind us that it was both an extremely frightening and difficult time, but also a time when FE and many other public services put in heroic, innovative, and highly professional efforts to maintain their support for their students and colleagues, and their commitment to their organisations to the best degree they possibly could.

The main section of the chapter uses research, reports, and sector stories to provide an analysis of the special challenges faced and the deep effects they had on learners, teachers, managers, and organisations. The chapter considers what damage was done, what, if any, benefits emerged, and what has happened in FE since the pandemic.

The two sector stories both come from the publication, 'Working and living in FE during the COVID-19 pandemic: 27 FE practitioners' voices' (2021).

The chapter concludes by asking if the sector has returned to the previous somewhat uncertain status quo, or if any of the positive or negative effects of COVID-19 have remained part of general practice in the FE sector.

COVID reminders – What happened, when did it happen, and what was the response?

The start of the COVID-19 pandemic was in January 2020, so it is no longer something in our immediate memory unless we suffered particular personal traumas at the time. The pandemic did, however, have very powerful impacts on FE at the time, and many of these impacts are still present. It is therefore essential in a book such as this to take account of those impacts and to discuss and analyse them.

The pandemic timeline

On 31 January 2020, the first two cases of coronavirus were confirmed, with the first death on 5 March 2020. In March 2020, nurseries, schools, and colleges in England were shut as part of the 'lockdown' procedure intended to stem the progress of the virus. Most pupils and students were at home, and online learning was their only available teaching. Children of key workers and

DOI: 10.4324/9781003468455-10

those considerable did still attend school and college. The national lockdown closed 'non-essential' high street businesses and public sector organisations, and all members of the community had to stay at home and could only leave for essential purposes such as food buying or medical reasons.

General Certificate of Secondary Education (GCSE) and A Level exams were cancelled, which had never happened before in the history of UK education. Grades were awarded based on predicted grades and teacher assessment. There were further lockdowns starting in November 2020 and January 2021. In December 2020, the 90-year-old Margaret Keenan became the first person to receive a vaccination outside a clinical trial. By July 2021, most COVID restrictions were lifted and in February 2022, and all remaining restrictions were lifted. In terms of statistics relating to the pandemic, they are below:

> By 30th November 2023, there had been 21,012,493 cases of Covid 19 in England.
> By 30th November 2023, there had been 197,010 deaths from Covid 19 in England.
> That is roughly the same as the population of the London borough of Kensington and Chelsea, and about 10,000 more than the population of the unitary authority of Bath and North East Somerset.
> By 30th November 2023, there had been 7,688,616 Covid 19 vaccinations in England.
>
> (UK Health Security Agency - UKHSA, 2023: 1)

What happened to FE? – In brief

The next section of the chapter features a selection of statements with particular relevance to FE and COVID in a series of categories, to draw the experience more directly to the forefront of the chapter. A fuller discussion of these categories is included in the main section of the chapter.

A vulnerable and stressed sector

Described by the Association of Colleges as uniquely vulnerable, the nature of the sector and its learners suggested that it could be particularly impacted by the pandemic in relation to the economic participation of young people, the process of becoming qualified, and the mental and physical wellbeing of learners who often come from low-income communities; the most vulnerable including those 'Not in Education, Employment or Training' (NEETs). The sector is also financially stressed (UCL Social Research Institute, 2021: 4).

> *Experiences of restrictions*
>
> Participants were asked about the restrictions put in place at school or college, and how these impacted their mental health and wellbeing. Mask-wearing, social distancing in schools and, for those that had left school for a new sixth-form college, not being able to mix in with their new peers in college impacted some participants' ability to build new social bonds with other students. This was unsettling and appears to have affected their confidence; many participants believed they had forgotten normal social skills, not having interacted with other young people face-to-face for so long.
>
> (Department for Education, 2022: 19)

Mental health and wellbeing

School and college restrictions meant that the wellbeing of many participants had suffered. Many said they missed out on traditional milestones such as the school prom or traditions such as signing shirts at the end of term, which was disappointing. Personalised support, where available, made a big difference to participants' mental health.

(*ibid.*: 22)

Disconnected and connected teachers and students.

Living and working through a pandemic meant employees were physically disconnected from each other and experienced a disruption to working patterns. In addition, there were concerns about job security, encroachment of work into homes both physically and psychologically, responsibilities of home schooling and/or caring for friends and relatives.

(Corbett et al., 2023: 2)

Voices from the front line

Suddenly, I hit a massive wall, realising the pace I had set for myself was unsustainable for the duration of the lockdown.

Used to working in an embodied way, we felt our bodies disappearing as we spent all day sitting still; disembodied heads on screens.

(Crawley et al., 2021: 8)

Questions for discussion

What happened to your education, or the education of members of your family, during the COVID-19 pandemic?
How did this affect your life, work, or education?

Sector story – Riding the coronacoaster

A number of groups of FE practitioners came forward with first-hand accounts of their experience of working during the pandemic. One project collected and published accounts of the experiences of 27 practitioners, and these accounts were edited by a group of other practitioners, and then published by Solihull College as Crawley *et al.* (2021). One particular account, by Amanda Turner, has been included in the summary as this sector story. Amanda is a teacher educator of teachers in FE and works at the University of Bolton. At the start of the pandemic, the account introduces the pressure and worry which many teachers must have felt when the lockdown took place. Amanda

.... Felt extremely unprepared. The immediate expectation was for all teaching to continue, through the use of virtual platforms and trainees were not to be disadvantaged. However, initially it was a time of heightened anxiety and fear, compounded by social media and the lack of normal contact with friends, family and colleagues. Established routines disappeared over night.

(*ibid.*: 87)

Immediate adaptation to the completely new and different situation was needed by all involved, whether students or teachers, and supporting the students, particularly in the process of online learning, meant that the teachers were not necessarily always very far ahead of their students in terms of their own digital literacy. At least partly due to the determination of all involved, the 'initial feelings of being stranded on a desert island were quickly replaced with the realisation that through the use of technology the world had become more connected than before, in a different way' (*ibid.*: 87).

Possibly one of the most appropriate and yet dramatic images of the COVID-19 pandemic from an FE practitioner was the notion of the 'coronacoaster', which Amanda coined as part of her account. Few passages can have summed up more effectively the experience of FE (and probably all parts of education, and many parts of society at the time):

> COVID-19 brought highs and lows, as we collectively rode the coronacoaster, in ever changing tides of emotions, from heightened anxiety through to elation. This is not a bleak picture, but one of positivity as trainees and staff developed true grit, resilience and determination. Teaching continued, but in a very different way. Students were supported more than ever as our patience and empathy towards one another, came into sharp focus.
>
> (*ibid.*: 87)

There will be further accounts from front line voices later in this chapter.

An analysis of what happened to FE

A vulnerable and stressed sector

As has been discussed in a number of previous chapters, before the pandemic FE was already in difficulty in terms of funding and inconsistent government policies.

> The Institute of Fiscal Studies (2020) calculated that funding per student in further education and sixth-form colleges in England fell by 12 per cent in real terms between 2010–11 and 2019–20 and adult learning and apprenticeships by 35 per cent.
>
> (UCL Social Research Institute, 2021: 4)

These structural issues then combined with the more direct differences which the pandemic brought, which are summed up by the UCL Social Research Institute:

> The FE Sector has been particularly impacted by the pandemic due a confluence of factors – its focus on vocational learning and the workplace that has been disrupted through successive lockdowns, the fact that it caters for more vulnerable sections of the population both young people and adults, and its financial stresses.
>
> (*ibid.*: 27)

FE also received less financial support from the government than schools during the pandemic, which added to the stresses already present. Local Government had been especially helpful in collaborating closely with colleges to mitigate the impacts of the pandemic'.

Spours et al. (2022) provide a very helpful summary of some of the key points from their own UCL Social Research Institute report of 2021. After reviewing evidence of the 'Mitigating impacts of the COVID-19 pandemic on the further education sector' they arrived at two lists, one of 'COVID Harms' and the other of 'Mitigation approaches'. The harms include:

- **Vocational disruption** – There were multiple disruptions including a 'decline in economic participation in apprenticeships' where 'the worst affected areas were health and social care, business management and hospitality'. There was also harm to college vocational learning with 'noticeable reversals for those taking vocational courses with declines most marked for those studying at the lower levels and for adults' (ibid.: 785). There was also a decline in enrolments and pass rates in functional skills, ESOL (English as a Second or Other Language), and basic maths and English.
- **Problematic transitions for students** – the drop in participation on vocational pathways appears to have harmed the prospects of transitions to further learning more in vocational provision than academic provision, exacerbating an already existing class gap.
- **Increased inequalities** – A predicted significant growth in the number of NEETs. Existing regional, social, and racial inequalities with 'minoritised groups, those from lower socio-economic positions and young people, struggling much more than those with greater social privilege (ibid.: 786).
- **A further 'stressed' FE sector** – the funding gap between schools and FE has remained and to some degree been reinforced. Staffing FE with suitably skilled staff has also become increasingly difficult, and 'in response, teachers have been working longer hours, worsening the situation of burnout prior to the pandemic' (ibid.: 787).

The COVID mitigation approaches which were intended to help offset the harms included:

- **Vocational disruption** – there are interventions which can mitigate the disruption, and they include emphasising how vocational programmes can have a positive effect on students' employment prospects; early intervention combined with ongoing personal support which can enhance the outcomes of disadvantaged groups; NEETs do respond to relevant and appropriate interventions when made directly available, and when they include 'targeted additional support for young people with additional needs' (ibid.: 788).
- **Problematic transitions for students** – research evidence indicates that 'integrated and aligned programmes for young people that emerge as personalised packages of skills, financial, emotional and practical support' (ibid.: 788) can make a difference.
- **Increased inequalities** – the evidence for mitigating interventions for this COVID harm was less directly available, but the research did suggest that more general strategies to reduce inequalities such as 'practices focused on individual vulnerable learners including accurate identification, effective engagement, effective assessment and profiling, a trusted, consistent advisor and delivery of personalised support' (ibid.: 788).
- **A further 'stressed' FE sector** – the research found difficulty identifying mitigating strategies for this harm, but there was a small note of optimism from the senior managers who were interviewed as part of the research when they stated that:

Staffing shortfalls in key areas were also worsened by the effects of the Omicron variant on sickness rates. Despite all of this, most of those interviewed considered that staff morale had been maintained, although many were exhausted with no end to the crisis in sight

(ibid.: 790)

COVID-19

The CollabGroup report (2021: 12) also managed to find some optimism for colleges when stating that 'colleges also played a critical role in supporting local communities throughout the pandemic. This support included fundraising activity to support community projects, volunteering space for vehicles and acting as temporary vaccination sites'.

Experiences of restrictions

The Department of Education's 2022 research about 16–19 learners' experiences of the pandemic features evidence about how much the COVID restrictions impacted their lives and their study. For students now being expected to study at home, the restrictions were challenging for:

> Participants within multi-generational households with many siblings, family life restricted the space that could be used to work from home, as well as access to available digital devices and access to the Internet, which made remote learning more difficult. Some BAME research participants also spoke about an additional pressure brought about by a perceived need to please their parents and meet their expectations. Participants felt that the legacy of lost learning was more pronounced for young people from disadvantaged backgrounds and locked down accentuated existing disadvantages.
>
> (*ibid.*: 11)

For those who needed additional support, they:

> ... Often used the SEND learning support that was available at their college, although this was not always available for the whole period of lockdown and participants would have liked support services to have remained open during lockdown. Participants found that it took time for specialised learning support to start again after returning to learning in person, which was a challenge. Staff changes during lockdown also meant teachers were sometimes unaware of young people's specific SEND needs.
>
> (*ibid.*: 23)

When students were allowed to return to their classroom or other learning site, they were 'pleased to return to the classroom but restrictions such as social distancing, mask-wearing and "learning bubbles" meant that it was harder to connect to peers' (*ibid.*: 28).

Despite the numerous restrictions, Raven's (2022) small study of FE students' views about the pandemic demonstrated:

> .... the resilience of the research participants and their determination to make the most of their situations. Various other studies have drawn attention to the positive outlook of those surveyed. What this study has shown is that this extends to a determination to succeed and, in at least some instances, to revise their ambitions in light of their experiences (*ibid.*: 204).

Mental health and wellbeing

The DfE (2022) research already referred to concentrated on the views of school and college 16–19 learners, and a number of issues with mental health and wellbeing were identified.

An example of this was that:

> .... Not seeing people in person or socialising with peers was difficult and had caused some to feel anxious and isolated. Many participants explained that they had to make a conscious effort to stay in touch with friends and remain social throughout lockdown.
>
> (*ibid.*: 17)

'The Covid-19 pandemic had also been challenging for participants' mental health and participants felt they would have benefited from more personalised wellbeing and academic support' (*ibid.*: 28).

Corbett *et al.* (2023) consider the wellbeing of the FE workforce with a study of 347 responses to questions about COVID from sector employees. The researchers firstly draw attention to a previous report about FE sector staff wellbeing from the Education and Training Foundation (2019). The key findings from this ETF report are:

> Staff wellbeing in post-14 education was found to be similar to the findings of other research studies in the wider education sector using the same approach. The wellbeing of staff working in the education sector as a whole was lower than that of the general population.
>
> (*ibid.*: 9)

The ETF report identified two 'pinch points', which were when 'starting out as a new teacher and when experiencing a change of role' and commented that the 'support offered to members of staff and to their personal growth as an individual during these points is weak' (*ibid.*: 9).

The ETF suggest that the ways forward with staff wellbeing include the following:

- **Collegial and effective management/leadership practice** – More needs to be done to ensure that staff in leadership and management positions in post-14 education develop a supportive working environment and communicate more effectively across their organisations, in order to create a positive workplace culture.
- **Autonomy and trust** – When staff felt they had the freedom (autonomy) to decide how to carry out their work and felt trusted (as opposed to experiencing 'micro-management' of their duties), this was considered to have a positive impact on their mental wellbeing. Managers need to consider how best to encourage such autonomy, and to build a sense of trust, in order to help their staff to flourish in their roles.
- **Additional support for newly qualified teachers and post-14 professionals undergoing a change of role** – Consideration needs to be given about how best to offer additional support to these two groups at these key points in their careers, as this will have a positive impact on their lives at times of great change and increase the likelihood that they will continue to work in the sector in the future (*ibid.*: 9–10)

Corbett *et al.*'s (2023) research confirmed most of the ETF recommendations, and the comparison between the two studies provided an opportunity to consider just how resilient the FE workforce is. They argue that they 'do not doubt the resilience of the FE workforce, but we would question if the continued change and tough demands have made the FE sector stronger or weaker' (*ibid.*: 9). Encouragingly, they found that respondents to their questions 'despite the apparent lack of financial or health-related enticements to work in the FE sector' still 'continues to demonstrate commitment to their work and positivity in supporting others' (*ibid.*: 9). Whilst supporting the recommendations from the ETF study, Corbett *et al.* (2023) argue that the changes to the sector should now go further, because there is a

> .... Need to rebuild workforce confidence, enable clarity and redress feelings of isolation (so) we believe a nuanced approach to drafting and implementing policy is required. We suggest FE institutions should redevelop their work-family policies in collaboration with all staff in their organisation not only HR, managers and senior leaders but the wider workforce too. This would begin to rebuild a sense of community and belonging within each organisation, something that has been eroded by the pandemic.
>
> (*ibid.*: 10)

They conclude that 'our study has highlighted the impact of the pandemic on wellbeing in the FE sector, however, many of the issues were present before the pandemic'. They suggest that it is time for the Cinderella sector to recognise that

> The value the FE sector gives to its students, employers and the economy is significant. Now it is time that it remembers its staff and seeks to re-establish itself as a sector of choice for employment. It's time to find the glass slipper.
>
> (*ibid.*: 11)

Disconnected and connected teachers and students

Because of necessity under lockdown, FE made great efforts to provide online learning for students, and also for continuing networking and support for teachers. The Edge Foundation produced a helpful report and commented that as would be expected with this happening so rapidly,

> There were a range of benefits and challenges of online learning. A majority of participants voiced they were keen to return to colleges and resume face-to-face teaching. Additionally, what could be seen as a benefit to one participant was sometimes a challenge to others.
>
> (Edge Foundation, 2022: 4)

The CollabGroup of senior college staff produced a discussion document to help them 'understand their experiences in navigating this uniquely challenging environment' (2021: 3) after one year of the pandemic. In terms of the use of online learning, they gave examples of ways in which FE sought to maintain connections between students and teachers and to rapidly adapt including the example below:

> Lecturers noticed that students were more comfortable using mobile phones, tablets, and gaming devices than they were using traditional laptops and desktops. To make students learning as accessible as possible, the college tried to deliver courses using these devices, with varying degrees of success. Students were more comfortable using these devices, but two-way communication was a huge hurdle due to these devices limited text capability.
>
> (*ibid.*: 5)

Mapletoft et al. (2022) carried out a study at a 'FE and higher education (HE) provider in England' which sought 'to help reduce digital poverty and support digital equity and inclusion amongst its learner base throughout the COVID-19 pandemic' (ibid.: 159). They used a variety of student enquiry, enrolment and data tracking learners, and conversations with the authors, who were four members of the senior management team at the provider. Their findings are grouped as opportunities and challenges, and the opportunities which were identified due to the COVID-19 pandemic were the following:

- Remote working provides 24/7 access for all, including, for example, staff and learners who may require reasonable adjustments.
- Learners have more time to study because they are not having to travel, providing an opportunity for those with multiple commitments.
- Socio-economic opportunities, for example, learners save money on travel expenses.
- The move to online provided opportunities to redesign curricula and advertising messages to appeal to potentially marginalised learners.
- There was the opportunity for technological adoption and innovation and training for staff and learners.
- Hybrid and flexible working can help staff and learners who have caring responsibilities (ibid.: 160).

The challenges were the following:

- Setup for working from home was a significant cost and required a good deal of managerial time, which led to a drop in enquirer engagement.
- Keeping learners engaged and staff motivated proved challenging.
- Staff willingness to work and deliver remotely, and their technical competency, were factors that affected their ability to deliver.
- Learners' who had low levels of digital literacy struggled with the online systems.
- Face-to-face assessment required full-site COVID-19 safety vetting, reduced numbers due to social distancing, and the need for large amounts of personal protective equipment (PPE).
- One of the biggest challenges was the inability of the awarding bodies to allow for changes to assessments.
- Remote invigilation presented several challenges.

The students in Raven's (2022: 201) study found that:

> Prominent among the challenges encountered were those associated with remote learning. These included technical difficulties with the online delivery of the curriculum. The main 'issues I have', one focus group member remarked, are 'IT. For someone like me, [who] doesn't know what they are doing, it is very stressful.' Similarly, a participant from the other group recalled being 'kicked off quite a few lessons because of 'Wi-Fi issues' – an experience shared by some of their fellow focus group members.
>
> (ibid.: 201)

The participants in the DfE 2020 research which has already been cited in this chapter:

> .... Reported finding online classes difficult and found that being at home was a challenging environment for remote learning. In some cases, there was too much noise or disruption to allow young people to concentrate. For others, there were too many distractions such as social media or family.
>
> *(ibid.: 7)*

> Those studying vocational courses also stated that 'there was only so much that could be learnt remotely or online before practical skills and techniques needed to be taught (vocational courses being studied included mechanical engineering, hairdressing and beauty)'.
>
> *(ibid.: 7)*

Despite there being a range of positive evidence regarding the uses of online learning to maintain connections between students and staff, students and students, and staff and staff, there is a broad agreement that those more generally disadvantaged students were also digitally disadvantaged.

The CollabGroup argued that:

> The pandemic has shone a light on inequality and the issue of digital poverty. With digital skills becoming more important and a requirement for many careers, the divide cannot be allowed to grow. In an increasingly interconnected and digitised world, the pandemic has shown that urgent action is needed to prevent inequalities widening.
>
> (CollabGroup, 2021: 9)

Question for discussion

If you were learning in an FE institution during COVID, now you can look back, how well was your study or work managed by other people during the pandemic?

Sector story: Voices from the front line – Working and living in FE during the pandemic

To complete this section of the chapter, the publication used for the first sector story of this chapter is used again, as it provides powerful accounts from the front line of FE during COVID. The author was part of the editorial team of this project and publication, and the 'themes' section at the end of the book provides our second sector story. The themes which emerged from the practitioner accounts are described as three phases, named 'Shockwaves', 'Riding the Coronacoaster', and 'The New Normal'. Where names are mentioned in this text, they are the practitioners who provided that comment in the publication, where the names are featured in the text. Discussing each of these in turn, the shockwaves happened because 'teaching and non-teaching staff were "ejected from the workplace mid-project" to "wait for further instruction". This was foreign territory (Kelly Casey)' (Crawley *et al.* 2021: 97). These shocks then produced powerful worries about 'can I do it' and:

> I am close to giving up, we have just had another hour-long meeting about something that we can't even do and never found a solution (Alistair Smith)
>
> > Was totally overwhelmed (Kerry Scattergood)
> > it was as if the stabilizers had been taken away. (Kevin Williams).
>
> (*ibid.*: 97)

Moving into the 'Riding the Coronacoaster' phase, it is remarkable how comments demonstrate a degree of creative thinking and application as professional strategies and motivations began to return to the fore:

> …. And professional coping strategies for self, students and colleagues were emerging, such as setting up a "Sunlight Station" at home which was intended to make use of the potential via technology to be "more connected" (Kelly Casey). Opportunities were found to make use of the "freedom to find 'light' in my work, my teaching, learning and assessment" (Annie Pendrey) and to immerse themselves in healthy practice that would elevate me to a place where I knew I could use this tragic circumstance and uncertainty for good (Kelly Casey).
>
> (*ibid.*: 99)

Attempts to adjust to and make positive use of the technology of which so much was expected also feature strongly in this phase.

> I had to learn rapidly how to use the platforms, teach the students how to use them and then teach staff at one of the colleges … I am now a lot braver and am much more likely to experiment with the use of technology.
>
> (Heather Booth-Martin)

> I had been on a huge learning curve without knowing it. I had accessed a rich seam of professional learning, some practical, some more philosophical. I had been witness to the building of community in online digital spaces.
>
> (Jo Fletcher-Saxon)

> The absolute highlight has been the connections and community I have found online and the transformative nature of that community (Isla Flood).
>
> (*ibid.*: 100)

The final part of this phase was practitioners feeling that they were trying to maintain home and work responsibilities in a significantly more difficult environment to do so. The most difficult thing about lockdown, as a mother, has been the constant feeling of being torn between being a good parent and a good teacher…I have often felt unable to give full focus to either role and the constant changing between them and (more than usual) multitasking has been exhausting.

(Isla Flood)

Importantly, Isla added that 'very few' colleagues 'seem to have been given any support or reassurance' (Isla Flood).

Our dining room became the space for working and my children's homeschooling, and being the best I could for my students, working around their home life and other pressures (Kathryn Pogson).

The third phase 'the new normal' was not of course at all a fully formed phase at this stage, but practitioners reflected on what the new normal may be as it was developing. Writing to COVID, one participant said:

> I wanted to thank you for giving me the gift of time. That gift has been used to experiment with digital tools and try new things in my teaching. I have also reignited my love of learning. ... You also gave me the confidence to 'put myself out there' by operating an online support network for colleagues (Amy Woodrow).

(*ibid.*: 101)

The stories of these practitioners during the pandemic are the stories of FE, and whatever the challenges and problems for FE which have in many ways been exacerbated by the pandemic, the positivity of the practitioners who featured in this project has to be admired.

> Human beings are adaptable and resilient. Our minds and bodies have an amazing design that enables us to face challenges and fight off illnesses ... it is important to model ourselves in strengthening our mind, body and soul so that we can look after each other better in the long term (Joyce Chen).

(*ibid.*: 104)

Conclusion

A number of helpful reports and pieces of research have given suggestions about the impact of the pandemic on FE and the way forward for FE. The Edge Foundation provides a positive vision when they state:

> Learning from the past two years, college leadership should reflect on their vision for the future; rethink student support, employability development, staff development and curriculum development, and pedagogy just to name a few. FE is now working in a new context, and this must be reflected in their vision. As classroom teaching resumes, the opportunity is unique to build on the best of both online and classroom teaching and learning.

(Edge Foundation, 2022: 31)

CollabGroup (2021: 17) conclude that the key lessons have included:

Online and blended learning options will likely be expanded due to the experience of the last 12 months; however, such options will not be appropriate and relevant in all contexts.

> Local economies have change drastically over the last year. While it is hoped that the economy will recover over the longer term, issues like youth unemployment and the disruption to industries like retail, hospitality and tourism will have effects for a long time yet. This is where

colleges are uniquely positioned to work with employers to help them plan for their short- and long-term skills needs.

It has been a very challenging year for the further education sector and society more broadly. But the contribution that further education colleges have made over the last year has been considerable. As we hope to move towards recovery, colleges will continue to play an indispensable role in helping employers, individuals and communities to build back and redress the impacts of this unique and challenging moment in history.

(*ibid.*: 18)

The Edge Foundation (2022: 4, 5) presents a positive forward vision that

FE is now working in a new context, and this must be reflected in their vision and in their practice. As classroom teaching resumes, the opportunity is unique to build on the best of both online and classroom teaching and learning.

Gadsby and Smith (2023) undertook a study of FE staff (making use of Microsoft Teams for interviews) during the pandemic and found that there were tensions between the teachers' professional aspiration of prioritising student needs and working collegially with colleagues, and the senior management's insistence on maintaining as near as possible 'business as usual'. They describe a

…. Tyranny of college cultures … during the pandemic. Institutional needs were prioritised and this colonised managers' thinking. The rhythms established pre-pandemic were fossilised and this meant staff needs were ignored. This fossilisation, according to the data, resulted in a huge increase in stress and feeling pressured on the part of staff.

(*ibid.*: 793)

Throughout the pandemic, the teachers wished to be supportive and empathetic in their work with their students in the same way as they were before the pandemic. Whilst teachers wish to 'attempt to tackle social inequality and realise purposes related to social justice' the stance of their management often means 'staff are positioned as agents of an instrumentalist and objectifying discourse' (*ibid.*: 798). Overall, despite a teacher vision of advancing social justice and equality, the pandemic often made that more difficult, and Gadsby and Smith (2023: 799) remind us that post pandemic we need to 'affirm a purpose of further education that is more human and more compassionate'.

Summary points
- The pandemic had many short- and long-term impacts on society and on FE.
- The FE sector was particularly vulnerable to and stressed by the pandemic.
- The COVID restrictions provided challenges to students, teachers, and institutions.
- The mental health and wellbeing of many staff and students worsened during the pandemic.
- The sudden growth of online learning not only provided important steps forward for this mode of teaching but also presented challenges to many students and staff.
- Teachers made significant efforts to maintain the learning and support of their students.
- Overall, the COVID-19 pandemic moved FE perhaps one or two steps forward, but this has not yet resulted in major change, and the sector may already have moved two steps backwards again.

Recommended reading

Crawley, J., Fletcher-Saxon, J., Powell, D. and Scattergood, K. (Eds) (2021) *Working and living in FE during the COVID-19 pandemic: 27 FE practitioners' voices*. Solihull: Solihull College.

References

CollabGroup (2021) *Reflections from further education leaders on the impact of Covid-19*. London: CollabGroup

Corbett, S., Johnston, K. and Bezuidenhout, A. (2023) Further education workforce wellbeing: Did Covid actually change anything? *Educational Management, Administration and Leadership*, pp. 1–13, DOI: 10.1177/17411432231153290

Crawley, J., Fletcher-Saxon, J., Powell, D. and Scattergood, K. (Eds) (2021) *Working and living in FE during the COVID-19 pandemic: 27 FE practitioners' voices*. Solihull: Solihull College.

Department for Education (2022) *16–19 Learners' experiences of the Covid-19 pandemic - Research report*. London: DfE

Edge Foundation (2022) *Responding to Covid-19: Experiences of vocational learning and teaching from colleges in the British Isles*. London: Edge Foundation.

Education and Training Foundation (2019) *Understanding the wellbeing of the post-14 education workforce*. London: ETF

Gadsby, J. and Smith, R. (2023) Further education and mental health during the pandemic: the moral impasse of meritocracy. *Research Papers in Education*, 38(5), pp. 783–803, DOI: 10.1080/02671522.2023.2212011

Institute of Fiscal Studies (2020) *2020 Annual report on education spending in England*. London: Institute of Fiscal Studies.

Mapletoft, N., Mapletoft, O., Henderson, T. and Pattison, K. (2022) Opportunities and challenges in widening participation through online learning: Comparison of findings in a further and higher education provider during COVID-19. *Widening Participation and Lifelong Learning*, 24(2), pp. 159–170.

Raven, N. (2022) Responding with resilience: The impact of the pandemic on the educational experiences and ambitions on FE students. *Widening Participation and Lifelong Learning*, 24(1), pp. 198–208.

Spours, K., Grainger, P. and Vigurs, C. (2022) 'We are all in the same storm but not in the same boat': The COVID pandemic and the further education sector. *Journal of Education and Work*, 35(8), pp. 782–797, DOI: 10.1080/13639080.2022.2149715

UCL Social Research Centre (2021) *Mitigating impacts of the COVID-67 pandemic on the further education sector. A rapid evidence review*. London: University College London (UCL) Social Research Institute.

UK Health Security Agency (2023) *England Summary: Coronavirus in the UK*. Available at: https://coronavirus.data.gov.uk/ (Accessed 4 December 2023).

11 14–19 education

Introduction

This chapter begins with an indication of the number of students involved in the '14–19 phase' in further education (FE), and then defines the provision which will be included in the chapter. It continues with extracts from the history of 14–19 provision, including the Tomlinson report of 2004, The Nuffield Review of 2009, and the Sainsbury Review of 2016.

The first sector story discusses a project seeking to encourage students in schools and colleges into careers in engineering, and further analysis of 14–19 in FE policy is presented. The chapter proceeds with examples of 14–16 programmes in FE, General Certificate of Secondary Education (GCSE) in FE, and a sector story about a successful student who was studying A-levels at a college. The chapter closes with a consideration of T-levels, their somewhat varied success and short life to date, and the announcement as this book was being written of yet another new 'gold standard' 16–19 qualification for FE.

What is the 14–19 provision in FE?

Because a significant number of the students in FE are in the 14–19 age group (665,000 out of 1.6 million, or 42 per cent, in 2022–23) (AoC, 2022: 7), and because they are involved in a wide selection of different types of provision, qualifications, and curriculum, the best place to start this chapter is with an outline of the numbers involved in the FE part of the '14–19 phase', as it has often been called.

14–19 student numbers in FE

Please note that these figures are from the Association of Colleges (AoC), so include only those studying in or with FE colleges. There are:

611,000 16–18-year-olds study in colleges.

(AoC, 2022: 7)

46,000 16-18-year-olds study as apprentices.

(*ibid.*: 7)

DOI: 10.4324/9781003468455-11

8,000 14–15-year-olds enrolled in colleges full or part time.

(*ibid.*: 7)

There were, therefore, 665,000 14–19 students in FE in 2022–23

One third of all English students aged 19 and under who enter higher education through UCAS studied at college.

(*ibid.*: 11).

179,000 students study GCSE English and/or maths.

(*ibid.*: 19)

124,000 students study A-Levels in colleges.

(*ibid.*: 19)

549,000 students study SfL (STEM - Science, Technology, English and Maths) courses.

(*ibid.*: 19)

(Adapted from AoC, 2022: 7–19)

Question for discussion

Is going to college at 14 too early?
 Consider the advantages and disadvantages of college at 14.

A definition of 14–19 provision in FE

As can be seen from the data above, 14–19-year-olds can be studying apprenticeships, which will also involve the study of skills for life; part-time and full-time vocational courses (diplomas, certificates, etc.); part-time and full-time academic courses (A-levels and GCSEs); and GCSE retakes and other STEM courses.

Other chapters have already considered SfL, apprenticeships, and vocational courses, so the range of the 14–19 subsector in FE which will be addressed specifically for this chapter is:

- 14–16-year-old programmes;
- A-Levels;
- GCSEs and GCSE retakes;
- T-Levels; and
- Vocational courses not covered in other chapters.

The history of 14–19 provision

14–19 Provision has been under the influence of the 'tripartite mentality', which divides young people between the three areas of 'academic', 'vocational/technical', and 'the rest' since the 1944

Education Act, and this has been a significant factor in policy determination and development which has outlasted a number of key historical events. There will be more analysis of the tripartite mentality later in the chapter.

The Tomlinson report – 2004

In 2003, Mike Tomlinson, a former chief inspector of Ofsted, was appointed to chair a working group which would 'examine how developments in vocational education, assessment and the qualifications framework could contribute to the successful and lasting transformation of 14–19 learning' (DfES, 2003: 7). Tomlinson identified the following problems:

- The low level of post-16 participation in education;
- Poor skill levels in 'functional mathematics, literacy and communication, and information and communications technology (ICT)';
- The low status of vocational courses and qualifications;
- The lack of challenge, especially for 'top performers';
- Exam overload; and
- The complexity and lack of transparency in the web of academic and vocational qualifications (Tomlinson, 2004: 4).

Tomlinson's recommendations included:

- Introducing a compulsory 'core' consisting of 'functional' subjects (maths, ICT, and communication skills) and 'wider activities' such as work experience, paid jobs, voluntary work, and family responsibilities (*ibid*.: 39);
- Replacing GCSEs, A-levels, and vocational qualifications with a new single modular diploma at four levels – entry, foundation, intermediate, and advanced (*ibid*.: 7);
- Cutting the number of exams (*ibid*.: 12); and
- Stretching the most able students with tougher additional A-level papers (*ibid*.: 90).

At the time, these recommendations appeared to offer what educators had been seeking with a phase from 14 to 19 which would not be interrupted by the assessments and results of GCSEs and A-levels. Tomlinson also recommended a ten-year implementation for most (though not all) of the recommendations. Almost immediately after the recommendations were made public, Tony Blair, the Prime Minster at the time, made a speech stating that A-levels would not be scrapped. The ten-year implementation schedule was also not popular with the government as it went beyond the five-year lifetime of a single term of government. It rapidly became clear that Tomlinson's recommendations would be rejected, and the approach of improving what was already there would be taken instead.

The Nuffield review – 2009

Also established in 2003 was the Nuffield Review of 14–19 education and training, which was financially supported by the Nuffield Foundation, based in Oxford. It was the largest review of 14–19 education since the Crowther Report of 1959 described in Chapter X. The final report, Education for All: The future of education and training for 14–19-year-olds, was published in June 2009 and argued for an understanding of education for all which would provide:

- The knowledge and understanding required for the 'intelligent management of life';
- Competence to make decisions about the future in the light of changing economic and social conditions;
- Practical capability – including preparation for employment;
- Moral seriousness with which to shape future choices and relationships; and
- A sense of responsibility for the community (Nuffield, 2009: 3).

The report demanded:

- *The re-assertion of a broader vision of education* in which there is a profound respect for the whole person (not just the narrowly conceived 'intellectual excellence' or 'skills for economic prosperity'), irrespective of ability or cultural and social background, in which there is a broader vision of learning and in which the learning contributes to a more just and cohesive society.
- *System performance indicators 'fit for purpose'*, in which the 'measures of success' reflect this range of educational aims, not simply those which are easy to measure or which please certain stakeholders only.
- *The re-distribution of power and decision-making* such that there can be greater room for the voice of the learner, for the expertise of the teacher, and for the concerns of other stakeholders in response to the learning needs of all young people in their different economic and social settings.
- *The creation of strongly collaborative local learning systems* in which schools, colleges, higher education institutions, the youth service, independent training providers, employers, and voluntary bodies can work together for the common good – in curriculum development, in provision of opportunities for all learners in a locality, and in ensuring appropriate progression into FE, training, and employment.
- *The development of a more unified system of qualifications* which meets the diverse talents of young people, the different levels and styles of learning, and the varied needs of the wider community, but which avoids the fragmentation, divisiveness, and inequalities to which the present system is prone (*ibid.*: 4).

Rarely in the history of educational reviews have the recommendations been as wide ranging, focussed on social justice, and presenting a positive vision of teaching and learning for the betterment of the community. Pring and colleagues were critical of performance management, the way teachers were treated, and government-centred thinking about curriculum and the organisation of learning, which was not necessarily helpful in the attempts to advance the implementation of their recommendations.

Richard Pring, one of the leaders of the Nuffield review (with Geoff Hayward), sums up well in a 2008 article that 'the legacy of the Blair years, therefore, with regard to 14–19' was to have produced 'a marked shift of emphasis upon a 14–19 phase of education and training, in which there should be provision and entitlement for all young people, irrespective of background or ability' (Pring, 2008: 687). He continues:

.... Second, to achieve this there has been a determined (and, in many ways, laudable) effort to reform the qualifications framework and system of apprenticeships, to provide a more interagency and holistic approach to the well-being of all young people, and to require greater collaboration between different providers'.

(*ibid*.: 687)

With a final sense of disappointment, however, Pring concludes that:

... The problems quite rightly identified (for example, the academic/vocational divide, the low status attached to vocational, the decline of apprenticeships and work-based learning) are deep rooted, economically and socially. And the solutions pursued with such vigour (for example, the proposed reform of qualification sand of apprenticeships) could well be but a continuation of a long line of "reforms" which do not work. In that respect, the most important legacy might be greater understanding of the problems, and a more humble approach to their long term solutions.

(*ibid*.: 687)

Sainsbury review – Independent Panel on Technical Education (2016)

The Independent Panel on Technical Education was established in November 2015 and chaired by David Sainsbury. The purpose of the Sainsbury Review was to advise 'ministers on actions to improve the quality of technical education in England and, in particular, to simplify the currently over-complex system and ensure the new system provides the skills most needed for the twenty-first century' (DfE, 2016: 2). It does need to be noted that this report was about 'post-16' provision so does not include all of the 14–19 phase but is very relevant to it. Sainsbury identified 'the four key features of technical education, and what the Government needs to do to put such a system in place:

i.) While Government has to design the overall system, industry experts must lay down the knowledge and skills, and methods of assessment, for each qualification.
ii.) The system should provide young people with clear educational routes, which lead to employment in specific occupations and must be sufficiently clear and simple that career advisers can easily explain to young people what options they have. Currently, there are 13,000 qualifications, many of them of little value, available to 16–18 year olds, and this makes career guidance extremely difficult.
iii.) Short, flexible bridging provisions should be developed to enable individuals who come to believe they have made the wrong decision to move between the academic and technical education options in either direction and to support adults returning to study.
iv.) Individuals who are not ready to access a technical education route at age 16 (or older if their education has been delayed) should be offered a flexible transition year tailored to their prior attainment and aspirations (*ibid*.: 6).

This was not, as we have seen in the historical analysis in this chapter and others, the first time that a number of these proposals had been made, particularly the desire to streamline the system of qualifications and make it more coherent. The Sainsbury review underlined where the difference was between their reforms and previous others by stating that these 'have all been unsuccessful because they tinkered with technical education and failed to learn from the successful systems in other countries' (*ibid.*: 6). Esmond (2019: 312) comments that 'these developments have made slow progress' and that reviving the term 'technical education' which had 'been little used since further education colleges developed broader missions in the 1970s and 1980s' (*ibid.*: 312). He continues to comment that the 'most immediately identifiable difference between these and earlier qualifications was the addition of substantial work placements of up to three months in duration' (*ibid.*: 312). Esmond (2019) also critiques the assertion that the new changes will move England nearer to the continental approach to skills and education and argues such a European system 'is far from being accomplished, despite longstanding discussion of a common European model' (*ibid.*: 313).

In his study comprising 'a series of qualitative case studies carried out at key points in the emergence of current skills policies' (*ibid.*: 311), Esmond found that the work-based routes of post-16 education 'will not provide opportunities to experience meaningful and fulfilling learning at work for substantial numbers of young people' (*ibid.*: 326), and that the 'implication of the Sainsbury Review that existing forms of vocational education would be superseded by an all-embracing technical education appears to be rapidly eroding' (*ibid.*: 326).

As has been seen by this section of the chapter, the 14–19 phase has had many reviews, proposals, and changes made over the years, but still remains a part of the education system which remains in need of further major changes. Esmond's concluding remarks offer possible ways forward.

> Workplaces are better able to support learning through suitable environments, planned activities and staff with training capabilities. Educational institutions and educators, currently expected mainly to meet targets and prepare students to behave during placements, will also play a more effective role if they engage directly with workplaces in the development of a more inclusive and equitable skill formation system.
>
> (*ibid.*: 327)

Sector story – Reading College – Learning to be an engineer

In 2017, the Royal Academy of Engineering initiated a major project intended to 'inspire young people throughout their education and improve the supply of engineering skills' (RAE, 2017: 1), because the 'engineering community is concerned that young people and the wider public do not understand engineering's valuable contribution to society and the exciting, diverse career opportunities it can offer' (*ibid.*: 1). The project involved 33 schools and 1 college, and the logic of only involving one college is not explained. The work with this college is a helpful piece of evidence of 14–19 in FE at work. The project utilised the 'six engineering habits of mind (EHoM): systems-thinking, adapting, problem-finding, creative problem-solving, visualising and improving' (*ibid.*: 2) and engaged the research participants in 'the use of EHoM to promote engineering in schools. Each intervention involved teacher professional development, curriculum planning and the use of one or more EHoM as a focus of activity with a particular group of learners.' (*ibid.*: 6).

The report describes a number of positive outcomes from the research including:

> .... Increased fluency in the key habits of mind, the development of 'growth mindsets', improvements in literacy, numeracy and oracy, enhanced self-management skills, and better

understanding of engineering. It describes many benefits to the capability and confidence of teachers, in particular their engagement with practising engineers'.

(*ibid.*: 2)

The project analysis and evaluation offers:

.... Four principles that underpin the kinds of teaching which are most likely to encourage young people to develop a passion for engineering in today's busy schools and colleges:

- Clear understanding of EHoM by teachers and learners.
- The creation of a culture in which these habits flourish.
- Selection of the best teaching and learning methods, the 'signature pedagogy' of engineering.
- An active engagement with learners as young engineers.

(*ibid.*: 2)

The one college involved, Reading College in Berkshire, has its own case study in the final report. Prior to the project, Reading College had found that 'even when students have elected to study engineering courses in FE, there is no guarantee that they will have a good understanding of what engineering is' (*ibid.*: 42). For the six teachers at the college who became involved, participation in the project provided an opportunity for them to 'reflect on their teaching and develop methods that might not only cultivate EHoM but also enhance students' understanding of engineering and develop their employability skills' (*ibid.*: 42). The strategy of the teachers was to embed the EHoM into their Business and Technology Education Council (BTEC) level 3 Diploma in Engineering, with the intention of improving the learning in particular of the 'disengaged young people who had been conditioned through their earlier education

experiences to reject learning approaches that required curiosity resourcefulness and resilience' (*ibid.*: 42). The results were positive, and the:

Combination of active learning strategies and real-world contexts proved engaging because learning had a purpose, it was relevant to the engineering workplace and students were working like professional engineers.

By standing back and giving students opportunities to tinker and ask questions, they fostered their problem solving ability, and their enthusiasm for thinking like an engineer.

(*ibid.*: 42)

Further analysis of 14–19 FE policy

This subsector of FE is of a particularly high level of importance for the nation, and the reviews of policy and their recommendations which the chapter has already considered were and still are seen as very important for the skills and communities of the future. Gibbons (2023: 196) states that the '14–19 phase' has come about:

.... As a result of the evolving expectation the young people would remain in education and training beyond the age of 16 and that it would be better to construct a coherent pathway rather than talk of pre- and post-16 experience. Policy change in this area has been rapid and repeated, and arguably the most recent developments mean that a return to speaking of pre- and post-16 education might actually be more meaningful.

He continues to argue that:

> .... The numerous policy developments and initiatives point to the pressing questions: what ought to be the central aims of this phase of education? How might these be reconciled with the perceived needs of individuals, society, employers and higher education establishments?

Hodgson and Spours are very experienced researchers and commentators in this field, and in 2008, they argued that to 'understand the main forces shaping 14 to 19 education training in England' it is necessary to recognise that 'there are sharply differing views about current policy and how mistakes might be avoided and the way in which policy needs to develop in the future' (*ibid.*: 19). Gibbons (2023: 197) summarises (2008) 'five legacies' from the Nuffield Review in the 14–19 phase as:

- The tripartite mentality, dividing young people between 'academic', 'vocational', 'technical', and 'the rest'.
- The failure to achieve parity of esteem between academic and vocational courses.
- Ambivalence towards the 'meaning of vocational'.
- Lack of recognition of new qualifications amongst employers and higher education.
- The transient nature of new qualifications.

Gibbons continues that:

> .... At post 16 the problem is perhaps particularly acute; There is little doubt that A level has the reputation as the "gold standard" amongst employers and university admissions tutors and it has been historically difficult for any alternative qualification to gain a meaningful foothold all the time its existence continues.
>
> (*ibid.*: 197)

The challenge of the 'academic/vocational divide', where the academic pathways have this more stable and valued position in the education hierarchy, has led to what Gibbons (2023: 197) calls 'a binary opposition'.

Richmond and Bailey (2023: 1) provide a powerful analysis of this divide when they state:

> .... The academic pathway from GCSEs to A-levels to an undergraduate degree at university is a well-trodden and well-understood route that attracts tens of thousands of young people in England every year. However, while this pathway receives considerable political and media interest, just 37 per cent of young people take three A-levels in their final years at school or college. In other words, over six in ten young people are not on a solely academic path. Even so, ever since then Prime Minister Tony Blair's infamous speech in 1999 that set a target of 50 per cent of young people entering Higher Education (HE), the academic pathway has been placed on a pedestal above all else.

The statistics lay bare the impact of so many young people being badly neglected. In 2022, 12.3 per cent of young people aged 16–24 in England were 'Not in Education, Employment and Training' (NEET) – the same proportion as when Tony Blair gave his aforementioned speech.

Their report on the reducing opportunities for young people continues to state that:

> .... Politicians frequently talk about the importance of creating a "ladder of opportunity" for young people, particularly for those from the least privileged backgrounds, but the stagnation of apprenticeships for young people and the enduring failure to tackle entrenched youth unemployment suggests that many young people are finding it very difficult to get onto the ladder – let alone progress up the ladder.
>
> (*ibid.*: 10)

Examples of practice in 14–19 provision in FE

14–16-year-old programmes taking place in designated colleges

Since its inception in 2013, provision for these learners has occupied a grey area between secondary education and further education, meaning they have routinely been underrepresented in government policy and funding.

> Over 100 further education (FE) colleges in England provide education for 14 to 16-year-olds. Approximately 10,000 14 to 16-year-olds access part or all of their education in colleges. This includes students on alternative provision (AP), many of whom are in danger of exclusion or have been excluded from school, electively home educated (EHE) learners who attend FE for up to 16 hours per week and full-time, Direct Entry, students who have chosen to study in FE.
>
> (AoC, 2023: 1)

The current 14–16 in FE part of the 14–19 phase has had little research undertaken, but there is some useful research about previous 'alternative provision' or AP available.

"My mates are dead jealous"

Between January and June 2002, the Learning and Skills Development Agency (LSDA) undertook a research project which 'focused on researching the extent of alternative educational provision for young people aged 14–16 years and on both their experiences and of the practitioners involved' (LSDA, 2003: 1). This project was ten years before the current form of 14 to 16 provision in colleges started and was at a time when colleges regularly made provision for 14–16-year-olds, often because the young people concerned were in danger of exclusion. The provision was described as 'alternative education for young people aged 14–16 years' (*ibid.*: 1). The project report defines this provision 'as that which was provided by schools, colleges, training providers and employers to young people aged 14 to16 who were not attending mainstream school full-time and following the National Curriculum' (*ibid.*: 4).

When this project took place, funding was made available from the 'Increased Flexibility Programme' funded by the recently created Learning and Skills Council (LSC). The type of provision ranged from full-time attendance at a college or training provider to one day a week, and a number of organisations were involved in addition to the colleges and Local Education Authorities (LEAs), which included schools, voluntary organisations, and careers services.

The researchers gathered data from relevant local organisational personnel, practitioners, documents, and over 80 young people who were involved 'with learning provision outside the school environment' (*ibid*.: 8). The project took place in a very brief time and the researchers called this a 'moment in time from which a number of issues and themes have been identified' (*ibid*.: 15). The young people involved commented positively on a number of aspects of the provision, such as having positive, more 'grown up' relationship with their tutors, including being able to call them by their first name. For example; 'College is loads better than school. They treat you like a grown-up. At college we can call the teachers by their first name. They don't talk to you like you're a kid, like they do at school' (*ibid*.: 8). The participants also enjoyed mixing with older students and working in a more realistic work environment. There were also some concerns including that the environment was too laid back; wearing school uniform in a college was an issue and being singled out as different from other college students. The comments which gave the research report its title were also made by one participant, with the statement 'my mates at school are dead jealous "cause they don't get to come here (college)"' (*ibid*.: 13). Overall:

> The young people had the view that if they were to continue into further education, they would stay with the same college, as they now knew their way around and felt comfortable. One individual was positive that his prior experience would be of great benefit, and that he would be "ahead of the game".
>
> (*ibid*.: 13)

The project came to a number of conclusions about 14–16 education in FE, including that participants started to develop more positive attitudes to vocational programmes; they enjoyed college life and the courses they studied and the second chance it appeared to give them, and they formed 'respectful and positive working relationships' (*ibid*.: 14) with adults and other participants. Practitioners were also positive but commented that more learning materials and funding would need to be available to be able to continue, and that more experience of working with the 14–16-year-olds who were involved would be useful in the future. Even 20 years since the publication of this report, its findings and analysis are still entirely relevant.

Orr (2010: 7) strongly critiques government policy related to 14–19 overall, arguing that 'the danger remains that weaker students from poorer backgrounds may continue to be directed towards vocational or 'applied' courses, while better-informed students.

May seek positional advantage in more traditional qualifications'. He also argues that 'those attending FE colleges aged 14–16 before the introduction of diplomas were the same students who have always attended, only a little earlier' (*ibid*.: 7–8). Orr interviewed 14–16-year-old students at a college with around '600 students aged 14–16 who normally attended two sessions each week and who are largely integrated within the rest of the college community' (*ibid*.: 10). Similarly to the project already discussed (LSDA, 2003), the students interviewed also felt they were treated like adults; appreciated the greater freedom of college; and 'appreciated their relationships with the teachers in college, and once again this was in contrast to their perceived relationships with teachers in school' (*ibid.*: 11).

The teachers interviewed for this project were a self-selecting group, but they all 'enjoyed working with the school links students and several had particular stories of those they had "turned around" or "managed to reach"' (*ibid.*: 13). Overall, this project identified the positives of 14–16 provision more clearly than the negatives, and Orr (2003: 115–116) concludes that:

> On the basis of these data, as well as that of other researchers, colleges are successfully including students who have been challenging or disaffected in schools, and in so doing have demonstrated to these young people that education can be attainable and even enjoyable. Despite the absence of coherent or consistent national policy, the attitude of staff and managers interviewed for this research project indicates a strong desire to provide young people in college with a worthwhile education.

GCSEs in FE

Anderson and Peart (2016) researched students involved in a 'GCSE Academy' at a large city FE college, which 'provides a fast-track 36-week GCSE programme to learners aged 16+ who have not yet achieved a full level 2 qualification' (*ibid.*: 197). The college academy has a strong record of success with this student group and has recruited 'students from schools identified as some of the poorest performing in the country, where behaviour has been reported as poor and underachievement is high' (*ibid.*: 198). Eight participants from the 120 students enrolled in the fast-track GCSE programme were interviewed about their experience for this small-scale study. The interviews were in groups to encourage more participation and discussion, and this strategy worked well. Anderson and Peart grouped the results into themes, which were:

1. *Motivation* – students had been demotivated at school and indicated this led them to a tendency to not complete work by deadlines. The structures, teaching styles, and support at college had helped encourage motivation to a much greater degree.
2. *Teacher–student relationship* – students found relationships with teachers at school varied from friendly and lacking discipline to over disciplined. Relationships with teachers at college were seen as more clearly defined and professional, open and that they 'treat you like people, not just a kid' (*ibid.*: 204).
3. *A second chance* – the students recognised this college course was a 'second chance' but also that their college teachers had high expectations of them. These understandings helped them to be strongly motivated to take that second chance.
4. *Classroom management and discipline* – the students recognised that their behaviour was often not good at school and that teachers found managing pupil behaviour difficult. At college, discipline systems seemed to be more directly, fairly, and consistently applied, and senior college management supported their teachers in keeping them on track. Students recognised in due course that staying within the boundaries of good behaviour with less disruption meant fewer interruptions and less disturbance of their overall study.
5. *Academic support* – support with work and classroom activities was more readily and consistently available at college than at school; the academic support at college was especially

helpful; and even 'reluctant learners become more motivated when they receive teacher support' (*ibid.*: 207).
6. *Class size* – Classes were smaller at the GCSE Academy at college (18 rather than between 20 and 30 at school), and this made it more straightforward for students to receive support and for teachers to provide it.

In their final conclusions from their research, Anderson and Peart (2016) commented that:

> The GCSE Academy adopted a behaviourist style, using both positive and negative reinforcement through reward, commendations and high expectations of behaviour, complemented by a comprehensive disciplinary process with senior management working closely with staff and students. However, student success was principally produced by the adoption of humanistic strategies revolving around positive supportive relationships with the teachers, independence and group belonging.
>
> (*ibid.*: 210)

Sector story – from grade Cs at school to student of the year – Emilia

Emilia was what would be described as an average student at school. She was a hard worker and had very good attendance and no behaviour problems and achieved grade Cs in most of her GCSEs at school. When considering her progression to further study, the school encouraged a Childcare course, and Emilia did start such a course, but did not find it interesting. She went to visit her local college and spoke to both the careers advisor and A-level tutors at an open day and discovered that she could take the opportunity to study A-level after all. Emilia decided to study for A-levels at college and enrolled in a two-year programme to study Sociology, Psychology, and Law. To her delight, and to some degree her surprise, she achieved A stars for all three A-levels at the end of her study.

In addition to much hard work, Emilia felt she had really good support from tutors and other staff at college, and this really helped her study, her motivation, and her consideration of further progression after A-levels. She appreciated the 'grown up' atmosphere at college, as we have seen from other 14–19 students in this chapter, and felt trusted to make her own decisions and live her life as an adult. She felt relaxed, but not in a way which would lead to becoming lazy about her study, or which would lead to losses of concentration. She felt that 'if you put in the work, you get good grades', and that the whole environment at college suited her really well as a person and as a student.

Her tutors also appreciated how hard Emilia worked, how much progress she made, and the choices she made in terms of seeking advice and support when she needed it. She also always tried to help other people in her classes at college, remembering when she needed help at school, but often didn't get it. This led to Emilia being nominated for a 'student of the year' award, which was a huge surprise to her as she had never been nominated for any awards at any time during her life so far. To her even greater surprise and delight, Emilia won the award for student of the year, and her only disappointment was that the ceremony was online because of COVID-19! She said in an interview with the local paper that the award 'shows just how far I've come since I've been here' and how succeeding at college and making friends there has worked as well for her as it possibly could. Emilia has now gained a place at university to study law and has a powerful confidence in her pathway to the future.

(Adapted from Barnet College case study, 2023: 7)

T- Levels – another short-lived qualification

T-level qualifications are level 3 qualifications for 16–19-year-olds introduced in England in 2020. The intention is for there to be a wide variety of T-levels available, with each one being relevant to one occupational area. One of the primary aspects of T-levels is for them to be developed in partnership with businesses and employers. Terry and Orr (2024: 560) interviewed 14 T-level teachers and found three subthemes which emerged from their data in relation to quality in T-levels, and these were 'rigour, assessment, and exclusivity; the absence of quality related to employer engagement; and quality related to progression, especially to university study' (*ibid.*: 562). The rigour of assessment had led to exclusivity in that the 'high stakes assessment' in T-levels meant colleges had to effectively 'cream off' the better students. Given the need for colleges to attract 'mainstream students' (*ibid.*: 565) to their provision, this would directly affect recruitment to T-levels in the long term. In terms of employer engagement, participants indicated that this had not been of a high quality, and although this may have been affected by COVID, it made it difficult to come to 'a justification of T levels' quality based on the involvement of employers because employers have only been peripherally involved in their delivery in these eleven colleges' (*ibid.*: 566). In terms of progression this was also considered to be an issue, as 'progression onto apprenticeships, employment with training or further study were described as differing according to the expectations and traditions of the industries associated with each T-level route; they do not differ according to the content of the qualification' (*ibid.*: 566–567). Terry and Orr conclude their study with the statement:

> .... For the designers of T levels, the pre-eminent criterion for quality is what one group of stakeholders wants or is perceived to want; that group is employers. However, as discussed above, the involvement of employers in the design of T levels is based on the involvement of few people who only represent few employers; and involvement of employers in their delivery is, on the basis of our interviews, negligible.
>
> (*ibid.*: 568)

In terms of numbers, a parliamentary update from the education minister, Gillian Keegan in March 2023 stated that:

> In September, 18 T Levels will be available, being delivered by hundreds of providers. The T Level Action Plan, which was published today, sets out that T Level starts doubled from around 5,000 to around 10,000 between 2021 and 2022. Most importantly, T Level students, teachers and employers continue to give us great feedback on the quality of T Level courses.
>
> (UK Parliament, 2023: 1)

This is a disappointingly low number for a new flagship qualification. Even as this chapter is being written, another new 16–19 qualification has been announced, to replace T-levels, and also to replace A-levels. In October 2023, the government published government of 'A World-Class Education system. The Advanced British Standard (DfE, 2023). In this publication, the Education Secretary optimistically states:

> .... We will create a new qualification that places equal value on technical and academic knowledge and skills by harnessing the best parts of both A levels and T levels. Under this qualification, known as the Advanced British Standard, students will be able to take a mix of technical and academic subjects, giving them a greater degree of flexibility over their future career options.
>
> (*ibid.*: 3)

The report further states that this qualification will be 'a new Baccalaureate-style qualification that takes the best of A levels and T levels and brings them together into a single qualification' (*ibid.*: 7). Most unusually, the government, in its plan, indicates that this reform could take some ten years.

From all the history, discussions, and analysis in this chapter, one would be forgiven for asking whether this is another attempt to update the tripartite system, or will it just be another false dawn. Only time will tell.

Question for discussion

Having read this chapter what would the first three things you would do about 14–19 provision in FE if you became the Minster for Education?

Conclusion

As has consistently been the case throughout the history of FE, the organisations and teachers of FE strive, often successfully, to make the best of inconsistent and difficult policy, performativity, and lack of equality in funding and the education system overall. 14–19 is another subsector where this is the case, as had been seen in this chapter.

Richmond and Bailey (2023) offer a concluding view for this chapter on policy, however, with which it is difficult to disagree.

> Young people who do not follow an academic pathway through and beyond secondary education deserve to be offered high-quality and respected courses and qualifications just as much as their academic counterparts. Regrettably, the instability and confusion created by government in recent years has been all too apparent, with apprenticeships drifting away from young people, various programmes coming and going, and research evidence frequently being ignored in favour of ideology. Not only has this instability been detrimental for young people, but employers will inevitably be less likely to engage with (and recruit) younger and less experienced workers if the education and skills system is being constantly redesigned.
>
> (*ibid.*: 4–5)

Summary points

- At least one in three students in FE are aged 14–19.
- 14–19 provision includes 14–16 provision, GCSEs and GCSE retakes, A-levels, T-levels, and other vocational qualifications.
- Despite regular reviews of 14–19 provision, England remains a country which appears to hang on to the tripartite system post school.
- FE colleges have good levels of success with 14–19 students, particularly those who have found school difficult.
- The history of 14–19 in FE policy suggests continuing change, turbulence, and challenge for the sector.

Recommended reading

Nuffield (2009) *Education for All: The future of education and training for 14–19 year olds summary, implications and recommendations*. Oxford: Nuffield Foundation.

References

Anderson, N. and Peart, S. (2016) Back on track: Exploring how a further education college re-motivates learners to re-sit previously failed qualifications at GCSE. *Research in Post-Compulsory Education*, 21(3), pp. 196–213, DOI: 10.1080/13596748.2016.1196978

Association of Colleges (2022) *College Key Facts 2022/23*. London: AOC.

Association of Colleges (2023) 14–16. Available at: https://www.aoc.co.uk/policy/education-policy/14-16-2 (Accessed 12 December 2023).

Barnet College (2023) *A-Level package. What our students think*. Available at: https://www.barnetsouthgate.ac.uk/a-level-package (Accessed 14 December 2023).

Department for Education (2016) *Report of the independent panel on technical education. (Sainsbury review.)* London: DfE.

Department for Education and Science (2003) *14–19: Opportunity and excellence*. London: DfES.

DfE (2023) *A World-Class Education system: The Advanced British Standard'*. London: Department for Education.

Esmond, B. (2019) Continental selections? Institutional actors and market mechanisms in post-16 education in England. *Research in Post-Compulsory Education*, 24(2–3), pp. 311–330, DOI: 10.1080/13596748.2019.1596434

Gibbons, S. (2023) 14–19 education: Education and training in school and beyond. In S. Gibbons, R. Brock, M. Glackin, E. Rushton, and E. Towers (Eds) *Becoming a teacher. Issues in secondary education* (6th ed.). Maidenhead: Open University Press.

Hodgson, A. and Spours, K. (2008) *Education and training 14–19: Curriculum, qualifications and organisation*. London: Sage.

LSDA (2003) *My mates are dead jealous' cause they don't get to come here!: An analysis of the provision of alternative, non-school-based learning activities for 14-16 year olds in the East Midlands*. London: Learning and Skills Development Agency.

Nuffield (2009) *Education for all: The future of education and training for 14–19 year olds summary, implications and recommendations*. Oxford: Nuffield Foundation.

Orr, K. (2010) *The entry of 14–16 students into colleges: Implications for further education initial teacher-training in England*. Huddersfield: University of Huddersfield.

Orr, K. (2003) The entry of 14-16 students into colleges: implications for Further Education initial teacher-training in England. *Journal of Further and Higher Education*, 34(1), pp. 47–57.

Pring, R. (2008) 14–19. *Oxford Review of Education*, 34(6), pp. 677–688.

Richmond, T. and Bailey, A. (2023) *Broken ladders. Why the 'ladder of opportunity' is broken for so many young people, and how to fix it*. London: EDSK (Education and Skills).

Royal Academy of Engineering (2017) *Learning to be an Engineer. Implications for the education system*. London: RAE

Terry, K. and Orr, K. (2024) Perceptions of quality and the shaping or misshaping of vocational education: The case of T level qualifications in England. In L.M. Herrera, M. Teras, P. Gougolakis, and J. Kointio (Eds) *Learning, teaching and policy making in VET. Emerging issues in research on vocational education and training, Vol 8.* Stockholm: Atlas forlag.

Tomlinson (2004) *14–19 Curriculum and qualifications reform final report of the working group on 14–19 reform.* London: Department for Education and Skills.

UK Parliament (2023) *T levels update: Statement made on 9 March 2023. Gillian Keegan. Secretary of State for Education.* London: UK Parliament.

12 Sustainability

Introduction

The chapter introduces an initial rationale for sustainability in the further education (FE) sector and introduces definitions of sustainability and sustainable development. The history and development of sustainability follows, including the first use of the word in the eighteenth century and its use in the Millennium Development Goals (MDGs), and then in the Sustainable Development Goals (SDGs) which replaced them in 2015. The next section discusses the current analysis, which is that progress with the SDGs has been limited by the COVID-19 pandemic, and other global factors, and that the lifelong learning part of SDG number four appears to be a lower priority than other areas of education.

The importance of the publication in England of the Stern Review in 2006, which assessed that evidence and built an understanding of the economics of climate change, is summarised in the next section, and the chapter progresses to consider progress towards sustainability in the FE sector. The first sector story is adapted from a case study about a 2023 award winner for their work in education for sustainable development (ESD) in FE. The later sections of the chapter focus on two pieces of FE research on sustainability and sustainable development and outline a sector-wide situation with a significant level of understanding of the challenges of ESD, but an early developing range of action, particularly with embedded ESD content in the curriculum of qualifications on offer.

The second sector story is about an example of embedding ESD into the FE curriculum; the conclusion of the chapter summarises current progress with sustainability in FE and makes recommendations for improvement.

What is sustainability in FE?

A publication specifically relating to sustainability in FE provides some helpful background, explanation, and definitions which are relevant. The London Sustainability Exchange and Learning and Skills Network publication (2021) aims to provide FE-specific guidance for:

> .... Embedding sustainability into every aspect of your organisation, with inspiring examples of what others are already doing. The Guide will provide a starting point, inspiration and signposts to places of more information if you wish to delve deeper. It can also be used by those already on the sustainability journey, as a way of reviewing where you are going, and where you may look next.

DOI: 10.4324/9781003468455-12

148 *Sustainability*

The same publication also provides definitions of sustainability and sustainable development as follows:

> *Sustainability* is an ideal state where human activity does not degrade the environment but maintains natural systems and resources for future generations.
> *Sustainable development* is the process that moves us closer to sustainability.
>
> (*ibid.*: 2)

London Sustainability Exchange and Learning and Skills Network (2021) continues to argue that it is logical, sensible, and desirable for FE as a business, to operate its buildings and estate with increasing efficiency, and to prioritise carbon reduction. The business argument is that early action will not only help sustainability but also make the operation of FE more sustainable. In terms of the educational focus of FE:

> It makes sense to introduce sustainable development into the curriculum to provide learners with the knowledge, skills and values that are needed to mitigate the effects of climate change. Students in FE need to be aware of and understand issues around sustainability, which are already important in the workplace, but will increasingly be so in the future. Students with the skills and competences gained through education in sustainability will have increased employment prospects and greater potential for career progression. Additionally, colleges have an important role to play in supporting local businesses and the wider community in their journey towards a more sustainable way of living.
>
> (*ibid.*: 3)

This is a powerful argument for FE being placed at a central position in the development of educational and community sustainability as no other sector of education than FE engages more broadly across the community.

History and development

The term sustainability has been in use since the early eighteenth century when Hans Carl von Carlowitz, a German forester, argued for 'sustainable use' of a forest after a major shortage of timber, which was used for Saxony's metallurgy and silver mining industries. Souto-Otero (2023: 183) argues that:

> It is highly significant that von Carlowitz's discussion of the term focused already on both natural (forest) and economic elements. Environmental and economic components continue to be at the core of discussions around sustainability today, but consideration to its social component has been added.

Souto-Otero continues that:

> While the intellectual history of sustainability can therefore be traced far back, the term sustainability (an objective) and sustainable development (the means to achieve that objective) did not

achieve wide currency until the second half of the 20th century, in the context of public debates about unsustainable patterns of production and consumption, limits to economic growth and the emergence of strong environmental movements.

(*ibid.*: 183)

The MDGs and the SDGs

The SDGs are a central part of the global efforts to achieve sustainability. Initially, at the start of the twenty-first century, eight MDGs were agreed at the United Nations (UN), and they 'focused on the many dimensions of extreme poverty, including low incomes, chronic hunger, gender inequality, lack of schooling, lack of access to health care, and deprivation of clean water and sanitation, among others' (United Nations Sustainable Development Solutions Network, 2015: 7). Despite some successes, including 'halving the likelihood of a child dying before their fifth birthday', new challenges were becoming more apparent, and by 2015:

> Around 700 million people still live below the World Bank's poverty line, and billions more suffer deprivations of one form or another. Many societies have experienced a rise of inequality even as they have achieved economic progress on average. Moreover, the entire world faces dire environmental threats of human-induced climate change and the loss of biodiversity. Poor governance, official corruption, and in dramatic cases overt conflict, afflict much of the world today.

(*ibid.*: 7)

In 2015, the seven MDGs were replaced by a set of 'SDGs' which placed:

> Sustainable development as the organizing principle for global cooperation, meaning the combination of economic development, social inclusion, and environmental sustainability. Hence, the overarching name "Sustainable Development Goals," as the key message to the world community. Furthermore, the SDGs and related agenda apply to all countries, developed and developing alike.

(*ibid.*: 17)

The current SDGs are the following:

Goal 1: End poverty in all its forms everywhere
Goal 2: End hunger, achieve food security and improved nutrition and promote sustainable agriculture.
Goal 3: Ensure healthy lives and promote well-being for all at all ages.
Goal 4: Ensure inclusive and equitable quality education and promote lifelong learning opportunities for all.
Goal 5: Achieve gender equality and empower all women and girls.
Goal 6: Ensure availability and sustainable management of water and sanitation for all.
Goal 7: Ensure access to affordable, reliable, sustainable and modern energy for all.
Goal 8: Promote sustained, inclusive and sustainable economic growth, full and productive employment and decent work for all.

Goal 9: Build resilient infrastructure, promote inclusive and sustainable industrialization and foster innovation.
Goal 10: Reduce inequality within and among countries.
Goal 11: Make cities and human settlements inclusive, safe, resilient and sustainable.
Goal 12: Ensure sustainable consumption and production patterns.
Goal 13: Take urgent action to combat climate change and its impacts.
Goal 14: Conserve and sustainably use the oceans, seas and marine resources for sustainable development.
Goal 15: Protect, restore and promote sustainable use of terrestrial ecosystems, sustainably manage forests, combat desertification, and halt and reverse land degradation and halt biodiversity loss.
Goal 16: Promote peaceful and inclusive societies for sustainable development, provide access to justice for all and build effective, accountable and inclusive institutions at all levels.
Goal 17: Strengthen the means of implementation and revitalize the global partnership for sustainable development.

(*ibid.*: 6)

As can be seen from the above list, Goal 4 is 'Ensure inclusive and equitable quality education and promote lifelong learning opportunities for all' (*ibid.*: 6).

Unfortunately, the most recently published UN update on progress with the SDGs gives an indication of how both the COVID-19 pandemic and other global factors have limited the progress towards many of the SDGs. The report states that:

> .... we are leaving more than half the world behind. Progress on more than 50 per cent of targets of the SDGs is weak and insufficient; on 30 per cent, it has stalled or gone into reverse. These include key targets on poverty, hunger and climate.
>
> (United Nations, 2023: 2)

The findings of the report on Goal 4 'Quality Education' are also pessimistic, reporting that:

> .... In education, the impacts of years of underinvestment and learning losses are such that, by 2030, some 84 million children will be out of school and 300 million children or young people attending school will leave unable to read and write.
>
> (*ibid.*: 4)

The 2023 UN progress report does offer some positives in that the 'share of government spending on essential services, such as education, health and social protection, is significantly higher in advanced economies than in emerging and developing economies' (*ibid.*: 12), and a 'surge in action and investment to enhance economic opportunities, improve education and extend social protection to all, particularly the most excluded, is crucial to delivering on the central commitment to end poverty and leave no one behind' (*ibid.*: 12). The SDGs have generally made more progress in countries with advanced economies, rather than in emerging and developing economies.

Unfortunately, the section in the 2023 report on Goal 4 does not mention colleges, vocational education, and training or lifelong learning at all, despite the full goal wording being 'Goal 4: Ensure inclusive and equitable quality education and promote lifelong learning opportunities for all' (UNSDSN, 2015: 6). This is extremely disappointing, but as has been discussed on a regular basis in this book, lifelong learning and FE do not appear to be considered by governments as important as other areas of education, and particularly in many areas of policy in England. The UN report unfortunately appears to broaden this lack of priority of FE and lifelong learning to a global situation.

There is an important comment in the 2023 report that 'education financing must become a national investment priority. Furthermore, measures such as making education free and compulsory, increasing the number of teachers, improving basic school infrastructure, and embracing digital transformation are essential' (*ibid.*: 20). This is important and would have been even more so had it included FE.

The Stern review (2006)

The Stern Review on the Economics of Climate Change was commissioned in 2005 'by the Chancellor of the Exchequer (Gordon Brown), reporting to both the Chancellor and to the Prime Minister (Tony Blair), as a contribution to assessing the evidence and building understanding of the economics of climate change' (HM Treasury, 2006b: i). The report concluded that:

- There is still time to avoid the worst impacts of climate change if we take strong action now;
- Climate change could have very serious impacts on growth and development;
- The costs of stabilising the climate are significant but manageable; delay would be dangerous and much more costly;
- Action on climate change is required across all countries, and it need not cap the aspirations for growth of rich or poor countries;
- A range of options exists to cut emissions; strong, deliberate policy action is required to motivate their take-up; and
- Climate change demands an international response, based on a shared understanding of long-term goals and agreement on frameworks for action. (HM Treasury, 2006b: vi–viii)

The Stern Review is one of the most significant reports in the UK on climate change, and the overall analysis that mitigation is the essential way forward is summarised as below:

> No-one can predict the consequences of climate change with complete certainty; but we now know enough to understand the risks. Mitigation - taking strong action to reduce emissions - must be viewed as an investment, a cost incurred now and in the coming few decades to avoid the risks of very severe consequences in the future. If these investments are made wisely, the costs will be manageable, and there will be a wide range of opportunities for growth and development along the way. For this to work well, policy must promote sound market signals, overcome market failures and have equity and risk mitigation at its core. That essentially is the conceptual framework of this Review.
>
> (HM Treasury, 2006a: i)

How has sustainability progressed in the FE sector?

The reasons why sustainability is 'particularly relevant' for FE (called the Learning and Skills Sector in this publication) include the following:

- FE colleges and other training providers are part of a wider community that is having to respond to new environmental, social, and economic challenges.
- The Learning and Skills sector has a duty to prepare its students for these challenges and for new ways of living and working. The curricula, management practices, and ethos of the organisation are equally important in performing this duty successfully.
- The business case for sustainability in the Learning and Skills sector is established and becoming stronger both for the organisation itself: as environmental legislation increases, there are more checks and measures needed to be put in place to ensure FE institutions comply; and this applies equally to the requirement for knowledge and skills for learners to take into the workplace where these environmental legislative requirements will also apply.
- Using sustainability as a framework can provide senior managers with a vision and a long-term strategy for their organisation.
- Organisations that create economic value, healthy ecosystems, and strong communities are more resilient to economic, environmental, and social stresses.
- Sustainability skills are important for students' employability!

(London Sustainability Exchange and Learning and Skills Network, 2021: 3)

As the chapters in this book have discussed previously, FE organisations and subsectors have a particular place in their communities and engage with all elements of those communities, including employers, other educational establishments, local councils, voluntary and community groups, and members of the community themselves. Investing in the role of colleges in terms of sustainability and sustainable development should be considered to be not just important, but essential.

FE is a founding partner of the 'Climate Commission for UK Higher & Further Education' and the intention of this commission is 'to develop an action plan in response to the UK government's stated climate emergency and draw together a strategic sector-wide approach to the Climate Framework on behalf of 410 institutions, 4.7m students, 540k staff and £43bn annual expenditure' (AoC, 2024: 1). The Climate Commission includes the Association of Colleges (AoC), Universities UK, and other related groupings, and the participants are senior staff from these organisations who act as the Commissioners. One of the current developments from the Climate Commission is the FE Climate Action Road Map, which has been adopted by over a third of FE colleges (AoC, 2024: 1).

The roadmap includes three 'levels' of colleges' approaches to sustainability, organised by different levels of maturity:

Emerging: colleges just beginning to address sustainability

- Established: colleges with an established approach to sustainability and structures in place to support it
- Leading: colleges which are models to others in sustainability

Each 'level' contains a series of initiatives colleges can implement to reach net zero emissions and improve their environmental impact.

These initiatives are categorised into:

- Leadership and Governance;
- Learning, Teaching, and Research;
- Estates and Operations; and
- Partnerships and Engagement.

The roadmap is intended to be used by college principals and their leadership teams, students, and other members of the college community. Although many of the initiatives require executive action or investment, students should be seen as partners in developing and implementing the college's approach to sustainability. The roadmap can also be shared by the college with other stakeholders – such as local authorities, or businesses – to explain their approach to reach net zero emissions (The Climate Commission for UK Higher & Further Education, 2020: 4).

As can be argued from this section of the chapter, a significant amount of thought, preparation, and advice for including sustainability in FE has taken place. The next section of the chapter after the first sector story discusses the progress towards the goal of sustainability to date.

Question for discussion

What would you prioritise in your organisation/institution/employer relating to sustainability over the next three years?

Sector Story 1 – Sustainable Development at Brighton Hove and Sussex Sixth Form College (BHASVIC) in partnership with FE Sussex

A recent award in the FE calendar is the 'Nous Group Award for Education for Sustainable Development', which is awarded each year, and sponsored by the Nous Group, a management consultancy. The winner in 2022/23 was BHASVIC in partnership with FE Sussex, and they won the award with their work with 'Sustainability and Carbon Literacy – A Collaborative Approach'. The project not only involved BHASVIC but also included a consortium of approximately ten colleges and sixth form colleges, known as 'FE Sussex'. The City of Brighton is something of a focus of green activity in England, and the group of colleges involved all agreed to adopt the objectives of the FE Climate Action Road Map and undertake action to support its implementation. The project included several strands, and one was a 'Carbon Literacy strand' with the objectives to:

- Embed carbon literacy into new and existing academic technical and vocational courses;
- Pilot the delivery of a level three carbon literacy short course qualification; and
- Facilitate project-based master classes to technical vocational and academic students across colleges.

(BHAVIC, 2023: 11)

Staff and students across the consortium enthusiastically took part in this project and its activities, and the outcomes across the consortium were the following:

154 *Sustainability*

- Over 1000 students engaged with **Carbon Literacy** and **Masterclass** activity, with many more involved in teaching and learning that was embedding this work.
- Thirteen **INSET** (In-Service Education and Training) sessions develop the confidence of over 475 staff to understand and begin to embed ESD into their work, sharing examples between college partners.
- Over 120 courses **embedding ESD**, engaging even more students, with these materials shared across the colleges reflecting the power of the collaborative approach. Eight employer-led **Masterclasses**, providing invaluable enrichment for students and staff and improve networks and contacts for careers and curriculum teams in our colleges.

(*ibid.*: 17)

This is an excellent example of a project which has moved forward in ESD in FE. It was not a coincidence that it was a very well-funded project, and this meant that an overall project manager across the consortium was appointed. This made sharing and collaboration work operate more effectively than if the management of the project had been an extra responsibility for other staff, which can often take place in short-term projects. It demonstrates what could be done if funding at a good level was available on an ongoing basis.

Moving forward with sustainability in FE

Two recent pieces of research by the Education and Training Foundation (ETF), are helpful in analysing where FE now stands with sustainability and ESD. One provides a helpful commentary on the development of sustainability in FE from the workforce perspective, and it states that:

> FE is the pipeline for the workforce of many industries, employers and sectors which have a critical role to play in sustainable development, including construction, manufacturing, agriculture, catering and transport. The sector reaches millions of learners from all walks of life. It employs over 100,000 staff and reaches communities in every town and city in the country. Imagine if everyone in the FE community – staff, learners, partners – had the knowledge, skills, attributes and agency required to be part of creating a sustainable and just future.
>
> (ETF, 2021a: 2)

They highlight a disappointing situation where:

> Despite the enormous potential reach of ESD (Education for Sustainable Development) in the FE and training sector, progress to date has been fragmented and slow, with ESD not yet seen as a central pillar of the sector and its work. It could be argued that we've gone backwards over the last decade, as competing priorities and reduced resources have meant that FE and training providers simply haven't had the motivation, capacity or space to progress their ESD work.
>
> (*ibid.*: 2)

The lack of success with ESD is reinforced by the statement that despite 'strong learner demand for ESD, exposure to ESD teaching, even on courses traditionally associated with sustainability (geography, the sciences etc.), is reported as low. FE and training providers are largely unprepared for the transition needed' (*ibid.*: 2).

This research undertaken by the ETF is a milestone in helping to understand the degree to which the FE sector has embedded sustainability across the sector, and it provides some very helpful baseline data. The ETF undertook the research because:

> We know that many FE colleagues want support to be able to equip their learners with the knowledge and competencies needed to meet these goals. Through this research we wanted to better understand opinions, barriers, opportunities and how we can help. This in turn will inform our approach and ensure we are best serving the sector's needs. We've chosen to publish the data to enable our peers and partners to also benefit from these insights, and to inform policy and decision makers about the needs of the sector.
>
> (*ibid.*: 3)

The ETF gained the support of the Society for Education and Training (SET), which is the professional association for staff in the sector, and other partners, and they surveyed '830 people who work in the FE and training sector' (*ibid.*: 4). They summarise the results as follows:

> Our data showed that while there was almost widespread recognition of the potential and importance of ESD, the extent to which it is being practiced at an individual and organisational level varies greatly. There are a range of barriers which we also explored, alongside solutions.
> Our findings broadly fall under one of five headlines:
>
> 1. Sustainability as a concept is broadly well understood.
> 2. There's a widespread belief that the sector is well placed to lead on sustainability solutions.
> 3. Diverse subject specialisms all have a role to play.
> 4. Different FE and training providers are at different stages of their ESD journey.
> 5. The FE workforce has had very little training on how to deliver quality, impactful ESD.
>
> (*ibid.*: 4)

A selection of the data from the survey is below:

- Seventy-four per cent of teaching staff feel that they haven't received adequate training to embed sustainability in their work nor to educate learners about sustainability or climate change.
- Eighty-five per cent agree that the FE and training sector have a valuable role to play in the achievement of sustainability goals.
- Sixty-eight per cent feel that the current UK post-16 education system does not adequately educate learners on sustainability issues.
- Ninety-four per cent of all respondents believe that all UK learners should be taught about sustainability issues – this is often referred to as an ESD curriculum entitlement.
- Forty-three per cent of people are familiar with the SDGs.
- Sixty-one per cent of respondents who teach a diverse range of subject specialisms report that they already actively incorporate sustainability themes into their teaching work to some extent.
- Only thirty-five per cent of respondents agree that the curriculum requirements support the delivery of sustainability issues.
- Twenty-four per cent of respondents didn't know what their organisational approach to sustainability is.
- Thirty per cent of respondents feel sustainability is an issue for all parts of their organisation.

(*ibid.*: 5)

156 *Sustainability*

Although the figures from the data are in some respects disappointing, ETF argues with conviction that the:

> …. insights from this work will enable the ETF to develop our strategy and initiatives to help support the sector's adoption of ESD to enhance teaching, learning, assessment and leadership. They will also enable us to benchmark current ESD practice across the FE training sector workforce, and give practitioners, providers and stakeholders data with which to plan their own ESD approaches.
>
> (*ibid.*: 4)

The second ETF report (2021b) is intended to establish:

- Which qualifications available to post-16 learners in England are enhancing their awareness of sustainable development.
- What proportion of learners have access to a broad ESD curriculum as part of the qualifications in their study programme.
- How educators and leaders from across the Further Education and Training (FE) sector are providing ESD.
- How leaders in the FE sector can best support greater uptake of ESD within their organisation.

(*ibid.*: 2)

The research involved:

- A detailed search of qualifications used by the FE sector;
- A curriculum audit; and
- Fourteen case studies of ESD in action.

The key findings included the following:

- English post-16 education is a long way from offering all learners the knowledge and skills needed to promote sustainable development, with fewer than 1 per cent of post-16 learners enrolled on qualifications with broad ESD content and only a few providers currently offering these opportunities.
- A very low proportion (0.5 per cent) of post-16 enrolments are on qualifications with broad ESD coverage. This represents 18,474 post-16 enrolments on 11 qualifications out of a baseline total of 3,466,069 enrolments on 10,815 qualifications.
- Qualifications with partial ESD coverage represent a further 116,833 enrolments on 46 qualifications. This brings the total to 135,307 enrolments or 3.9 per cent of all post-16 enrolments.
- The proportion of providers offering qualifications with broad ESD coverage is relatively low (the highest proportion for any single qualification is 62 per cent of colleges offering A-Level Geography).

(*ibid.*: 3–4)

The ETF analysis of the results is encouraging, but the challenge for the FE sector and related organisations such as awarding bodies is clearly significant. The ETF comments that:

Case studies

The case studies showed that where sustainability in the curriculum is at its most effective, it is characterised by engagement with external community and corporate organisations which bring the learning to life. There are examples of this approach resulting in learners using their knowledge and understanding to positively influence sustainability within their communities, the workplace and the home. Many teachers see it as their responsibility to prepare their learners to be empowered and to eventually act as leaders, influencers and advocates for sustainability when they progress into the workplace.

Qualifications

There are too few discrete ESD qualifications available to teachers. As a result, they are finding and amplifying relevant content from within other qualifications to meet what they report as a burgeoning interest and commitment to the principles and practices around sustainable development amongst learners.

Recommendations

The recommendations suggest a range of approaches which could be adopted by leaders, educators, FE providers and sector bodies to ensure that the teaching of ESD reaches more post-16 learners, including the embedding of ESD into existing qualifications as well as developing and promoting qualifications with ESD at their core.

(ibid.: 4–5)

Overall, the two pieces of ETF research provide a disappointing analysis of the current situation of ESD in FE, but with elements of good practice which could be shared and used across the sector, given sufficient funding and government priority. A selection of the recommendations from the reports will feature in the conclusion of this chapter.

Sector Story 2 – Erica Bergstadt – Lecturer in travel and tourism

Erica is a 33-year-old lecturer in travel and tourism in a medium-sized sixth form college in the north east of England. She started her interest in sustainability in her home country, the Netherlands, as she volunteered in the national landscape protection programme while at university and became involved in several sustainability projects. These included monitoring tourism in low-lying areas of the country, which are particularly at risk from climate change for evidence of responsible tourism and its mitigating effects. She is particularly interested in advancing awareness and the potential for action on sustainability and in particular responsible tourism in her college teaching. Her level 3 Travel and Tourism diploma includes an extended project based on a scenario where students are asked to:

- Reflect on your current travel and travel you have made recently to consider the positive and negative impacts which tourism can have.
- Note your concerns and how they could be addressed.
- Create an article which showcases your knowledge of responsible tourism and the impact of tourism on destinations.

158 *Sustainability*

- Cover the degree to which those involved in tourism locally and travel agents recognise their responsibilities relating to sustainability.
- Ensure you include analytical thinking, examples, and comparisons, and a list of your sources and references.

Erica has devised a series of sessions, activities, and resources to assist the students in their project, and this includes discussions, debates, group work, and mini presentations by her students. They also access reports, destination information, and ESD content online to support their projects. The work is popular with students who find that:

> This project really broadened out my understanding of responsible tourism, and I learned a lot about how to help develop travel which helps sustainability.
>
> I changed my opinion about tourism and now support the ideas of carbon offsetting and recycling strategies to promote responsible tourism.

(Adapted from ETF, 2021b)

Question for discussion

In your education to date, what have you learned about sustainability and sustainable development?

Conclusion

This chapter has considered the current situation with the cross-sector theme of sustainability, and it is arguably the most important theme for the whole FE sector, the education sector as a whole, and indeed the whole world, as ESD is the place where the new generation of citizens who prioritise sustainability enough to change the world will be educated. As far as the FE sector is concerned, the key issues are recognised, and some good practice is in place, but the rate of progress has been slow, and the impact on the sector is limited. There are, however, strong suggestions and recommendations for moving forward and these are now summarised.

From ETF (2021b)

Recommendations for FE providers and their leaders and educators

- Ensure ESD work is central to a whole institution approach and include it in organisation strategic goals.
- Assess the training need across the FE workforce for embedding ESD into their teaching and learning practice.
- Develop a series of training programmes based on existing ESD good practice and include them in staff meetings, workshops, teacher education, and seminars.
- Map existing ESD practice across your own provision, including enrichment, tutorials, careers advice, guidance etc.

- Consult with and build partnerships with relevant stakeholders to develop ESD practice.
- Add ESD to existing curriculum planning templates for schemes of work and lesson plans.
- Discussion ESD with your contacts within awarding organisations.

Recommendations for sector bodies who can promote and enable ESD uptake

- **Awarding bodies** should map ESD outcomes within their own portfolio and develop their ESD provision to ensure ESD is embedded.
- **Employers** contributing to the development of new apprenticeships and technical qualifications should seek to ensure ESD competencies are included.
- **Funders and regulators** should:
    - Work with relevant sector stakeholders to review all qualification specifications and ensure that ESD is addressed and opportunities teach it are signposted.
    - Set targets for all students to experience some ESD during their post-16 studies and require all study programmes to address ESD, including financially incentivising providers to offer qualifications which have a strong ESD focus.
    - Make access to ESD an entitlement for all post-16 learners.
    - Fund the necessary training and support to enhance the knowledge and confidence of leaders and educators across the FE workforce.
    - Include ESD provision within the regulatory frameworks used by the sector.

(Adapted from *ibid.*: 9–11)

This comprehensive range of recommendations offers real hope for the future of sustainability in FE, but unless it is strongly accepted and funded by the government, it could be another opportunity to prioritise FE which will be missed, or only taken up in a limited way.

Summary points

- The need to embed sustainability in FE has been growing since the start of the twenty-first century.
- Sustainability should be seen as good business practice in addition to good educational practice.
- There has been progress with ESD in FE, but it has been slow and limited.
- Students and staff willingly engage with sustainability themes, but institutions need to increase the prioritisation of sustainability.
- There are useful recommendations which offer hope for the future of sustainability in FE, but they need to be positively accepted and funded by government and embraced by providers, awarding organisations, employers, and communities.

Recommended reading

London Sustainability Exchange and Learning and Skills Network (2021) *SORTED guide to sustainability in further education*. London: London Sustainability Exchange and Learning and Skills Network.

References

Association of Colleges (2024). *The climate commission for UK higher & further education.* Available at: https://www.aoc.co.uk/corporate-services/sustainability-climate-action-hub/the-climate-commission-for-uk-higher-further-education (Accessed 2 January 2024).

Brighton Hove and Sussex Sixth Form College (BHAVIC) (2023) *Sustainability and carbon literacy – A collaborative approach.* Brighton: BHAVIC.

Education and Training Foundation (2021a) *Experiences of education for sustainable development in the further education and training sector.* London: ETF.

Education and Training Foundation (2021b) *Leadership for ESD in the FE curriculum. A review of Education for Sustainable Development (ESD) approaches and curriculum content in post-16 qualifications in England.* London: ETF.

HM Treasury (2006a) *Stern review report on the economics of climate change: Executive summary.* London: HM Treasury.

HM Treasury (2006b) *Stern review report on the economics of climate change: Summary of conclusions.* London: HM Treasury.

London Sustainability Exchange and Learning and Skills Network (2021) *SORTED guide to sustainability in further education.* London: London Sustainability Exchange and Learning and Skills Network.

Souto-Otero, M. (2023) Six principles to advance technical and vocational education for sustainable development. *Panorama*, Vol. 1 pp. 183–195.

The Climate Commission for UK Higher & Further Education (2020) *A climate action roadmap for FE colleges.* London: The Climate Commission for UK Higher & Further Education.

United Nations (2023) *The sustainable development goals report 2023: Special edition. Towards a rescue plan for people and planet.* New York: UN.

United Nations Sustainable Development Solutions Network (2015) *Getting started with the sustainable development goals.* New York: UNSDSN.

13 Specialist colleges

Introduction

There are 67 colleges which are not general further education colleges, but specialist institutions, and they include sixth-form colleges, land-based colleges, art, design, and performing arts colleges, and specialist-designated colleges/institutes of adult learning. This chapter summarises the provision, responsibilities, and circumstances of these colleges, how they do (or do not) fit into the broader approaches and principles of the further education (FE) sector, and what their current situation is.

The chapter starts by asking 'what are specialist colleges' and provides an indication of the size and scope of the subsector. The chapter then proceeds with a section for each type of specialist colleges, starting with sixth-form colleges. This section contains some history and background, a sector story about St Brendan's Sixth Form College in Bristol, and examples of sixth-form colleges in action, including research about sixth-form college tutors and student independent learning at a sixth-form college.

Land-based colleges feature next, with a brief history, then an example of a land-based college: Capel Manor College. The chapter proceeds with a summary of research on middle managers in land-based colleges and finds similarities between the findings and research into leaders in general FE colleges. There are just two art, design, and performing arts colleges, and one of them, The Northern School of Art is featured as an example. The second sector study features a collaborative project on student wellbeing carried out by The Northern School of Art. One or two specialist-designated colleges have already been featured in other chapters within this book, so the last section on colleges in action just features reminders of those chapters.

The chapter concludes with an analysis of the differences and similarities between this specialist FE subsector and other FE subsectors.

What are specialist colleges?

Specialist colleges have one obvious characteristic which is that they either only provide sixth-form, land-based, art design, and performing arts or specialist-designated provision. This chapter will consider, discuss, and analyse whether that is the main difference, or possibly the only difference, between these colleges and general FE colleges, or whether all specialist colleges, or each individually have other characteristics which make them different or even unique.

DOI: 10.4324/9781003468455-13

162 *Specialist colleges*

There are 228 colleges in England (AoC, 2022: 4)

161	general further education colleges
44	sixth form colleges
11	land-based colleges
2	art, design and performing arts colleges.
10	specialist designated colleges/institutes of adult learning.

Specialist colleges are an under-researched part of FE and, as a result, some of the examples of specialist colleges in action which are used in this chapter are less current. As has been found in other chapters, however, issues, characteristics, and circumstances of FE subsectors and provisions often overlap, cross over, and remain current and relevant over a considerable period of time.

> **Question for discussion**
>
> What do you think would be the main reasons for a prospective student choosing a specialist college for their study?

Sixth-form colleges

History and background

Shorter (1994: 461) provides a helpful early history of sixth-form colleges. He introduces this by stating that:

> The concept of the sixth-form college probably owes most to R. Wearing King, Chief Education Officer of Croydon in the 1950s. King's unsuccessful scheme for the reorganisation of small grammar school sixth forms in that borough was for a prototype sixth-form college, more or less in the image of a traditional Grammar School. King continued to argue for the idea of the sixth-form college: describing it in 1968 as 'the only way' … The north of England made its initial contribution to this movement in 1964 with the opening of Mexborough Sixth Form College in Yorkshire. However, although Mexborough was the first institution to use this title, it was still closely attached to a school, and might now be seen as more equivalent to a sixth-form centre.

The first genuinely operational sixth-form college was opened in Luton in 1966, and Southampton was next. Shorter continues:

> Soon a patchwork of colleges was visible across the country as this new form of organisation was adopted in part or whole by various LEAs. Motives ranged from an obvious concern for the economies of scale in post-16 education, which led sometimes to well-resourced, purpose-built new creations, to a pragmatic (and cheaper) response to the strength of local lobbies who wished to retain elements of the Grammar School tradition. This sometimes led to decisions which perhaps lacked clear coherence: in the relatively small town of Huddersfield, for instance, three sixth-form colleges were originally set up in competition with each other and

an established Technical College. Within a few years 'market forces' impelled the LEA to reduce the number of sixth-form colleges to a more manageable two.

(*ibid.*: 462)

In terms of early numbers, Shorter continues that by '1992 there were 117 colleges in existence with 85,000 students–almost 25% of the country's sixth formers' (*ibid.*: 462). This did not last, however, as

> .... Their "historical moment" was brief, broadly spanning the decades from the 1970s to the 1990s (and much shorter for many individual institutions). Their separate existence was literally ended by the 1992 Further and Higher Education Act, which made them legislatively indistinguishable from all Further Education Colleges in the new market-based model of post-16 education.
>
> (*ibid.*: 462)

The sixth-form colleges were not, of course, indistinguishable from other FE institutions in terms of their own particular provision, although by definition they offered a narrower range of provision (but still as many 16–19 options in their specialism as they could) and more age-restricted enrolment.

Schofield (2007) also provides helpful background to the history of sixth-form colleges after the 1992 Education Act which introduced the independence of colleges through incorporation.

> Sixth Form Colleges as centres for Further Education first arose in 1967 and came to prominence in the 1990s with the introduction of the Further and Higher Education Act 1992. This Act broadened the programme of study and increased the number of vocational courses available to 16–19-year-old students. Since then the number of students in Sixth Form Colleges has increased significantly and has become a popular choice for students in post compulsory education.
>
> (*ibid.*: 26)

The Association of Colleges (AoC) now publishes a small amount of up-to-date information about all specialist colleges including sixth-form colleges; it describes them below:

> Sixth Form Colleges offer general academic and technical education, mainly for 16 to 18-year-olds. There are currently 47 sixth form colleges in England, educating thousands of students.
>
> Sixth form colleges tend to focus on level 3 provision and to be highly focused on preparing students for progression to higher education. They also offer technical and vocational courses, including T levels and applied general qualifications, and often offer students a combination of A levels and applied generals. Some FE colleges have dedicated sixth form centres or campuses and some Sixth Form Colleges have merged with General FE Colleges. Others have chosen to convert to academy status, becoming a type of 16–19 Academy.
>
> (AoC, 2023b: 1)

Since 2015, sixth-form colleges have been able to convert to a '16–19 academy' and this has been a popular choice. By 2023, '29 sixth form colleges have converted to become 16–19 academies

(17 in 2017, 3 in 2018, 5 in 2019, 1 in 2020, 3 in 2021)' (AoC, 2023a: 1). In order to convert, the colleges have to dissolve their organisation as a college and adopt the governance requirements of an academy.

Sector story – St Brendan's Sixth Form College, Bristol

As has previously been the case with other sector stories, its Ofsted report is helpful in providing a clear description of the college, how it works, and what it does. In the provider information, the college description starts:

> St Brendan's Sixth Form College (St Brendan's) is a Catholic college located to the south of Bristol. It sits in the Clifton Diocese and is the only Catholic sixth form in the south west and one of 14 in England and Wales. Students from the city and a wide surrounding area, including Bath, south Gloucestershire and north Somerset, attend the college. St Brendan's is based on one campus and provides education for around 1,800 students aged 16 to 18 years. Around 95% of students study level 3 courses, choosing between three A levels, level 3 vocational qualifications equivalent to three A levels, or a mix of A levels and vocational qualifications. Over half of students study a mixed programme, and the very large majority study at least one A level.
>
> Around 90 students study an access to level 3 programme, which consists of level 2 vocational courses and/or GCSEs, including English and mathematics. All students follow a tutorial programme and a compulsory religion, philosophy and ethics programme.
>
> (Ofsted, 2023: 1).

When inspected in 2023, the college was graded 'good' in all areas, and the report states that:

> …. students enjoy their lessons because teachers have created a positive learning environment. Teachers value students' contributions to class discussions and encourage full participation in learning activities. As a result, students become more confident and proud of their learning over time.
>
> Students behave well in lessons and when using communal areas because leaders and managers set high expectations that are upheld by staff.
>
> Teachers set high expectations for completion of work and for meeting deadlines. When students fall behind, they are supported appropriately to improve their attitudes towards learning.

The atmosphere of the college is 'non-judgemental, inclusive', and students:

> …. Feel that they can be themselves and are respected as individuals. Students from a wide diversity of backgrounds, including those of various faiths, those with special educational needs and/or disabilities and students from the LGBTQ+ community, feel welcomed and valued at the college. For example, leaders provide designated prayer rooms for Muslim students to practise their faith.
>
> Students further develop their understanding of what it means to be a good citizen through their learning of the compulsory religion, philosophy and ethics curriculum. They learn about the importance of developing positive relationships in a community and how to resolve conflict through communication.

> Students rarely experience bullying, harassment or discrimination, and if they do, they are comfortable to talk to staff, who deal with concerns sensitively and quickly.
>
> Students have a limited knowledge of the dangers of radicalisation and extremism. While they are taught this in the tutorial programme, this knowledge is not revisited and is often not remembered.
>
> Most students have limited work experience. Students are not taught how to link the skills they develop to the workplace. In business and psychology, students can take optional activities that do not form a structured part of their curriculum. Students with high needs do not receive careers guidance early enough in their programme and are not always well prepared for their next steps.
>
> (ibid.: 2)

In terms of the teaching and learning in the college, the report comments:

> Teachers use a variety of teaching strategies well to help students to learn the new knowledge and skills they need. For example, teachers of GCSE mathematics use effective questioning techniques by giving students thinking time and guiding them to work out answers for themselves. Teachers of vocational business courses use exercises in class to revisit previous knowledge and link new and previous learning through clear explanations. The large majority of teachers and learning support assistants support students with high needs with appropriate strategies.
>
> (ibid.: 3)

Overall, this Ofsted report provides evidence that this sixth-form college is demonstrating the same effective, student-centred teaching and learning which has been shown to exist in most other sub-sectors of FE, and that this is also supported by managers at the college. The emphasis on equality, diversity, tolerance, and communities is also welcome, and the overall impression is of an FE college which has much to be proud of.

Sixth-form colleges in action

The role of a sixth-form college tutor

Although the research was carried out in 2007, Schofield's study of students and tutors at a sixth-form college is still a helpful contribution to a sixth-form college in action, researching the role of the college tutor.

> Sixth Form Colleges can offer a unique experience, giving students a degree of independence and responsibility not always possible in a school environment. It can prepare students for the next step in life while still being supported, in the majority of cases, by a network of family and friends from home. However, students face academic pressures on entering a college, coupled with personal and social concerns.
>
> (ibid.: 26)

166 *Specialist colleges*

Students also face

> new teaching styles, loss of existing peer support groups and high expectations (both parental and student) are all associated with this change. Providing the appropriate academic and emotional support is therefore essential, and is integral to the role of the tutor
>
> (*ibid.*: 26–27)

Schofield's mixed methods study used interviews, questionnaires, and focus groups which combined to give a good understanding of both student and tutor perceptions of tutor support in this particular sixth-form college. The key evidence from the study concluded that students:

- Recognised the value of the emotional support provided by tutors, although they felt not enough time was available for tutorials.
- Emphasised the administrative role of the tutors, and how helpful that was, particularly in their Universities and Colleges Admissions System (UCAS) applications.
- Agreed that tutors monitoring progress with them in their subjects was essential.
- Felt they knew and trusted their tutor.

The evidence from the tutors indicated that they:

- Agreed about the value of providing emotional support to their students.
- Had not recognised as clearly as the students the importance of the administrative part of their roles.
- They felt they did not have enough time to fulfil their roles as tutor as well as possible.

This quote from one student sums it up well:

> It is a big change from GCSE where we were kids. We would get told off. Now it's kind of strange coming into a place where we are treated more as adults and our views are respected and important and it's hard to get out of the "we are not important and we can't express a view" (Year 13 student).
>
> (*ibid.*: 31)

Student independent learning at a sixth-form college

Stoten (2014: 452) undertook a small study to identify 'progress in promoting independent learning in a Sixth Form College'. Stoten undertook a mixed methods study including focus groups and a questionnaire with some 50 students at a medium-sized sixth-form college. The students were asked to respond to a series of statements about their approaches to study, their confidence in their study, and their worries and concerns about success or failure. The college and its staff gave a high priority to target and goal setting with the students, but the students did not appear to recognise this to a particularly strong degree. Although students did consider themselves organised, they appeared to find a teacher-centred approach more to their preference than becoming more independent learners. The college had introduced an initiative to promote independent learning, but this research suggested that it had not as yet been successful. Stoten argued that the findings from the study 'suggest that there may well be resistance to change, especially from students whose experience of teaching has been largely teacher led' (*ibid.*: 455).

Given that a significant proportion of the students at the sixth-form college had studied at schools before joining the college, it is probable that Stoten is correct, but also appears likely to be the case that the college, in this instance, mistakenly believed that a strong emphasis on numerical target-setting would promote independent learning, rather than a more direct personal, face-to-face level teaching approach, and a range of increased support from tutors.

Land-based colleges

History and background

The organisation which first represented the interests of land-based colleges, Napaeo, was founded in 1950; in 2006, the current organisation, Landex (Land-based Colleges aspiring to excellence) took over, and in 2023, Landex has 39 members, supports 53,000+students and offers 800+ courses (Landex, 2023: 6). There are only 11 land-based colleges (AoC, 2022: 4) so it is likely that some of their 39 members are other organisations other than colleges. In 1993, when incorporation of colleges took place, there were 36 'independent, land-based colleges' (Lloyd, 2018: 19). By 2015, there were 14, with 'the rest having merged with General Further Education Colleges or Higher Education Institutes' (*ibid.*: 19), and there were 11 in 2023. This is a reduction of 60 per cent since 1993. Lloyd provides a very useful further set of background information relating to land-based colleges including:

> Land-based colleges are often in rural settings and have large estates, farms, animal collections and equestrian centres that provide the breadth of practical resources needed to develop skills for employment. In many cases they may once have formed part of a large country estate and often retain assets such as a large period country house. They may also run commercial enterprises such as garden centres, livery stables and dog grooming parlours.
>
> (*ibid.*: 20)

Land-based colleges also manage large tracts of land (12,000 hectares of educational campus with 10,000 of that being farmed land in 2018). Lloyd continues to explain that 'in comparison with many other subject areas it is evident that land-based education requires large and diverse physical resources which are expensive to provide and maintain' (*ibid.*: 21). In terms of the curriculum,

> As well as the traditional subjects of agriculture and horticulture, the sector subject area includes study for qualifications in environmental conservation; countryside and wildlife management; floristry; arboriculture; equine studies and animal care, collectively these subject areas are referred to as land-based provision.
>
> (*ibid.*: 21)

To take one land-based college as an example, Capel Manor College, is:

> .... A specialist land-based college situated on five sites across London. The largest site is in Enfield, with other campuses in Regent's Park, Crystal Palace, Mottingham and Gunnersbury Park.

Students study qualifications from entry level to level 4 in foundation learning, animal management, horticulture, garden design and floristry. Approximately half of the students study at level 2 with the remaining students split equally between level 1 and level 3. A small proportion of students study at level 4 in floristry and animal management.

There were 911 students aged 16 to 18 and 1,165 adult students. Nine hundred and ninety-seven adult students study on part-time courses and 168 study fulltime. There were 207 apprentices on apprenticeship standards in level 2 horticulture and golf greenkeeper and in level 3 landscape technician, keeper and aquarist, and advanced golf greenkeeper. Most apprentices were over 19, with a small proportion of apprentices aged 16 to 18.

There were 215 students with high needs and 673 students with special educational needs or learning difficulties or disabilities. There were 42 students aged 14 to 16 studying part time at the college.

(Ofsted, 2023: 1)

Despite being specialist, this land-based college does have a similar diversity of students to a general FE college, more so than a sixth-form college, and within its specialist subject, there are many courses and combinations on offer. On the college website, there are 13 subject areas from Agriculture and Animal Management to Saddlery and Shoemaking and Wildlife and Environmental Conservation. The area of study characterised as 'land-based' includes a broader and more varied curriculum than may have been expected. The college also has an important place in the community:

We ensure that we play an active role within the local communities around our five campuses across the capital. Between them, our campuses include 30-acres of gardens, two zoos, a farm, a dog grooming parlour and flower shop, all of which are open to the public. We host regular events throughout the year for families to enjoy, and some of our campuses are available for function and event hire. We are proud to provide visitors with the opportunity to enjoy our animals and natural environments just as much as our students and staff do.

(Capel Manor College, 2023: 1)

Middle managers in land-based education

Lloyd's (2018) research investigated 'the role of middle managers within land-based colleges' (*ibid.*: 3). Lloyd used 'semi-structured interviews and analysis of job descriptions and organisational charts' (*ibid.*: 61) to collect data about middle managers and their situation. Of the 14 colleges contacted, 50 per cent responded positively and five were visited to collect data. Two of the five then did not continue, leaving five colleges as the colleges for data collection, of which three were still specialist colleges, and two merged, although until very recently they had been land-based specialist colleges. The turbulence of the FE sector, and this particular subsector, can be seen in Lloyd's somewhat difficult progress with gaining a good sample of research participants. Twelve middle managers participated in the study, and the findings and conclusions included:

- Building leadership capacity at all levels is considered to be a key factor in enabling colleges to meet the current and future challenges (*ibid.*: 137).

- Despite the current challenges within the sector and the consequent impact of these on the middle managers, the overall impression was that they retained a strong moral purpose and focus on the learner (*ibid.*: 138).
- The managers demonstrated a strong vocational calling and commitment to their subject areas, balancing the requirements of the college courses with the professional standards of the occupations the students hoped to enter. This strength of connection was also evident through their involvement with the resources required to deliver their subject areas (*ibid.*: 138).
- There was evidence that they concentrated their efforts on areas where they could make a difference, particularly in regard to the curriculum and learners (*ibid.*: 139).
- 'Role overload' ... 'continues to be an issue for those in the middle of an organisation' (*ibid.*: 140)
- For all the managers, a key part of the role was being able to identify and respond to these continually shifting priorities in order to secure the success of their department and the college as a whole (*ibid.*: 142).

At the beginning of this chapter, the question 'are specialist colleges particularly different from other FE colleges' was asked, and this research, although undertaken in specialist land-based colleges, has very similar results to the Azumah Dennis *et al.* (2019) study which features in Chapter 3, Managing and Working in Further Education. The views and actions of the college leaders in that study make almost the same points as those in this study. The specialist nature of the colleges here makes a difference to the specific context, curriculum, and circumstances of the research, but the working situation of these middle managers appears to be representative of those across the sector. It would be surprising if the broad range of issues and challenges which feature in the FE sector as a whole did not also affect the specialist colleges in the sector. The views of leaders in both studies are almost interchangeable, but Lloyd's research did not ask the question about the potential uniqueness of land-based education in comparison to the rest of FE, as this was not a key focus of her research.

Art, design, and performing arts colleges

As there are only two art, design, and performing arts colleges, this section of the chapter will provide details of one by way of example, based on their Ofsted reports and their presence online at the time of writing, as no specific research featuring either college is available.

The Northern School of Art

Background and history

This specialist college is located in campuses in Middlesborough and Hartlepool and started its life as Middlesborough School of Art in 1870. Between 1974 and 1996, the college operated as Cleveland College of Art and Design, and in 2018, it changed its name to The Northern School of Art. In 2023, it offers both FE and Higher Education (HE) courses, from Level 1 to postgraduate level, and also offers an access to HE diploma in Art and Design. HE qualifications are validated by the Arts University Bournemouth. The 'only large-scale commercial television and film studio in the

North East' (Northern School of Art, 2023a: 11), which is Northern Studios, is available as part of the provision of a range of the courses on offer. The plans for the future of the college are summarised on their website in 2023 (Northern School of Art, 2023b: 1).

> Our ambition is to become a university for the creative industries. We have a well-established track record of delivering the highest quality teaching and learning to our higher education students. The organisational changes we are proposing are one essential step on this journey. We have already applied for degree awarding powers which we should have by late summer 2024. By establishing ourselves as a Higher Education Institution (HEI) we will unlock the door to subsequently applying for university title.
>
> Our further education provision has been judged Outstanding by Ofsted since 2009. We are committed to enhancing our outstanding further education provision at our new Middlesbrough Campus with its excellent results and progression for students. We see this as fundamental to our mission to provide opportunities for the whole community. In recent years our Newport Road Campus has seen significant growth in student numbers and our Saturday Clubs are also thriving and growing. Similarly, we are dedicated to providing an accessible route into higher education at our Hartlepool campus.
>
> The additional resources which will result from our proposed changes will enable us to continue to invest to improve our further education provision. Close association with a higher education institution – ultimately a university – will bring additional benefits for our further education students.

Northern School of Art in action

The college Ofsted report from 2022 describes the college as follows:

> Further education provision is delivered at a purpose-built facility that opened in September 2021. At the time of the inspection, there were 450 learners studying creative arts programmes which include vocational qualifications, A levels and access to higher education courses in art and design. Of these, 434 learners were on education programmes for young people. Sixteen were on adult learning programmes, and there were 22 learners with high needs.
>
> (Ofsted, 2022: 1)

The college is rated outstanding in every area apart from one, and comments include:

> Leaders and managers provide an exceptionally current and relevant curriculum that enables learners to develop specialist knowledge and skills in creative arts. They have invested in a new, purpose-built arts centre which provides learners with access to highly specialised equipment and resources that enhances their studies. As a result, learners are well prepared for progression into careers in the creative arts industries and higher education. For example, learners aged 16 to 18 studying photography benefit from accessing specialist resources such as a photoshoot gallery, dark rooms and specialist commercial printers to support their learning. On completion of their final major projects, they are highly competent in creating a range of professional photographic images.
>
> (*ibid.*: 2)

In terms of the teaching:

> Lecturers are highly skilled and expert in their arts specialisms. They participate in relevant professional development activities by attending workshops, exhibitions and conferences. Many continue to work in the creative industries outside of their teaching roles to maintain their design expertise. Leaders host an annual further and higher education conference that allows staff to share best teaching and industry practice.
>
> (ibid.: 3)

And 'Lecturers sequence their teaching exceptionally well to help learners learn and recall key artistic concepts before moving onto more complex art projects that further develop learners' knowledge and skills' (ibid.: 3). With such high-quality teaching and support:

> Learners respond very positively to the high expectations set by their lecturers. They approach challenging, employer-led projects enthusiastically and creatively. Learners demonstrate a good understanding of wider social issues and the beneficial impact that the creative industries have on society. They take on active roles in artistic projects set by lecturers and employers that enable them to contribute to improving their local communities.
>
> (ibid.: 3)

Northern School of Art has a number of clear advantages in terms of a range of purpose-built campuses and facilities which some colleges would very much appreciate, but don't have; however, they are also operating in a location with multiple disadvantages and levels of deprivation in some of the local communities. To have achieved so well as a specialist college appears to make Northern School of Art and example which other colleges could aspire to.

Sector story – Northern School of Art – College collaboration fund project – Wellbeing

The college collaboration fund (CCF) was a peer-support programme to help FE colleges to collaboratively address shared quality improvement priorities and share good practice. The CCF ran from 2020 to 2022 and supported a range of projects. (Gov.uk, 2022: 1), and the summary of the project which involved Northern Art School is described below:

The project aims to:

- Enhance support for learners' mental health and wellbeing;
- Improve teaching and support staff's understanding of mental health and wellbeing;
- Develop strategies to improve learners' resilience and positive attitudes and behaviours.

The objectives are to:

- Improve understanding of the challenges learners face by extending the 'learner voice' and enhancing the curriculum, tutorial, and enrichment offer;
- Extend and amplify staff understanding of mental wellbeing and growth mindsets through staff training;

172 *Specialist colleges*

- Develop a suite of resources to enhance learners' determination, independence, and creative problem solving through multidimensional learning.

(DfE, 2022: 10)

The Northern School of Art has subsequently published a case study of their work on the project, and it included details of

- A survey of all FE students about their wellbeing where the results indicated that students wished to have more contact with other students and more physical activity. The project organised a number of activities including yoga and dog-walking, and the students found these worked really well to build their own confidence and appreciate more fully college life.
- An opportunity for first-year film students to film the work of the project during a wellbeing week which was also organised as part of the project. The film made a useful record of the project, and it also helped those who took part in the film and in making the film gain confidence and improve their life and work skills by doing so.

Overall, this project involved students and staff, and all gained from their participation whether it was an enhanced feeling of wellbeing, new skills including leadership skills, or playing a part in creating project learning resources which would be shared across the participating colleges and made freely available to all online.

Specialist-designated colleges/institutes of adult learning

These colleges are all related to adult learning and are either residential colleges or adult education institutes or colleges. The Marine Society College of the Sea, one of this group, is a college for those who are employed in jobs which take place at sea and offer courses by distance learning.

Two of this group of specialist colleges have been featured in other chapters, with the City Literature Institute (City Lit) featuring in Chapter 8 on 'social justice, equality and diversity', the Workers' Educational Association (WEA) in Chapter 6, 'widening participation and access to higher education', and briefly also in Chapter 8 on 'social justice, equality, and diversity'. They all provide a range of courses to a field which is not a subject specialism, as is the case with the other specialist colleges, but which is a specialist because of their target age group, i.e., 'adults'.

Question for discussion
Why do we need specialist colleges?

Conclusion

Specialist colleges are a diminishing subsector within FE, with mergers, sixth-form academies, and moves towards becoming a higher education institution potentially reducing the numbers in this subsector further. Data on enrolments across this subsector is not available, but given that there are 67 of them out of 228 colleges overall (29 per cent of the total), it would be reasonable to estimate there would be in the region of 80,000 students involved. The discussion and analysis in this chapter have identified that the key difference between specialist FE colleges and other FE colleges is indeed their specialism. Here it has been possible to compare subsector-specific research with other research featured in this book, considerably more similarities than differences emerge from that analysis. This leads to the conclusion that specialist colleges are special but are not unique.

Summary points

- Specialist colleges are a significant but shrinking part of the FE sector.
- Sixth-form colleges are the largest group within this subsector and are a popular choice for 16–19 study and training.
- Land-based colleges have particular organisational challenges associated with the land, which is associated with their provision.
- Land-based middle managers experience similar positive experiences and challenges as those in general FE colleges.
- Art, design, and performing arts colleges are a small but strongly performing small group within this subsector.
- Specialist-designated colleges make a significant contribution to adult and community learning.
- From the analysis in this chapter, it can be argued that specialist colleges are special, but are not unique.

Recommended reading

Lloyd, C. (2018) *The role of middle managers in land based further education. Doctoral thesis (Ed. D.)*. London: University College London.

References

Association of Colleges (2022) *College key facts 2022/23*. London: AoC.
Association of Colleges (2023a) *Sixth form colleges*. Available at: https://www.aoc.co.uk/about/sixth-form-colleges (Accessed 17 December 2023).
Association of Colleges (2023b) *College mergers*. Available at: https://www.aoc.co.uk/about/college-mergers (Accessed 18 December 2023).
Azumah Dennis, C., Springbett, O. and Walker, L. (2019) Further education leaders: Securing the sector's future. *Futures*, 110, pp. 1–10.
Capel Manor College (2023) *Community*. Available at: https://www.capel.ac.uk/community/ (Accessed 19 December 2023).
Department for Education (2022) *Promotional material: Round 2 project summaries: College collaboration fund (CCF)*. Available at: https://www.gov.uk/government/publications/college-collaboration-fund-ccf-projects/round-2-project-summaries-college-collaboration-fund-ccf (Accessed 21 December 2023).
Gov.uk. (2022) *Guidance: College Collaboration Fund (CCF)*. Available at: https://www.gov.uk/guidance/college-collaboration-fund-ccf#successful-applicants (Accessed 21 December 2023).
Landex – Land-based colleges aspiring to excellence (2023) *About landex*. Available at: https://landex.org.uk/about/ (Accessed 19 December 2023).
Lloyd, C. (2018) *The role of middle managers in land based further education. Doctoral thesis (Ed. D.)*. London: University College London.
Northern School of Art (2023a) *Sector transfer consultation*. Available at: https://northernart.ac.uk/sector-transfer/ (Accessed 21 December 2023).
Northern School of Art (2023b) *Higher education prospectus*. Middlesborough: Northern School of Art.
Office for Standards in Education (2022) *Inspection of Northern School of Art*. Manchester: Ofsted.
Office for Standards in Education (2023a) *Inspection of Capel Manor College*. Manchester: Ofsted.

Office for Standards in Education (2023b) *Inspection of St Brendan's Sixth Form College.* Manchester: Ofsted.

Schofield, T. (2007) Student and tutor perceptions of the role of the tutor in a sixth form college. *Pastoral Care in Education,* 25(1), pp. 26–32.

Shorter, P. (1994) Sixth-form colleges and incorporation: Some evidence from case studies in the north of England. *Oxford Review of Education,* 20(4), pp. 461–474.

Stoten, D.W. (2014) Are we there yet? Progress in promoting independent learning in a Sixth Form College. *Educational Studies,* 40(4), pp. 452–455, DOI: 10.1080/03055698.2014.930342.

14 Offender learning

Introduction

This little-known subsector involves learning which takes place in institutions where offenders are located, or in the community after they have been convicted. Examples of the best practices in offender learning will be included, and discussion and analysis of the challenges of producing the same quality of learning experience for offenders in institutions as for those in the rest of the further education (FE) sector. The chapter opens with an explanation of the objectives of offender learning and a definition of this FE subsector. The history and background section of the chapter discusses the evolution of offender learning against a background of whether punishment or rehabilitation should be its central intention.

The chapter then outlines the significant amount of learning which takes place within this FE subsector using available data. The ongoing development of a policy over-emphasis on skills for life, particularly maths and English, is also discussed. The first sector story for the chapter features days in the life of an offender learning organiser and an offender who is participating in offender learning, and the second sector story showcases an imaginative piece of project-based offender learning.

The situation of teachers in offender learning, their experiences, and how they can be caught between three types and levels of management is also analysed. A consideration of the further potential for rehabilitation in the current subsector is featured, and the chapter concludes with a selection of recommendations for how this subsector could be helped to improve in the future.

What is offender learning?

The organisation which has overall responsibility for offender learning in 2023 is the newly created (during 2023), Prisoner Education Service, and its objectives are to:

- Appoint 'Education Skills and Work' roles in every prison to work with governors to enhance learning in their institution;
- Undertake earlier assessments of the learning and training needs of offenders;
- Enhance the vocational skills and employability of offenders;
- Refocus attention on improving the literacy and numeracy skills of offenders;
- More successfully rehabilitate offenders;
- Reduce repeat offending;
- Reduce crime in the community.

DOI: 10.4324/9781003468455-14

176 Offender learning

Most offender learning takes place in prisons, and it has been an FE subsector which has often experienced even more challenges in relation to the influence of government policy than the other subsectors already featured in this book. For the purpose of this chapter, and in this book, offender learning is defined as a structured process and series of interventions which can 'change individual offender behaviour' and 'reduce the risks of people engaging in criminal activity and reoffending'. In addition, increasing 'human capital through skills and qualifications must go with building social capital, building useful networks and peer/family support: and with building appropriate self-esteem and the belief in a better life ahead' (NIACE, 2009: 5).

NIACE (2009) extends this definition by emphasising that:

> Learning will only have significant effect if linked with other policies, particularly on employment and accommodation. This is crucial at key transition points, particularly at the point of release. There is a strong case for all prisoners to be given access to education or training as a matter of course immediately when they leave prison, combined with pre-release preparation for it.
>
> (*ibid.*: 5)

History and background

The first person to propose education in prisons was an eighteenth-century philanthropist called John Howard in 1777, and in 1779, two prisons were constructed using his theories. This early vision of prison education was harsh, as it included a regime of hard labour, time in solitary confinement, and religious instruction; this was in tune with the philosophy of harsh punishments and penitence, which was that such regimes could reform prisoners. The 'Gaols Act 1823'

> …. Introduced 'a reformatory pace in criminal justice and a change in attitude, from retribution through harsh punishments, to reform through work and education that would give prisoners the practical skills they would need to gain employment on their release. However, the rising crime rates in the mid-nineteenth century meant that this reformatory regime was soon replaced with a more retributive penal approach that focused on occupying prisoners in dull, monotonous labour such as oakum picking.
>
> (Wilkinson, 2020: 220)

In 1895, the Gladstone Report proposed:

> … That the purpose of imprisonment should be a combination of deterrence and reformation, and that the role of education was to provide prisoners with the basic skills in English and maths, so that on their release they will be able to undertake useful labour.
>
> This regime continued into the twentieth century until the appointment in 1921 of a new Prison Commissioner, Sir Alexander Patterson, who proposed that education in prisons should be used to encourage creative expression through music, art, discussions and play readings, as well as lessons in basic skills.
>
> (*ibid.*: 220)

Local authorities were given responsibility for offender learning in 1947, and the prison educators, who had been volunteers up to that point, became paid employees of the local authority. This not only created some improvements to the system but also created a further need for training and development of those teachers. When the 1992 Education Act was introduced, the offender learning system became fragmented as FE colleges and local authority adult education services both found themselves with some responsibility for offender learning. At the start of the twenty-first century, government began the process, which continues to this day, of competitive tendering of offender learning services. Initially, these changes meant that all of offender learning was managed by FE colleges, and this did bring all offender learning into the FE sector. In a review of offender learning commissioned by the then Secretary of State for Justice, Michael Gove, published in 2016, the recommendations included 'more personal and social development (PSD) courses and more arts, music and sports activities alongside the basics of maths and English' (*ibid.*: 221). As has often been seen in terms of FE policy, however, a ministerial change in 2016 then led to a further change which prioritised maths and English as central to the purpose of offender learning. This still prevails at the time of writing.

How much offender learning is there?

In contrast with a number of other FE subsectors, the data relating to Offender Learning is somewhat more comprehensive, and extracts from that data follow.

In terms of the number of people in prison, the Institute for Government states that:

> Between April 2021 and December 2022, the prison population increased at an average rate of 220 people per month. Between December 2022 and mid-October 2023, this increased to 605 per month, helping the total prison population reach 88,225 – the highest level since at least January 2011.
>
> (Institute for Government, 2023: 1)

The Ministry of Justice Statistics Bulletin for April 2022 to March 2023 (Ministry of Justice, 2023: 1) includes these figures **(for England and Wales)**:

Main points

- 59,480 prisoners completed an initial Maths or English assessment.
    Of these prisoners, 56,548 took at least one Maths assessment and 57,002 took at least one English assessment.
- Prisoners took 58,321 Maths and 58,907 English initial assessments.
    Most initial assessment results were at entry level 1–3, with 68 per cent in Maths and 65 per cent in English.
- Overall, 28 per cent of prisoners who took an initial assessment had a learning difficulty/disability (LDD) confirmed through an LDD assessment.
    This varied across ethnic groups and was highest for prisoners from white groups at 30% and lowest for those from the other ethnic group at 17 per cent.
- 63,744 prisoners participated in courses.
    This was a 28 per cent increase on the 49,855 prisoners participating in courses last year.
- 28,832 prisoners participated in functional skills courses from 1 April 2022 to 31 March 2023. Over the same time period 19,329 prisoners achieved at least a partial grade.

From 1 April 2022 to 31 March 2023, the number of prison learners participating in a functional skills course increased by 71 per cent, from 16,866 to 28,832. Prisoners achieving a full or partial grade increased by 80 per cent from 10,755 to 19,329.
- The number of starts for Accredited Programmes in custody increased.
  From 1 April 2022 to 31 March 2023, there were 4,820 Accredited Programme starts, a 110 per cent increase when compared with the previous 12-month period.
- The number of completions for Accredited Programmes in custody increased.
  From 1 April 2022 to 31 March 2023, 4,135 accredited programmes were completed by offenders, representing an increase of 124 per cent compared with the previous 12-month period.

(*ibid*.: 1)

When considering these two sets of figures, it would appear that a significant proportion of the prison population is engaged in offender learning. The figures include Wales and England which would make some difference, and the completion rate for 'Accredited Programmes' is just 4,135, which is small, despite it increasing significantly over the previous period. From the Ministry of Justice data, however, it is clear that a significant number of offenders are undertaking assessments, which is encouraging.

Sector story – A day in the life of an offender learning organiser and a learner who is an offender

Denzil – The learning organiser

Denzil works as the learning and skill co-ordinator at a medium-sized prison in the midlands and starts work every day at eight am, significantly earlier than most Department for Education (DfE) staff would officially begin their working day. He does sometimes teach sessions, but his overall job is to liaise, collaborate, and co-operate with all parties in the prison to ensure offender learning takes place in ways which assist and support the offenders, and which also meet prison and government targets. He also needs to ensure that FE standards for teaching and learning are maintained. On some days, when he arrives, the inmates are still locked in their cells because there has been a disturbance, difficult incident, or serious example of rule breaking, and there is a 'lockdown'. This means Denzil can't get into the teaching spaces or his office, which is inside the prison's main area, and that any prisoners will be tense and lack concentration for their learning when the lockdown has ended. Denzil has worked hard to get good relationships with both the offenders and the other professionals in the prison and undertakes appropriate risk assessments when such situations arise to ascertain what education can be offered and where it can take place once the cells are unlocked. This usually results in some activities being able to take place and this could include library work, recycling, waste management, and classes and workshops in their spaces within the prison. On a normal day, there is a good range of learning opportunities taking place within the prison, which has a workshop, classrooms, a computer room, and small discussion/tutorial spaces. The training includes building and construction, information technology (IT), maths and English and catering, and a range of other subjects.

There are a significant number of foreign nationals in Denzil's prison, so there are several organisations with whom he works, which are part of the operation to keep foreign nationals secure and to support their ongoing needs. These include the National Careers Service (NCS), Shannon Trust, Migrant Help, and the St Giles Trust. Overall, Denzil sees his key purpose as helping to ensure that the inmates gain skills and confidence, which will help them live a purposeful life in England or in the country of their origin. Despite the particular challenges of working in offender learning, Denzil appreciates the successes and regularly sees major changes and improvements in the lives of the inmates after they have taken part in successful educational experiences.

David – The offender who is learning

David is 75 per cent of the way through his sentence at the prison where Denzil works, and over the years, he has been there he has taken on a range of learning opportunities as his attitude towards learning opportunities became more positive. Initial and regular ongoing conversations with Denzil, teachers and the prison careers officer steadily convinced him it was worth pursuing educational opportunities. He developed an action plan during his first course, which was a 'getting into learning' programme. The first stage of the plan was boosting his literacy and numeracy, and he undertook and gained level 2 qualifications in both. As he undertook further courses and made progress with his learning and confidence, his enthusiasm for training, and his opinion of its value grew considerably. He participated in classes with other inmates, received good support from his tutors, and started to develop an interest in advice and guidance and working in the prison system himself. He enrolled on a level 3 and then level 4 qualification in advice and guidance and undertook work experience for the courses (strictly supervised), where he gave advice and guidance to some other inmates. He has become really enthusiastic about the courses on offer in the prison and has assisted other inmates to enrol in building and painting and decoration courses. As he approaches the end of his sentence, he is hopeful that he will be able to continue the advice and guidance work with inmates, and that this could even lead to employment within the prison service.

> ### Question for discussion
> Why should people who have committed crimes have access to learning?

Offender learning policy

Offender learning teachers are in a different and more complicated situation than most other teachers in FE as 'they are governed by FE, prison education and penal policies simultaneously' (Wilkinson, 2020: 225). Wilkinson continues that:

> These policies determine the purpose of prison education, its content, mode of delivery, and the type and calibre of the people employed to deliver it. Being subject to these different sets of policies puts prison teachers in a position that is underpinned by the fact that although they work in a prison setting, they are not employed by the prison service. They are expected to deliver all the policy requirements of their employers whilst being restricted by the policies and practises of the prison system. They are part of, but set apart from, the

system, often geographically distant from the education provider and ideologically different from the prison system.

(ibid.: 225)

To explain this situation, most contracts to organise and deliver offender learning are gained by FE colleges, so the staff who teach in prisons are FE college teachers, and they need to have the same level of qualification as all FE teaching staff in a college should have, which is generally to possess or take part in an FE teacher training programme. Although most of the qualifications which offenders would undertake would be ones also offered in colleges, the oversight of everything which takes place in a prison is managed by the governor. Prison governors are senior civil servants and so are themselves subject to government policy. The prison in which a teacher carries out their teaching may also be geographically distant from the employing college of that teacher, as the contracts may cover prisons some distance from the FE college. Because of this, the offender learning teacher will need to navigate between their college, their prison, and government policy as a regular part of their job.

Other key differences between working in a mainstream FE college and offender learning include the following:

- FE college funding comes almost entirely from the Department for Education, and funding for offender learning entirely from the Ministry of Justice.
- Seventeen per cent of FE college students have a learning difficulty or disability and approximately 33 per cent in offender learning.
- The environment in FE colleges focusses on education and training and for offender learning it is security and containment.
- The curriculum of FE colleges is extremely diverse, ranging from level one to level seven in many courses and qualifications. The curriculum of offender learning focusses on Maths, English, ICT, and ESOL to level 2, and a small range of vocational qualifications, also to level 2.

Adapted from Wilkinson (2020: 226–227)

Flynn and Higdon (2022: 197) also argue that government policy has meant that 'the role afforded prison education has been tied to reducing reoffending', and that overall, 'education conceived as an activity with the potential to engender critical awareness and agency unrelated to the reform of criminal conduct as an end in itself has been marginalised' (*ibid.*: 197). This is one subsector of FE where the learners involved are even more disadvantaged than those who are involved in other subsectors of FE. Significant numbers of offenders were excluded from school, have a learning difficulty or disability, and have 'negative, unconfident perceptions of education generally. Incarcerated individuals often express a sense of futility about their position at the bottom of the educational ladder' (*ibid.*: 199). There is value in the learning prioritised by government policy in prison, and 'the most significant learning they receive in prison may well be in basic literacy, or training in industry/production work. But it should not end there' (*ibid.*: 199). Flynn and Higdon strongly argue for more focus in offender learning to be on 'Citizenship education' when they conclude:

> Basic-level prison education is limited to training prisoners for low-skill and low-paid jobs, and learning their place within society. Therefore, it is all too readily rejected. And higher-level

prison education, engaged in as it is by only a very few high-performing prisoners, necessarily means the neglect of others. Citizenship education is not a panacea. However, as a process of development built from the bottom up, it offers a potential for reconstructing the content, delivery, and environment of prison education in a way that is meaningful to participants. Education in prison that is recognised and assessed as a lived experience and social activity that encourages prisoners to express agency in relation to their needs is long overdue.

(ibid.: 211–212)

Offender learning in action

The experiences of prison educators

In 2021, the University and College Union (UCU) and the Prison Learning Alliance (PLA) published an important piece of research about 'the experience of teachers working in prisons' (UCU/PLA, 2021: 1). At the time, they cited the numbers of offender learning teachers as 'approximately 1,640 full-time equivalent (FTE) teachers' (ibid.: 3). The researchers carried out a survey of teachers in prison education and received 412 replies. UCU did not

> Claim that this data is representative of the entire prison educator population, but we believe that the numbers are sufficient and the findings relevant to provide evidence which highlights the experiences of prison educators and demonstrates the case for change.
>
> (ibid.: 3)

The research produced a range of conclusions including:

- In many prisons, the regime does not prioritise or even facilitate education. Many prison teachers feel a lack of support from the prison staff they work with and in some places, morale is low, which, in turn, impacts on learners' experience of education and their outcomes.
- Generally, prison educators are experienced teachers, with most having substantial teaching experience both inside and outside prison. Almost half of the survey respondents have worked in prison education for over a decade. Many are unhappy with the current commissioning arrangements for prison education and would like this to be reviewed.
- Teaching in prison is a highly specialised role. Despite this, support for prison teachers is generally inadequate, and just under one in ten (9.7 per cent) of our survey respondents believed that support for new teachers was good enough. Some teachers have paid for their own professional development because they were unable to secure opportunities through their employers.
- Prison educators are motivated by spending time with learners and the transformational impact that education can have on people's lives. Teachers understand the rehabilitative impact of education, and they value the process of supporting people in prison to make changes that will lead to better outcomes on release.
- Education staff would welcome more input from prison management and officers. There is an appetite for additional training on the operational and cultural aspects of prison life. Prison

teachers would welcome regular communication and updates from the prisons they work in, and to feel more integrated into the prison.
- Teachers responding to the survey expressed a need for further professional development, opportunities for mentoring, shadowing, networking, sharing good practice, and developing specialisms. There is also a need to support teachers' well-being much more effectively, including providing therapeutic support.
- Many prison teachers feel doubly disadvantaged through not feeling part of the further education sector or part of the prison sector. There is a belief that their concerns are hidden, that their views are not sought, and that their voices are not heard (*ibid.*: 21–22).

Do prisons rehabilitate – The offender view

Bullock and Bunce (2020) gather accounts from prisoners about their experiences of offender learning and comment that previous research has already argued that:

> …. Despite rhetoric which stresses the desirability of the prison as a place of reform and rehabilitation, official reports also draw attention to how as an institution it is failing to embed the cultures, relational processes and practices that have been found to facilitate effective implementation of rehabilitative regimes.
>
> (*ibid.*: 112)

They collected 27 'in-depth accounts' from offenders through semi-structured interviews, and there were 20 male and 70 female participants. The prisoners' reflections on their experiences included:

- A lack of support with attempts to plan for release and potential employment.
- Some mandatory programmes appeared to be ticking boxes for the institution and the offenders that they had done as required.
- Programmes with a positive and personal focus which engaged the offenders as learners and human beings could be beneficial and enjoyable.
- Prisons are not serious about rehabilitation.
- Work experience tended to be mundane and repetitive.
- Prison staff were often not helpful and positive about rehabilitation.

(Bullock and Bunce, 2020)

Overall, Bullock and Bunce conclude:

> In sum, while penal policy is optimistic, a body of research is drawing attention to the challenges faced by those aiming to deliver the ideal of rehabilitative prisons in practice. For the implementation and impact of any rehabilitative interventions cannot be separated from the wider prison environment in which they operate. The institution of the prison does little to promote a positive climate within which to motivate prisoners to reconsider their attitudes towards crime, and make genuine plans to change their lifestyle.
>
> (*ibid.*: 123)

Sector story – Creative projects in offender learning

A medium-sized prison in the South East of England was presented with an opportunity to collaborate with a well-known museum in London, when they were asked to design posters and leaflets for a planned new exhibition, working with museum staff and a team of offender learning teachers. The exhibition theme was street art in London and its origins and included creating a piece of street art with an expert in the field as part of the advertising for the project. The museum provided a clear and detailed brief for participants, which involved participants pitching ideas, researching, and gathering historical information and budgeting for the different parts of the exhibition, and also provided a street artist who would work towards creating a piece of street art with a team of five offenders, which would be placed outside the museum before and during the exhibition. The staff from the museum had done this kind of project very successfully before, and the offender learning teachers took on the brief with great enthusiasm. The work for the offenders involved planning and problem solving, literacy and numeracy, creative arts, and opportunities to develop and pursue their own interests in the field. This was a major challenge for many of them, but the project team of teachers and the museum worked hard to devise accessible, step-by-step tasks, and activities for the learning objectives of the project. Skills for life were also carefully embedded into the work that offenders did to take part in the project by the offender learning teachers, and this helped a number of participants move closer to gaining their level 2 qualifications in English, Maths, and ICT. The piece of street art produced for the exhibition was created in one of the prison workshops with the help and supervision of the street artist; it was displayed outside the museum before the exhibition started, and while it was on. The five participants who created the piece of street art were featured in the local and national press (with their permission), and this all helped to build confidence and promote the exhibition which proved to be very successful.

A considerable amount of preparation with offenders took place, and 15 became the regular project-participant team. As could be imagined, progress was not always rapid, but enough regular participants met and worked together over the weeks to ensure that an exhibition poster and leaflet and the piece of street art were created (just) in time for the exhibition. Learners in the project commented that this project had helped them to build and improve on a good range of skills and gain or get nearer to gaining their qualifications. Participation had also helped them feel they had given something back to the community, and that taking part in this project could help them to get employment on release. The museum was very happy with the project team's contribution, and they were mentioned in the exhibition publicity. A short video showcasing the exhibition and the project's piece of street art was produced to both publicise the exhibition and enable the participating offenders and others to see the exhibition they had helped to create.

The project demonstrates that, with an imaginative project-based learning approach, it can be possible to engage offenders in meaningful learning which focusses on, but also goes beyond, skills for life and gives the community a somewhat more positive view of offenders and offender learning.

Question for discussion

What would you include as the main skills and knowledge involved in an offender learning curriculum?

Conclusion

Positive proposals for the development and improvement of offender learning have been made, and to conclude the chapter, an example of those ideas is included. A summary of the recommendations from the UCU/PLA research (2021) is included as it offers a number of positive ways forward.

Recommendations

For the Ministry of Justice

- Commissioning processes for education should ensure that conditions, salaries (including clear and transparent incremental progression for service), and pension entitlements for prison educators are at the very minimum equivalent to further education in the community.
- Contracts should include adequate time for administration work, class preparation, training, and development of prison teachers.
- The Ministry of Justice should work with Post Graduate Certificate in Education (PGCE) providers to develop a specific unit on teaching in prisons.
- The Ministry of Justice needs to develop a coherent, sustainable strategy to recruit and retain prison educators, working with education providers but ensuring that there is also ownership and input from senior prison teams.
- Resources for prison education need to be sufficient to ensure that appropriate technology and facilities are provided.

For HM (His Majesty's) prison and probation service

- The prison service should develop a formal induction process for prison teachers, to be carried out by the host prison and that enables them to develop a good understanding and knowledge of prison operations.
- The regime should be changed to facilitate better engagement with education and class lengths should be equivalent to those in the community.

For education providers

- Teachers need sufficient time for class preparation and administration tasks and more input into the curriculum.
- More support and/or oversight is needed for some managers, and concerns from teachers should be given full consideration and fully investigated.
- Providers should develop incentives for teachers, including progression routes, training, mentoring, and shadowing schemes.
- Consideration should be given to employing more admin staff in education departments to support monitoring and recording functions and free up teaching time.
- Prison teachers should be offered opportunities for clinical supervision and therapeutic support.
- Opportunities to network and share good practice between prisons and with the wider further education community should be increased.

For governors

- Governors should include prison teachers in induction processes and develop regular training opportunities involving both prison officers and teachers.
- Governors should implement processes that consult and involve education staff more in regime delivery and planning.
- Governors should promote opportunities for officers and teachers to work together on projects and for teachers to communicate with keyworkers about learners' needs and progress.

(UCU/PLA, 2021: 22–23)

Summary points

- Offender learning at its best makes a strong contribution to rehabilitation and enhanced employability.
- Offender learning at its weakest makes little contribution to rehabilitation.
- Producing the same quality of learning experience for offenders in institutions as those in the rest of the FE sector presents a significant challenge for all concerned.
- The history and background of offender learning tends to focus on whether punishment or rehabilitation is the central intention of policy and practice.
- Recent policy relating to offender learning tends to over-emphasise improvements to skills for life as the main intention, particularly Maths and English.
- Teachers in offender learning can be caught between three types and levels of management, their FE employer, the prison governor's rules and regulations, and the government of the day's requirements.
- Recommendations for how this subsector could be helped to improve in the future include enhancing the staffing situation, revising the curriculum, and engaging the professionals working

Recommended reading

University and College Union and the Prisoner Learning Alliance (2021) *Hidden Voices. The experience of teachers working in prison.* London: UCU and PLA.

References

Bullock, K. and Bunce, A. (2020) 'The prison don't talk to you about getting out of prison': On why prisons in England and Wales fail to rehabilitate prisoners. *Criminology & Criminal Justice,* 20(1), pp. 111–127.

Flynn, N. and Higdon, R. (2022). Prison education: Beyond review and evaluation. *The Prison Journal,* 102(2), pp. 196–216.

Institute for Government (2023) *Performance tracker, 2023: Prisons.* Available at: https://www.instituteforgovernment.org.uk/publication/performance-tracker-2023/prisons#:~:text=The%20prison%20population%20has%20grown%20rapidly%20in%202023&text=Between%20December%202022%20and%20mid,since%20at%20least%20January%202011 (Accessed 31 December 2023).

Ministry of Justice (2023) *Prison education statistics and accredited programmes in custody April 2022 to March 2023.* London: Ministry of Justice.

NIACE (National Institute of Adult and Continuing Education) (2009) *Crime and lifelong learning.* Leicester: NIACE.

University and College Union and the Prisoner Learning Alliance (2021) *Hidden voices. The experience of teachers working in prison.* London: UCU and PLA.

Wilkinson, S. (2020) Offender learning and prison education. In J. Tummons (Ed.) *PCET: Learning and teaching in the post compulsory sector.* London: Sage.

15 Making connections – The future of further education

Introduction

The extensive range of chapters in this book has provided the reader with a comprehensive and detailed picture of the further education (FE) sector which will be helpful whether studying FE, studying *in* FE, or *working* in FE. This final chapter draws the book to a conclusion by reflecting on the themes and writings which have featured through the different chapters and makes connections between them as recurring characteristics, achievements, issues, and challenges. Although FE is under-researched in comparison to other education sectors, many worthwhile publications, and their ideas about the present and the future of FE, have been written, and a selection of those ideas will be drawn together to suggest how FE could become a stronger, more equal, and better-recognised sector in the future. The author will close the book with a brief summary of his engagement with appreciation of and hopes for the future of FE.

Breadth and diversity

The breadth and diversity of the FE sector become clear just from the content of the first three chapters of this book. With 2 million students, multiple learning sites or locations, multiple subsectors, and links and connections with all areas of the community, FE has real breadth and real diversity. These characteristics do, however, bring with them a number of challenges, and the sector is more complex because of this breadth and diversity. Hodgson *et al.* (2018: 3) state that 'there is no single system' of FE in the four countries of the UK, and that this not only presents 'challenges of coherence' but also offers 'a unique opportunity' (*ibid.*: 3). The breadth and diversity of the sector does make naming, describing, and understanding FE difficult. If you are working in FE, you will firstly develop your own particular professional understanding of the sector which will start with your immediate work role in your home organisation. This understanding will develop, through conversations, staff development, personal study or research, membership of professional associations such as the Society for Education and Training, and activities with professional networks such as the Learning and Skills Research Network. Over time, you will develop your own broader particular professional and personal sense of the sector as a whole. That may well be similar in many ways to another person working in the sector, but it could also be distinctly different.

When it comes to governing the sector, a minister who may well have no experience at all of FE will not find many other minsters who do, and although there are experienced and expert advisors and civil servants to assist, it is not entirely surprising that ministers find it difficult to make their

DOI: 10.4324/9781003468455-15

mark, and perhaps try too hard to introduce changes which will make their name rather than which support the best practice in the sector and help it to develop. Overall, therefore the breadth and diversity of the sector does, as Hodgson *et al.* (2018) state, offer a 'unique opportunity' by providing a very comprehensive educational offer, but this very breadth and diversity can also present challenges of understanding. Developing a coherent, comprehensive vision of the sector has defeated many, and will no doubt make it difficult for many more.

Policy churn

'Education for other people's children' is a term coined about FE in an article which argued that FE colleges 'are often poorly understood by policymakers who have had little if any experience of these institutions which cater mainly to the less privileged in society' (Orr, 2018: 253). This has led to 'constant churn of both government initiatives and skills ministers' and highlighted 'the lack of institutional memory hampering good and informed decision making' (City and Guilds, 2019: 2). The Edge Foundation (2020: 5) comments that

> Since the 1980s there have been 48 different Secretaries of State for Education and 28 major pieces of legislation covering the FE sector, during the same period, responsibility for the FE sector has moved between six separate government departments.

This number of changes would be dismissed as at least unlikely, and probably as impossible over such a short period of time, but the fact that they have happened is evidence which 'reflects not only the shifting perspectives and priorities of policymakers in England, but also a sector almost permanently in search of itself, struggling to define its mission and purpose in a context of near-constant reform and regular political upheaval', Keep *et al.* (2021: 5). Pring joined this chorus of disappointment with his judgement about 14–19 reform, where:

> .... The solutions pursued with such vigour (for example, the proposed reform of qualifications and of apprenticeships) could well be but a continuation of a long line of 'reforms' which do not work. In that respect, the most important legacy might be greater understanding of the problems, and a more humble approach to their long term solutions.
>
> (Pring, 2008: 687)

Since the Education Act of 1992, this policy churn has combined with a period of tight financial control, target-setting, required savings, and a growth in government control which have created a harsh, performance-driven regime described as the 'terrors of performativity' (Ball, 2003: 215).

The Edge Foundation's (2020) report summarises some of the challenges currently faced by FE due to government policy:

- With a lack of stability in both policy and funding, the FE sector has struggled to dictate the direction of its own future.
- England has seen attempts to implement different funding models, from the output model of the 1990s through to performance-based from 2002 to 2006 before moving to employer-based funding.

- A continuous decline in funding both 16–18 and post-18 has caused significant challenges for the FE sector.
- Colleges are facing a staff recruitment and retention crisis reinforced by the increased marketisation of the sector.
- The breadth of provision offered alongside a stretched workforce often means FE providers take on more than they have the capacity to handle.
- Class sizes have increased and learning hours per student decreased to compensate for cuts in funding.
- Mergers have attempted to respond to funding and governance challenges across the sector, but the emerging evidence to date suggests this had limited success (*ibid.*: 20).

Purpose of FE

Despite the challenges discussed in the previous section, a sense of the purpose of FE is still present at many levels, even if this does not always coalesce into a coherent vision across the sector. Azumah Dennis *et al.* (2019), in interviews with college leaders, found they expressed a powerful sense of purpose for FE and stated that it was:

1. To provide opportunities for the development of individual learners;
2. To make an active contribution to society (*ibid.*: 2019: 4).

Their research concluded that:

> … While leadership actions may contribute to the further political devaluing of the sector and its designation as a labour-market skills provider, some attempts are made to preserve its wider contribution to society, offering a basis for the creation of a more socially just future for FE.
>
> (*ibid.*: 1)

This social purpose is endorsed by the FETL (2020) when they state that:

> …. Further education learning environments work to promote an ethos of egalitarianism – usually explicitly. Students' backgrounds are taken into account, while their thoughts, views and practices are valued and seen as an important curriculum resource from which to move forward. In such a context, teachers emerge as transformative leaders, subverting the 'symbolic violence' inflicted on their students in their earlier experience of education'.
>
> (*ibid.*: 32)

and

> …. In a college setting in which social justice values are most fully realised, the pedagogical goals reach beyond college walls. There is a selflessness and altruism in the everyday cultural practices of the college. The college is, in that sense, primarily a vehicle for bringing about change at the level of the individual but also in society more broadly.
>
> (*ibid.*: 124)

Returning to Azumah Dennis et al. (2019) they emphasise that there is still some autonomy even within the most apparently constricted circumstances because what

> .... Colleges achieve occurs despite of rather than because of the intentions and incentives set by national policy. Colleges are, to some extent at least, masters or mistresses of their own destinies, and they build upon histories and institutional legacies and trajectories that are very varied.
>
> (ibid.: 6)

Despite considerable pressure to follow only the purpose and direction laid out by funding and government direction, FE as a sector still manages to work towards reducing disadvantage, increasing equality, and helping create a better world for the future, which is a major achievement given the ongoing working environment.

Sector-wide data

If the FE sector wishes to aspire to presenting a clear and coherent vision of its services, provision, and achievements to the public, employers, organisations, and to governments, it must be easier to find out whole-sector data, and that must be easily accessible from one starting point. Much helpful data has been located about the sector during the writing of this book, but locating that data is often difficult, and data about different aspects and subsectors of FE is often found in different places, rather than a central source. The situation regarding sector-wide data is improving, but it still has a long way to go, and this has been a goal of organisations and governments for some years, and, although it has improved over the last ten years, it is still by no means comprehensive nor easily accessible. An urgent review of sector-wide data is needed, and a high-priority objective is set to develop a central access point for all FE sector data.

Positive professionalism

When organisations are under pressure, their staff are too. This causes ongoing difficulties across FE. There are numerous examples in the 'in action' sections of chapters in the book where teachers have found positive, supportive, student-centred ways of teaching which have brought successful results for their students and improved Ofsted inspection results for their institution. There are professional approaches which can mitigate the challenges, as cited earlier in the book.

> Machiavelli (1908: 7) argued that those who remain 'poor and scattered are never able to injure' the prince. 'Poor and scattered' is a description which just about sums up the professional situation of many working in FE. Machiavelli also believed that a prince who had held power for some time was more likely to have loyal and well-disposed subjects than a 'new prince'.
>
> (Crawley, 2017: 115)

In addition, Daley et al. (2015) encouraged those working in FE not to be destroyed by the power of 'princes' but to join together in what has been called 'the making and taking of professionalism' (Gleeson et al., 2005). A possible model which could help teachers make and take professionalism in the future is introduced in Chapter 3, and it is that of the 'connected professional', with four 'connections' which combine to make a 'connected professional', and they are:

1. The Practical Connection – The practical underpinning of teaching skills, knowledge, understanding, and application which are essential for all teachers to be able to carry out their role.
2. The Democratic Connection – The active involvement in democratic action where practitioners work together with other colleagues towards achieving agreed common goals.
3. The Civic Connection – The active engagement in civic action with the wider community to support and enact development with and for that community. This involves moving outside of the day-to-day interactions of education and pursuing goals, activities, and developments for and with the broader community.
4. The Networked Connection – The cultivation, involvement, and sustaining of the means of active engagement with other professionals and the wider community.

As argued in Chapter 3,

> If we do not try to move towards acts of connection, being connected professionals and building principalities of people however, our future will continue to be disconnected and unfulfilled, and ultimately we will be unable to serve our students in the way they deserve.
>
> (Crawley, 2017: 122)

The academic/vocational divide

Gibbons (2023: 197), when discussing legacies from the Nuffield Review in the 14–19 phase, highlights the 'tripartite mentality', which divides young people between 'academic', 'vocational/technical', and 'the rest'.

Gibbons continues that:

> …. At post 16 the problem is perhaps particularly acute; there is little doubt that A level has the reputation as the "gold standard" amongst employers and university admissions tutors and it has been historically difficult for any alternative qualification to gain a meaningful foothold all the time its existence continues.
>
> (*ibid.*: 197)

The 'academic/vocational divide', where the academic pathways have this more stable and valued position in the education hierarchy, and vocational programmes are always second best, has led to a situation Richmond and Bailey (2023: 1) describe as follows:

> …. The academic pathway from GCSEs to A-levels to an undergraduate degree at university is a well-trodden and well-understood route that attracts tens of thousands of young people in England every year. However, while this pathway receives considerable political and media interest, just 37 per cent of young people take three A-levels in their final years at school or college. In other words, over six in ten young people are not on a solely academic path. Even so, ever

since then Prime Minister Tony Blair's infamous speech in 1999 that set a target of 50 per cent of young people entering Higher Education (HE), the academic pathway has been placed on a pedestal above all else.

Their report on the reducing opportunities for young people mentions the often-stated desire of governments 'to create a "ladder of opportunity" for young people particularly for those from the least privileged backgrounds' often results in 'the enduring failure to tackle entrenched youth unemployment', which 'suggests that many young people are finding it very difficult to get onto the ladder – let alone progress up the ladder' (ibid.: 10).

This is such an entrenched situation across governments for years, and although some progress has been made in strengthening the vocational side of FE, it is still seen by many as second choice.

A particularly powerful judgement on the value of vocational education and training can be found in Thomas Ralph's 2024 book about 'the motivations behind disruptive school behaviour' (ibid.: i). Although this is the voice of 'disruptive school pupils', and not from FE, it reveals much about educational attitudes in England and how pupils can leave school feeling second best. The quotes below are from a conversation about woodworking classes:

Martin: Coz we're vocational we get treated differently. We get shit wood. We don't do work experience, nothing.
Jemma: We're outcasts.

> The use of the word 'outcasts' makes clear their perspective that they were not valued in the same way as other members of the school student population. They respect each other's work, clearly locating the blame for the poor quality of the outcome with the school. The view that the school considered them to be second class also extended to other areas such as the motor mechanics room. Despite evidently being very absorbed by the work that could potentially be done in this room they felt that the resource is in the room were being kept for the mainstream students.
>
> (ibid.: 186)

Sustainability

This cross-sector theme is particularly important, as it is the students of today who will help, we hope, to save the world tomorrow. The FE sector as a whole, and the associated organisations, at the time of writing this book, still has some distance to go in achieving progress on sustainability and education for sustainable development.

ETF (2021) make this clear with their recent research and state:

> Despite the enormous potential reach of ESD (Education for Sustainable Development) in the FE and training sector, progress to date has been fragmented and slow, with ESD not yet seen as a central pillar of the sector and its work. It could be argued that we've gone backwards over the last decade, as competing priorities and reduced resources have meant that FE and training providers simply haven't had the motivation, capacity or space to progress their ESD work.
>
> (ibid.: 2)

There is optimism that the sector is beyond the starting point and this is endorsed by the ETF, who state:

> We know that many FE colleagues want support to be able to equip their learners with the knowledge and competencies needed to meet these goals. Through this research we wanted to better understand opinions, barriers, opportunities and how we can help. This in turn will inform our approach and ensure we are best serving the sector's needs. We've chosen to publish the data to enable our peers and partners to also benefit from these insights, and to inform policy and decision makers about the needs of the sector.
>
> (*ibid.*: 3)

This section of the chapter firstly introduces and analyses two reports from well-respected FE organisations which were published in 2020, and which offer recommendations for the future of FE. During and after the COVID-19 pandemic, people and organisations were naturally reflecting on life in the future, at a time when life in the present was under threat. This included a number of reports about FE, and a report by the Edge Foundation (2020) about the future of FE is included, which makes three key recommendations. They are divided into three headings which are the following.

Defined

Key recommendation: Edge encourages the FE sector to establish a clear definition for itself, with a focus on what it is as opposed to what it is not. This could provide greater clarity across the system. Edge recommends individual FE providers continue to define their own identity and missions within this to ensure that their local offer is equally clear (*ibid.*: 42).

This is a sensible and straightforward recommendation, which would be helpful for all in FE and many beyond FE, but as has been discussed earlier in this chapter, it is not as easy to achieve as it may seem.

Career and skill focussed

Key recommendation: To develop a skilled UK workforce, the FE sector needs to attract, develop, and recognise its own teaching staff. Edge supports the formation of an independent panel for FE pay, which would help establish transparency, fairness, and impartiality. The panel would consider pay and conditions in other sectors from which FE staff may be drawn to ensure parity and fairness across the country (*ibid.*: 42).

This recommendation, if actioned, would be a potentially significant move forward for FE teachers whose incomes have fallen further behind school teachers in recent times. A 2023 Institute for Fiscal Studies report states that:

1. The recommended pay of college teachers has declined by 18 per cent in real terms since 2010–11. In the same period, teacher pay scales have fallen by between 5 per cent and 13 per cent. There have been especially sharp declines in recent years due to high levels of inflation – recommended college teacher pay has fallen by 9 per cent in the last two years.
2. The gap between the average salary of school and college teachers has grown over time. In 2010–11, the median salary (in today's prices) was around £48,000 for a school

teacher and £42,500 for a college teacher. Median pay is now around £41,500 for a school teacher and £34,500 for a college teacher. This means that between 2010–11 and 2022–23, the median salary for a school teacher fell by 14 per cent, while the median salary for a college teacher fell by 19 per cent.

(*ibid.*: 2)

This recommendation could start to rectify that situation for FE teachers.

Collaboration

Key recommendation: Colleges and education departments across the four nations are encouraged to focus on forming collaborative groupings, bringing together schools, independent training providers, and higher education institutions. With support from organisations like Edge, sharing best practices can be facilitated right across the UK (*ibid.*: 43).

This is another helpful and important recommendation, and with the use of existing examples of good practice in collaboration which already exist across the FE sector, a number of which have been featured in this book; this would be very helpful if implemented. Overall, these suggestions are not especially original or different, but would offer hope for the future of FE if they were adopted by the government.

FETL/EDSK (2020) is a report from one particular organisation, the Further Education Trust for Leadership (in partnership with Education and Skills EDSK), who has expressed a more independent voice than a number of organisations have been able to. This report (which is only about colleges) proposes a better future for colleges in particular and argues:

> ....That the only way the FE sector will become a respected and ambitious choice for young people and adults is by arranging itself in such a way that there is complete clarity about what it can offer learners. Bundling every student and course under the single banner of a 'college' will never deliver this goal.
>
> (*ibid.*: 4).

The report offers a large number of recommendations which are grouped together here to make them more readily accessible.

Newly named and organized institutions

FE colleges should be split into separate institutions that reflect their distinctive purposes for different groups of learners:

Community Colleges – basic skills courses, community learning and other entry level programmes (including ESOL)

Sixth Form Colleges – A-levels and other classroom-based Level 2 and 3 courses

Technology Colleges – vocational and technical training (including apprenticeships) up to Levels 4 and 5

The terms 'Community College' and 'Technology College' should be converted into protected titles, similar to the status given to the term 'university'.

(*ibid.*: 4)

Implementing this proposal would be a huge change for the sector, but there is a compelling argument that it would make provision, and potentially the sector much clearer overall.

Colleges and A-Levels

FE colleges that wish to offer A-levels should be required to convert their academic 16-19 provision into a Sixth Form College (*ibid.*: 4).

This would require a disaggregation of A-levels from existing provisions at colleges, where most of them currently offer A-levels and vocational/community learning. It is difficult to see how this could be implemented as losing their A-levels, however good their other provision is, would probably be a step too far for most colleges.

Area FE Directors

In each area of the country – a new 'FE Director' should be appointed by the sector as the representative for all the colleges within their geographical area. The FE Director (FED) will act as the convener and ambassador for their local FE institutions on both strategic and financial issues.

(*ibid.*: 5)

The FEDs will be tasked with mapping and subsequently arranging provision across their Community Colleges, Sixth Form Colleges and Technology Colleges in line with local social and economic needs as well as eliminating duplication of courses and promoting specialisation. This includes every FED having the ability to determine how the AEB is distributed among colleges.

(*ibid.*: 7)

With the right people in these roles, and other regional staff to support them in their work, this proposal could provide an extremely helpful impetus and organising focus for localised provision. It does mirror some of the approaches used by organisations such as the Learning and Skills Research Network and would be supported by sector professionals if the role was facilitative and supportive rather than monitoring and controlling.

Funding

- Increased funding for collaborative activities.
- The single-year funding allocations for the Adult Education Budget should be replaced by a three-year funding cycle for the FE sector.
- A dedicated capital investment in FE colleges from government of £1.5 billion should be delivered over an agreed period of time.
- The 'base rate' of funding for 16–19-year-olds should be increased by approximately £200 (4 per cent) per student in every year of Parliament to improve teaching and learning as well as the staff salaries available in colleges.
- The government should introduce a tertiary education funding model based on 'Individual Education Budgets' for every learner.
- All learners should be given access to a new 'lifetime loan limit' of £75,000, which they can use to engage in education and training at any time throughout their career.

Making connections – The future of further education 195

- Institutes of Technology should be established in every area so that all learners have access to higher-level technical education within a reasonable distance.
- Higher-level technical qualifications should be funded by the government if they are publicly endorsed by employers, professional bodies, or Institutes of Technology.
- Provision of Level 4 and 5 technical qualifications should be led in future by Technology Colleges.

(Adapted from FETL/EDSK, 2020)

This is a comprehensive and significant set of recommendations relating to funding, which would have the potential to enhance certain aspects of FE provision considerably. Overall, this report does contain a number of fair, imaginative, and potentially achievable recommendations. Realistically, however, this report offers a number of suggestions which could mean significant change for many FE organisations, but it does include strategies which could work, given a considerable and carefully planned development and implementation period.

> **Question for discussion**
> How has this book affected your view of the FE sector?

Conclusion

This final section of the book uses writings from experienced practitioners in FE and their reflections on the present and potential future of FE. Husband and Mycroft (2020) concluding the book about FE (PCET: Learning and Teaching in the post compulsory sector), which has been referred to often in this volume, offer messages of hope and resistance:

> However, it is time to get up and move on. This is a call to arms. The opposite of inertia is momentum, and in FE this takes the form of an affirmative sector-wide movement focused on robust self-owned evidence, which attempts to remove itself from the constraints of bureaucracy, endless reform and policy shift. A movement that attends to the constant and never-changing purpose of FE. Those working as educators know FE's value, it's potential, and moreover its future.
>
> (*ibid.*: 351)

> It is time to ditch the self-fulfilling prophecy that will inevitably consume any remaining aspirations of learning for the greater good and remove the pressure from FE. let the sector develop is partnerships, pathways, methods and processes without continued reform. FE need time and space to recover and regroup we boldly call on policy makers to leave the sector alone for *three years* and see what it formulates in response to its obligations. Thinkers need time to think so that action can develop that is meaningful.
>
> (*ibid.*: 352)

> We are caught in a round of endless, meaningless sticking plaster change. It is time to be incisive, to encourage FE's wounds to be exposed and allow time for them to heal. The cycle of victimhood needs to come to an end and the sector allowed to coalesce and speak for

itself. In the course of our work, we meet countless bright, talented, frustrated FE people and this convinces us that our profession has all the results is it needs to carry out this life-saving endeavour.

(*ibid.*: 352)

Another companion on the journey through this book has been the 'Dancing Princesses' book about FE, which concludes with this statement:

The 12 princesses may have been dancing secretly for years, with FE teachers publicly acquiescing to being locked within policy and managerial confines, while persisting in doing their own thing surreptitiously, but this clandestine dancing must come to an end. It is high time the princesses defy the king, own up to their subversive activity and out themselves as the great dancers they are. It is time we restore our autonomy and voice, rather than persisting in living this double life that is keeping us under the metaphorical lock and key, and eroding our professionalism. The king will never allow the princesses out to dance and we need to stop waiting for his permission. It's gone past the time of subversion. It's high time for revolution. It's time to take over the castle!

(Hillier, 2015: 164)

Of all the publications about FE, one particularly powerful critique was the publication from 2008 by Frank Coffield entitled, 'Just suppose teaching and learning became the first priority…' Coffield's research and commentary absolutely eviscerates the managerial, performative FE of that time, and appears to still retain many of the characteristics from then at the present time. He concludes, though, with an emotional and personal tribute to the spirit of education, and he has been allowed the last but one word in this book with his closing comment:

Moreover, something vital to the whole enterprise is being forgotten. I learned from my father, as he learned from his, to hear the music, the excitement and the hope in the word 'education'. I also learned that it is the job of teachers to help other people's children to hear and respond to that music. We do it because teaching is a noble profession, which dedicates itself to the lot of those who have not had our advantages. We do it because we believe in social justice and, like our parents and grandparents, we want a better world for ourselves, our children and all children. That is the meaning of our lives as teachers.

(Coffield, 2008: 61)

As the author of this book, and as a professional who has worked in or with FE for almost 50 years, the final word must be mine. Being someone who works in FE can be a mess, a struggle, and an unremitting swim against the current to help your students, your colleagues, and your organisation succeed and improve themselves. It can exhaust you, disappoint you, and make you very angry. Over the time of my working life, however, I have seen, and in some cases helped it to happen, thousands of lives transformed, achievements by students which they never imagined they could make and organisations and individuals working, teaching, and researching very hard for the common good. It is an absolutely brilliant part of English education, and deserves a much more respected and valued place in our society.

Summary points

- The breadth and diversity of FE can be an advantage and a disadvantage;
- Ongoing policy churn is an ongoing issue for FE;
- Despite many challenges FE maintains a positive purpose;
- Coherent, comprehensive, and accessible sector data is urgently needed;
- Models of positive professionalism do exist in FE;
- The academic/vocational divide is a systemic problem for FE;
- More progress needs to be made in the FE sector on sustainability and education for sustainable development;
- There are many positive recommendations about the future of FE, but a significant change in the government approach is needed.

Recommended reading

Coffield, F. (2008) *Just suppose teaching and learning became the first priority...* London: Learning and Skills Network.

References

Ball, S. (2003) The teacher's soul and the terrors of performativity. *Journal of Education Policy*, 18(2), pp. 215–228.

Azumah Dennis, C., Springbett, O. and Walker, L. (2019) Further education leaders: Securing the sector's future. *Futures*, 110, pp. 1–10.

City and Guilds (2019) *Sense and instability: Executive summary*. London: City and Guilds.

Coffield, F. (2008) *Just suppose teaching and learning became the first priority...* London: Learning and Skills Network.

Crawley, J. (2017) Principalities of people – Destabilising the prince's power through 'acts of connection'. In M. Daley, K. Orr and J. Petrie (Eds) *The principal: Power and professionalism in FE*. London: IOE Press.

Daley, M., Orr, K., & Petrie, J. (2015). *Further education and the twelve dancing princesses*. London Institute of Education Press.

Edge Foundation (2020) *Our plan for further education. Defined, career and skills focused, collaborative*. London: Edge Foundation.

Education and Training Foundation (2021) *Experiences of education for sustainable development in the further education and training sector*. London: ETF.

FETL (Further Education Trust for Leadership) (2020) *Leadership, further education and social justice*. London: FETL.

FETL / EDSK (2020) *Further consideration: Creating a new role, purpose and direction for the FE sector*. London: Further Education Trust for Leadership/Education and skills.

Gibbons, S. (2023) 14–19 Education: Education and training in school and beyond. In S. Gibbons, R. Brock, M. Glackin, E. Rushton and E. Towers (Eds) *Becoming a teacher. Issues in secondary education* (6th ed.). Maidenhead: Open University Press.

Gleeson, D., Davies, J. and Wheeler, E. (2005) On the making and taking of professionalism in the further education workplace. *British Journal of Sociology of Education*, 26(4), pp. 445–460.

Hillier, Y. (2015) Conclusion: Leading a merry dance through times of change and challenge. In M. Daley, K. Orr and J. Petrie (Eds) *Further education and the twelve dancing princesses*. London: Institute of Education Press.

Hodgson, A., Gallacher, J., Irwin, T., James, D. and Spours, K. (2018) *FE and skills across the four countries of the UK: New opportunities for policy learning*. London: Edge Foundation.

Husband, G. and Mycroft, L. (2020) The cost of everything and the values of nothing: What's next for the FE sector? In J. Tummons (Ed.) *Professionalism in post-compulsory education and training. empirical and theoretical perspectives*. Abingdon: Routledge.

Institute for Fiscal Studies (2023) *What has happened to college teacher pay in England?* London: IFS.

Keep, E., Richmond, T. and Silver, R. (2021) *Honourable histories. From the local management of colleges via incorporation to the present day: 30 years of reform in Further Education.* London: Further Education Trust for Leadership.

Machiavelli, N. (1908) *The Prince.* Translated by W.K. Marriott. London: EP Dutton & Company.

Orr, K. (2018) Further education colleges in the United Kingdom: Providing education for other people's children. In R. Latiner Raby and E.J. Valeau (Eds) *Handbook of comparative studies on community colleges and global counterparts* (1st ed.). (Springer International Handbooks of Education). Cham: Springer International Publishing AG, DOI: 10.1007/978-3-319-50911-2_42

Pring, R. (2008) 14–19. *Oxford Review of Education,* 34(6), pp. 677–688.

Ralph, T. (2024) *Student voice, behaviour, and resistance in the classroom environment: Lessons from disruptive and disaffected school children.* Abingdon: Routledge.

Richmond, T. and Bailey, A. (2023) *Broken ladders. Why the 'ladder of opportunity' is broken for so many young people, and how to fix it.* London: EDSK (Education and Skills).

Index

14-19 education 8, 103, 131, 187, 190; 14-16 programmes 139–141; in action 139–142; data 131–132; definition 132; history 132–136; policy 133–135, 137–139, 143–145

academic staff governor 24, 29–30
academic/vocational divide 112
access to higher education 1, 21, 69–71, 83, 170, 172; in action 70–71, 83, 170; benefits 69; characteristics 69–70, 72; data 69, 71; definition 69; history 69–70; policy 69–70; student support 69; teaching on 70
action for ESOL 109–110
adult and community learning 1, 50, 173; in action 53–60, 70, 96–97; data 53–54, 58–59; definition 50–53; history 55–58; policy 58–59, 60–61
Adult Basic Education 83, 106, 107
Adult Literacy and Basic Skills Unit 106
Adult Participation in Learning Survey 53
adult schools 56
A-levels 133, 142, 156
Allison, J. 9
Anderson, N. 141, 142
apprentices 6, 7, 16, 29, 39–41, 46–47, 53, 93, 107, 113–114, 131, 168; apprenticeships xiv, 2, 3, 7, 14, 16, 37–39, 40–42, 47, 58–59, 93, 120–121, 132, 135, 139, 143–144, 159, 168, 187, 193
Apprentify 46–47
area adult education officer 58
Armitage, A. 7
art, design and performing arts college 161, 169–172
Association of Colleges (AoC) xiii, xiv, 3, 9, 14–15, 30, 31, 39, 75, 92, 118, 131–132, 139, 152, 162, 163, 164, 167
Atkins, L. 8, 88
Audit Commission 17–18
Avila, T.B. 97
Avis, J. 80, 88, 91
Azumah Dennis, C. 14, 27–28, 169, 188–189

Bailey, A. 138, 144, 190
Bailey, B. 23
Basic Skills Unit 106
Ball, S. 8, 187
Barnet College 142–143
Bath College 5, 15–16, 21
Bathmaker, A-M. 29
Beck, D. 52
Bellini, S. 99
Bernhardt, A.C. 26
Blair, E. 10
Blair, T. 133–134, 138–139, 151, 191
Booth-Martin, H 127
Bradbury, A. 40
Brighton Hove and Sussex Sixth Form College 153–154
Brine, F. 69
Brown, G. 151
Brown, S. 104–105
Bullock, K. 182
Bunce, A. 182
Busher, H. 69–70
Business Register and Employment Survey 38

Cantor, L.M. 7, 17, 76
Casey, Kelly 126, 127
Chen, Joyce 128
citizenship education 180–181
City and Guilds 9–10, 40, 83, 187
City Literary Institute 87, 94–96
Climate Commission for UK Higher and Further Education 152–153
Coffield, F. 196
CollabGroup 122, 124, 126, 128
community 51–52; definition 51
community college 13, 19–20, 22, 193, 194
competence-based 42, 104, 105, 134, 148
connection 34; act of connection 34; acts of 34–35; civic connection; democratic connection; making connections 6, 34–35; networked connection 34; practical connection 34
Corbett, S. 119, 123, 124

Covid-19 2, 15, 22, 97, 101, 117–129; in action 119–126; data 118
Craig, G. 51
Crawley, J. 33–35, 119, 126, 189–190
Crowther Report (1959) 17

Dalby, D. 112
Daley, M. 34, 189
Davison, E. 78
Dearing, R. 76–77, 84
Dearing Report (1997) 74, 76–77, 84
defining principles 1
Department for Education 118, 178, 180
Department for Education and Skills 146
disability/disabilities 2, 3, 14, 15, 25, 30, 57, 68, 90–93, 95, 98, 99, 164, 168, 177, 180
disabled xv, 10, 51, 57, 87, 100
Duckworth, V. 94

Edge Foundation 6, 124, 128–129, 187, 192
Education Act (1944) 7, 17, 76, 133, 163, 177
Education and Skills (EDSK) 193–194
Education and Training Foundation 13–14, 77–78, 123–124, 154–157, 158
Education USA 19–20
Employer Skills Survey 38
Engineering Habits of Mind 136–137
English for Speakers of Other Languages 52, 103, 104–105; in action 109–110; action for campaign 109–110; data 110–111; definition 104–105; history 106–107; policy 105–106, 109–110
equality and diversity 25, 29–30, 87–88, 89–91, 100, 172; in action 89–90, 93–94, 94–96, 96–99; data 30–31, 91–92, 95, 100; history 30–31, 89–90; policy 89–91, 100
Esmond, B. 136

Fisher, R. 6
Fletcher, R. 7
Fletcher-Saxon, J. 127
Flood, I. 127, 128
Flynn, N. 180
Formosa, M. 57
foundation degree 74, 75, 77, 78
Fuller, A. 37, 44–47
Fuller and Unwin restricted and expansive learning 37, 44–47
functional analysis 42
functional skills 103, 107, 112
Further and Adult Education 88
Further and Adult Education Certificate 83, 88
Further and Higher Education Act (1992) 8, 18, 90, 163

Further Education Climate Action Road Map 152–153
further education college 5, 14–15, 17, 22, 35, 41, 69; in action 15–17, 20–21, 58, 69, 83–84, 95, 99, 141, 165, 180; data 14–15, 17, 22, 35, 41, 69, 79, 83; definition 13–14; history 17, 58; policy 17–19
Further Education Funding Council 18, 90
Further Education Trust for Leadership 87–88, 193–194

Gadsby, J. 129
The Gaols Act (1823) 176
General Certificate of Education 16, 19, 52, 112, 118, 132, 133, 138, 141–142, 164, 165, 166, 190
Gibbons, S. 137, 138, 190
Gillard, D. 89
Gleeson, D. 34, 189
governance 24–26, 30, 149, 153, 188
Greenwood, M. 74

Hayward, G. 134
Higdon, R. 180
Higher Education in Further Education 74–75, 76–78, 82–85; in action 83–84; data 75–76; definition 74–75; HEness 82–83, 84, 85; history 76–78; hybrid provision; policy 76–78, 84
Higher Education Statistics Agency 75, 76, 81
Higher National Certificate 75, 77
Higher National Diploma 75, 77
Hillier, Y. 17, 32, 196
HM Treasury 151
Hodgson, A. 6, 17, 40, 43–44, 138, 186–187
House of Commons Education Committee 52
Hudson, A. 70
Husband, G. 195
Hyland, T. 42

inclusion xiv, xv, 4, 25, 92, 95, 105, 125, 149
incorporation 18, 66, 163, 167
independent training provider 3, 31, 46–47, 134, 193
Industrial Training Board 8
Inner London Education Authority 107
Institute for Government 6, 177
Institute for Fiscal Studies 58–59, 192–193
Inter-Agency Group on Technical and Vocational Education and Training 38

James, N. 69–70
Jephcote, M. 20
Johnson, R. 64
Jones, D. 66
Jones, H.M.F. 107–108

Kaufmann-Kuchta, K. 26
Keep, E. 1, 10, 18–19, 187
Kennedy, H. 66–67, 90
Kennedy Report (1997) 66–67, 90
King, M. 83

land-based colleges 161, 167; in action 168–169; data 162, 167; history 167–168; policy 167–168
Latiner Raby, R. 20
Lavender, K. 77, 79, 81
Lea, J. 82–83
leadership styles 28–29, 36
Learning and Skills Council 8, 107, 140
Learning and Skills Development Agency 139
Learning and Skills Research Network 31–32, 186, 194
Learning and Work Institute 53–54, 107, 110–111, 115
The Learning Curve Group 4–5, 31
learning difficulties xv, 14, 15, 87, 90, 92, 100, 168
Leitch, A. 41
Leitch Review of Skills 41
Lewis, L. 96–97
Lloyd, C. 167, 168–169
The London Sustainability Exchange 147–148
Lord Taunton 89
Lovett, T. 64

Machiavelli, N. 33–34, 189
management 4, 18, 24–26, 30, 65, 70, 90, 123, 125, 129, 134, 142, 152, 181
Manpower Services Commission 17
Mapletoft, N. 125
Marriott, S. 107–108
McGiveney, V. 67–68
Mechanics Institute 7, 37, 40, 47
Millenium Development Goals 149
Mintz, J. 106
Moser report (1999) 103, 106, 108–109, 111
Munday, D. 90
Mycroft, L. 195

National Association for Teaching English and Other Community Languages 109
National Council for Vocational Qualifications 37, 42, 47, 48
National Institute for Adult and Continuing Education 104, 176
National Star College 87, 93–94
National Vocational Qualification 37, 42
NEET – young people not in education, employment, or training 97, 118, 121, 139
New Labour 8
Norton Radstock College 20–21

Noyes, A. 112
Nuffield Review (2009) 133–135, 138, 190

offender learning data 3, 177–178; in action 178–179; definition 175–176; history 176–177, 181–183; policy 175–176, 179–181
Office for National Statistics 2, 3, 4, 30, 31, 38, 92
Office for standards in education 4, 8, 15–16, 19, 21, 22, 44, 46, 47, 59–60, 93, 133, 164–165, 168, 169, 170, 189
Office for Students 81
On the Move 103, 107–108
Orr, K. 1, 10, 26, 80, 140–141, 143, 187
other people's children xiii, 1, 10, 37, 187

Pangrazio, F. 105
Peart, S. 141–142
Pendrey, A. 127
Pennacchia, J. 29
Percy Report (1944) 76
performativity 8, 187
Peutrell, R. 109–110
Pogson, Kathryn 128
polytechnic 18, 76
Pring, R. 134–135, 187
Prison Learning Alliance 181
professionalism 31, 33, 34–35, 108, 110, 189–190, 196
Purcell, M. 60–61
Purcell, R. 52

Quality Assurance Agency 69

Ralph, T. 191
Raven, N. 80, 122, 125
Reading College 136–137
really useful knowledge 64, 80
Reddy, S. 41
regional college 17, 76
return to work courses 65–66
Richmond, T. 138, 144, 190
Roberts, I. F. 7, 17, 76
Robinson, P. 69
Rose, J. 97
Royal Academy of Engineering 136

Sainsbury Review (2016) 135–136
Saxby-Smith, S. 65–66
Scattergood, K. 127
Schofield, T. 163, 165–166
Scottish Executive 105
sector story 4–5, 9, 15–16, 19, 20–21, 29–30, 31–33, 41–42, 46–47, 54–56, 78, 83–84, 93–94, 94–95, 111–112, 114, 119–120, 126–127, 136–137, 142–143,

153–154, 157–158, 164–165, 171–172, 178–179, 183
Shepherd, J. 65, 98–99
Sheridan, L. 65
Shorter, P. 162–163
Simmons, J. 82
Simmons, R. 6
sixth form college 153–157, 162–167, 194; in action 153–154, 157, 164–165, 165–167; data 162–164; definition 161, 162–163; history 162–164; policy 162–164, 194
skills for life 104–111; in action 106–114; data 108–109, 110; definition 104–106; history 106–111; policy 106–111
Sligo, F. 113
Smith, A. 56, 127
Smith, M. 104
Smith, M.K. 56
Smith, R. 94, 129
Smithers, A. 69
social justice 80, 89–100, 113–114, 129, 134, 188, 196; in action 93–95, 96–97, 99, 105, 113, 114; data 92; definition 88–89; history 89–91; policy 89–91, 99, 100; transitions 98–99
social mobility 26, 88–89, 91–92, 97, 99, 100, 108
Social Mobility Commission 91–92
Somerset Skills and Leisure 59–60
South West Foundation 54–56
Souto-Otero, M. 148
special educational needs 15, 25, 92, 164, 168
specialist college 3, 4, 161, 168, 169, 171, 172; in action 169, 171; data 3, 162, 163; definition 161–162
Spours, K. 121, 138
Stern Review (2006) 151
Stoten, D.W. 79, 166–167
sustainability 154–157, 191–192; in action 152–153, 153–154, 154–157; data 154–157, 158–159; definition 147–148; education for sustainable development; history 148–151, 154–157; policy 149–150, 151, 154–157, 158–159, 191–192
Sustainable Development Goals 149–151
The Sutton Trust 88, 99–100, 106

Taunton Report 87, 89, 101
teacher education 9, 21, 32, 83, 158
Terry, K. 143

Thomas, L. 66, 68
Thompson, D.W. 68
Tight, M. 67, 187
T-level 143–144
Tomlinson, I 133–135
Tomlinson, M. 87, 90–91
Tomlinson Report (1994-6) 87, 90–91
Tomlinson Report (2004) 133–135
tripartite mentality 132, 138; system 144
Tuckett, A. 57, 58
Tummons, J. 31
Turner, Amanda 119–120

U3A 50, 56–57
UK Health Security Agency 118
UK Parliament 143
United Nations 149–150
United Nations Sustainable Development Solutions Network 149–150
University and College Union 181
University College London Social Research Institute 118, 120–122
Unwin, L. 37, 44–46, 48

vocational education and training 42–43, 74, 91, 101, 151, 191
von Carlowitz, C. 148

Walker, M. 40
Waller, R. 69
Widdowson, J. 83
widening participation 63, 67–68, 77, 78, 80; in action 67–68, 69–70, 71; data 65, 66, 67, 71; definition 63–64; history 64–67; policy 64–67, 69–70
Wilkinson, S. 176, 179–180
Williams, K. 127
Wolf, A. 8–9
Wolf report (2010) 8–9
women returner courses 65–66
Woodrow, A. 128
work-based learning 37, 38–39, 40–41; in action 42, 44–46; data 38–39; definition 37–38; history 40–41, 42–44; policy 40–41, 42–44
Workers Education Association 64
workforce data 3–4
Worth, E. 65
Wynne, V. 40–41

Youth Media Project (1976) 111–112

For Product Safety Concerns and Information please contact our EU
representative GPSR@taylorandfrancis.com
Taylor & Francis Verlag GmbH, Kaufingerstraße 24, 80331 München, Germany

www.ingramcontent.com/pod-product-compliance
Lightning Source LLC
Chambersburg PA
CBHW080924300426
44115CB00018B/2933